IARIA

ICDS 2016

The Tenth International Conference on Digital Society

April 24 - 28, 2016

Venice, Italy

ICDS 2016 Editors

Lasse Berntzen, Buskerud and Vestfold University College, Norway
Mark Perry, University of New England, Australia

Printed from e-media with permission by:

Curran Associates, Inc.
57 Morehouse Lane
Red Hook, NY 12571

Some format issues inherent in the e-media version may also appear in this print version.

Printed by Curran Associates, Inc. (2016)

International Academy, Research, and Industry Association (IARIA)
412 Derby Way
Wilmington, DE 19810

Phone: (408) 893-6407
Fax: (408) 527-6351

petre@iaria.org

Additional copies of this publication are available from:

Curran Associates, Inc.
57 Morehouse Lane
Red Hook, NY 12571 USA
Phone: 845-758-0400
Fax: 845-758-2633
Email: curran@proceedings.com
Web: www.proceedings.com

TABLE OF CONTENTS

ICDS 1: NETWORKING AND TELECOMMUNICATIONS

ICDS 2: EGOVERNMENT SERVICES IN THE CONTEXT OF DIGITAL SOCIETY

ICDS 3: SOCIAL NETWORKING

ICDS 4: CONSUMER-ORIENTED DEVICES AND SERVICES

ICDS 2016

Forward

The Tenth International Conference on Digital Society and eGovernments (ICDS 2016), held between April 24 and April 28, 2016 in Venice, Italy, continued a series of international events covering a large spectrum of topics related to advanced networking, applications, and systems technologies in a digital society.

Nowadays, most of the economic activities and business models are driven by the unprecedented evolution of theories and technologies. The impregnation of these achievements into our society is present everywhere, and it is only question of user education and business models optimization towards a digital society.

Digital devices conquer from kitchen to space vessels most of the functionality commonly performed by human beings. Telecommunications, advanced computation, miniaturization, and high speed devices make tele-presence easy. Wireless and mobility allow ubiquitous systems to be developed. Progress in image processing and exchanging facilitate e-health and virtual doctor teams for patient surgeries.

Naturally, issues on how to monitor, control and manage these systems become crucial to guarantee user privacy and safety. Not only devices, but also special software features must be enforced and guaranteed in a digital society.

The variety of the systems and applications and the heterogeneous nature of information and knowledge representation require special technologies to capture, manage, store, preserve, interpret and deliver the content and documents related to a particular target.

In response to this challenge, Intrusion Prevention and Detection Systems have now grown in prominence to such an extent that they are now considered a vital component for any enterprise organisation serious about network defense. However the numerous recorded attacks against high profile organizations is continuing evidence that many of these controls are not, at present, a panacea for dealing with the threats. Having themselves learnt the mechanisms employed by IPDS malicious parties are becoming particularly adept at evading them through inventive obfuscation techniques. These challenges need to be addressed using increasingly more innovative, creative and measurable IPDS mechanisms and methods.

Progress in cognitive science, knowledge acquisition, representation, and processing helped to deal with imprecise, uncertain or incomplete information. Management of geographical and temporal information becomes a challenge, in terms of volume, speed, semantic, decision, and delivery.

Information technologies allow optimization in searching an interpreting data, yet special constraints imposed by the digital society require on-demand, ethics, and legal aspects, as well as user privacy and safety.

Nowadays, there is notable progress in designing and deploying information and organizational management systems, experts systems, tutoring systems, decision support systems, and in general, industrial systems.

The progress in different domains, such as image processing, wireless communications, computer vision, cardiology, and information storage and management assure a virtual team to access online to the latest achievements.

Processing medical data benefits now from advanced techniques for color imaging, visualization of multi-dimensional projections, Internet imaging localization archiving and as well as from high resolution of medical devices.

Collecting, storing, and handling patient data requires robust processing systems, safe communications and storage, and easy and authenticated online access.

National and cross-national governments' decisions for using the digital advances require e-Government activities on developmental trends, adoption, architecture, transformation, barrier removals, and global success factors. There are challenges for government efficiency in using these technologies such as e-Voting, eHealth record cards, citizen identity digital cards, citizen-centric services, social e-financing projects, and so on.

We believe that the ICDS 2015 contributions offered a panel of solutions to key problems in all areas of digital needs of today's society.

The conference had the following tracks:

- Networking and telecommunications
- eGovernment services in the context of digital society
- Social networking
- Consumer-oriented devices and services

We take here the opportunity to warmly thank all the members of the ICDS 2016 technical program committee, as well as the numerous reviewers. The creation of such a high quality conference program would not have been possible without their involvement. We also kindly thank all the authors that dedicated much of their time and effort to contribute to ICDS 2016. We truly believe that, thanks to all these efforts, the final conference program consisted of top quality contributions.

Also, this event could not have been a reality without the support of many individuals, organizations and sponsors. We also gratefully thank the members of the ICDS 2016 organizing committee for their help in handling the logistics and for their work that made this professional meeting a success.

We hope ICDS 2016 was a successful international forum for the exchange of ideas and results between academia and industry and to promote further progress in the field of digital society and eGovernments. We also hope that Venice, Italy, provided a pleasant environment during the conference and everyone saved some time to enjoy the unique charm of the city.

ICDS Advisory Committee

Lasse Berntzen, Buskerud and Vestfold University College, Norway
Åsa Smedberg, DSV, Stockholm University/KTH, Sweden
Freimut Bodendorf, University of Erlangen, Germany
Andranik Tangian, Wirtschafts- und Sozialwissenschaftliches Institut - Düsseldorf | Karlsruhe Institute of Technology, Germany

ICDS 2016

Committee

ICDS Advisory Committee

Lasse Berntzen, Buskerud and Vestfold University College, Norway
Åsa Smedberg, DSV, Stockholm University/KTH, Sweden
Freimut Bodendorf, University of Erlangen, Germany
Andranik Tangian, Wirtschafts- und Sozialwissenschaftliches Institut - Düsseldorf | Karlsruhe Institute of Technology, Germany

ICDS 2016 Technical Program Committee

Habtamu Abie, Norwegian Computing Center, Norway
Mir Abolfazl Mostafavi, Université Laval - Québec, Canada
Witold Abramowicz, The Poznan University of Economics, Poland
Gil Ad Ariely, Interdisciplinary Center Herzliya (IDC), Israel
Masanori Akiyoshi, Kanagawa University, Japan
Mutaz M. Al-Debei, University of Jordan, Jordan
Ali Ahmad Alawneh, Philadelphia University, Jordan
Adolfo Albaladejo Blázquez, Universidad de Alicante, Spain
Cristina Alcaraz, University of Malaga, Spain
Salvador Alcaraz Carrasco, Universidad Miguel Hernández, Spain
Eugenia Alexandropoulou, University of Macedonia, Greece
Giner Alor Hernández, Instituto Tecnológico de Orizaba-Veracruz, México
Aini Aman, Universiti Kebangsaan Malaysia, Malaysia
Pasquale Ardimento, University of Bari, Italy
Masrah Azrifah Azmi Murad, Universiti Putra Malaysia, Malaysia
Saïd Assar, Institut Mines-Telecom - Ecole de Management, France
Charles K. Ayo, Covenant University, Nigeria
Ambrose A. Azeta, Covenant University, Nigeria
Gilbert Babin, HEC Montréal, Canada
Kambiz Badie, Research Institute for ICT, Iran
Ilija Basicevic, University of Novi Sad, Serbia
Michaela Baumann, Institute for Computer Science - University of Bayreuth, Germany
Najib Belkhayat, ENCG Marrakech (Business School), Morocco
Farid E. Ben Amor, University of Southern California / DIRECTV, USA
Khalid Benali, LORIA -Université de Lorraine, France
Martina Benvenuti, University of Bologna, Italy
Eleni Berki, University of Tampere, Finland
Lasse Berntzen, Buskerud and Vestfold University College, Norway

Aljoša Jerman Blažič, SETCCE - Ljubljana, Slovenia
Marco Block-Berlitz, Hochschule für Technik und Wirtschaft Dresden, Germany
Freimut Bodendorf, University of Erlangen, Germany
Nicola Boffoli, University of Bari, Italy
Sabrina Bonomi, e-Campus University, Italy
Mahmoud Boufaida, Mentouri University of Constantine, Algeria
Danielle Boulanger, University of Lyon-Jean Moulin, France
Mahmoud Brahimi, University of Msila, Algeria
Diana Bri Molinero, Universitat Politècnica de València, Spain
Anna Brunstrom, Karlstad University, Sweden
Alberto Caballero Martínez, Universidad Católica San Antonio de Murcia, Spain
Luis M. Camarinha-Matos, New University of Lisbon, Portugal
Omar Andres Carmona Cortes, Instituto Federal do Maranhão, Brazil
María Luisa Carrió-Pastor, Universitat Politècnica de València, Spain
Lemuria Carter, Virginia Commonwealth University, USA
Maria Chiara Caschera, IRPPS-CNR - Rome, Italy
Oscar Castillo, Tijuana Institute of Technology, Mexico
Walter Castelnovo, University of Insubria, Italy
Sudip Chakraborty, Valdosta State University, USA
Ramaswamy Chandramouli, NIST, USA
Sung-Bae Cho, Yonsei University, Korea
Kim-Kwang Raymond Choo, University of South Australia, Australia
Kalloniatis Christos, University of the Aegean, Greece
Yul Chu, University of Texas Pan American, USA
Arthur Csetenyi, Budapest Corvinus University, Hungary
Glenn S. Dardick, Longwood University, USA
David Day, Sheffield Hallam University, UK
Peter Day, University of Brighton, UK
Marco De Marco, Università Marconi, Italy
Gert-Jan de Vreede, University of Nebraska at Omaha, USA
Jana Dittmann, University of Magdeburg, Germany
Jerome Donet, Université de Lorraine, France
Prokopios Drogkaris, University of the Aegean - Karlovasi, Greece
Gerard M De Leoz, Baylor University in Waco, USA
Pedro Felipe do Prado, University of São Paulo, Brazil
Joël Dumoulin, HumanTech Institute, Switzerland
Martin Ebner, Graz University of Technology, Austria
Noella Edelmann, Danube University Krems, Austria
Ahmed El Oualkadi, Abdelmalek Essaadi University, Morocco
El-Sayed Mohamed El-Alfy, King Fahd University of Petroleum and Minerals, Saudi Arabia
Jacques Fayolle, Télécom Saint-Etienne | Université Jean Monnet, France
Matthias Finger, SwissFederal Institute of Technology, Switzerland
Karla Felix Navarro, University of Technology, Sydney
Adina Magda Florea, University Politehnica of Bucharest, Romania

Larisa Shwartz, IBM T. J. Watson Research Center, USA
Patrick Siarry, Université de Paris 12 – Creteil, France
Pushpendra B. Singh, MindTree - Bangalore, India
Georgios Ch. Sirakoulis, Democritus University of Thrace, Greece
Åsa Smedberg, Stockholm University, Sweden
Kingkarn Sookhanaphibarn, Bangkok University, Thailand
Maria T. Soto-Sanfiel, Autonomous University of Barcelona, Spain
Wellington Souza, Federal University of Rio Grande do Norte, Brazil
Sasikumaran Sreedharan, King Khalid University, Saudi Arabia
Yannis Stamatiou, University of Patras, Greece
Dalibor Stanimirović, University of Ljubljana, Slovenia
Peter L. Stanchev, Kettering University - Flint, USA
Dimitrios Stratogiannis, National Technical University of Athens, Greece
Ivan Strugar, University of Zagreb, Croatia
Chandrasekaran Subramaniam, Velammal Engineering College, India
Dennis Tachiki, Tamagawa University, Japan
Andranik Tangian, Wirtschafts- und Sozialwissenschaftliches Institut - Düsseldorf | Karlsruhe Institute of Technology, Germany
Shigeaki Tanimoto, Chiba Institute of Technology, Japan
Maryam Tayefeh Mahmoudi, Research Institute for ICT - Alzahra University, Iran
Joe M. Tekli, Lebanese American University, Lebanon
Sampo Teräs, Aalto University, Finland
Steffen Thiel, Furtwangen University of Applied Sciences, Germany
Ashley Thomas, Dell Secureworks, USA
Mohamed Fahmy Tolba, Ain Shams University, Egypt
Ioan Toma, STI, Austria
Jesus Tomas, Universidad Politecnica de Valencia, Spain
Juan-Manuel Tores, Université d'Avignon, France
Chrisa Tsinaraki, EU JRC, Italy
Julien Tscherrig, HumanTech Institute, Switzerland
Umut Turksen, University of the West of England, UK
Klaus Turowski, Otto-von-Guericke University Magdeburg, Germany
Jengnan Tzeng, National Chengchi University - Taipei, Taiwan
Theodoros Tzouramanis, University of the Aegean, Greece
Meike Ullrich, Karlsruhe Institute of Technology (KIT), Germany
Abel Usoro, University of the West of Scotland, UK
Emmanouel Varvarigos, University of Patras, Greece
Seppo Väyrynen, University of Oulu, Finland
Nikos Vrakas, University of Piraeus, Greece
Dawid Grzegorz Weckowski, Poznan University of Economics, Poland
Alex Wiesmaier, AGT Germany, Germany
Adam Wojciechowski, Poznan University of Technology, Poland
Xiaoli (Lucy) Yang, Purdue University - Calumet, USA
Yingjie Yang, De Montfort University, UK

Copyright Information

SDN-based Implementation of P2P Streaming Networks with Dynamic Reconfiguration

Ryo Shibasaki, Noriko Matsumoto, Norihiko Yoshida
Graduate School of Science and Engineering
Saitama University
Saitama, Japan
Emails: {shibasaki, noriko, yoshida}@ss.ics.saitama-u.ac.jp

Abstract—**The Software Defined Networking (SDN) technology is one of the major technical infrastructures for the digital society. This paper focuses on a dynamic streaming network and its efficient implementation. A Peer to Peer (P2P) streaming network tends to be unbalanced because of the dynamic nature of its nodes to join and leave, and often suffers from delivery delay. Therefore, it is required to reconfigure the network dynamically to keep it balanced. This paper proposes an SDN-based scheme for adaptive reconfiguration of the structure and routing in a P2P streaming network. This scheme enables fully decentralized delivery under a centralized control. Some simulation-based experiments confirmed that this scheme worked effectively.**

Keywords—P2P streaming; SDN

I. Introduction

Streaming is used to download a multimedia content while playing it. In this delivery method, the content is divided into units called segments. Segments are transferred from the server to the clients in turn. Typically, the Client/Server (C/S) model is available for streaming. However, the C/S model has problems such as the increase of the server load and maintenance costs according to the increase of the number of clients. Peer-to-Peer (P2P) Streaming has attracted attention in order to solve these problems. However, P2P streaming also has shortcomings such as failures due to concentration of the connection to a specific node and delays in receiving contents due to the increase of the number of hops from the source node. In order to prevent these shortcomings, it is important to reconfigure the P2P streaming network dynamically to keep it balanced [1]. Traditionally, each node in a P2P network performs data transfer and routing in an autonomous distributed manner. Load balancing could be achieved by each node independently, however it would be inefficient. Therefore, we propose a centralized control scheme for such decentralized P2P networks.

Recently, Software Defined Networking (SDN) is attracted attention as a concept of centralized control of network devices. SDN can control network devices flexibly using software. SDN has already been used in Google's data center [2] for example. In addition to this, SDN is expected to realize new technologies such as Network Function Virtualization (NFV) and Information Centric Network (ICN) [3]. OpenFlow [4] is a typical implementation technology of SDN. The OpenFlow specifies network devices from the datalink layer to the transport layer. However, a conventional P2P network is implemented as an overlay network at the application layer.

In this paper, we propose a scheme to configure a P2P streaming network at the IP layer using OpenFlow. In our proposal, the OpenFlow configures a P2P streaming network and a centralized routing control for network devices. The structure of this paper is as follows: Section II introduces a routing method of P2P network using OpenFlow. Section III describes our proposal. Section IV shows some results of simulation-based experiments and related considerations. Finally, Section V includes some concluding remarks and future work.

II. Related Works

OpenFlow consists of a controller, OpenFlow switches and OpenFlow Protocol. The OpenFlow switches forward or discard packets according to "flows" which are given from the controller. The OpenFlow Protocol is used to communicate between the controller and switches. The controller is implemented in software, and can update flows for the switches dynamically. The network topology and its routing mechanism is reconfigured flexibly and dynamically under the centralized control in this manner. The routing method for the P2P network using OpenFlow will be presented later.

In streaming delivery, delay or loss in the reception of the segments leads to interruption of playback of contents. Trajikovska et al. [5] proposed SDN based Quality-of-Service (QoS) control in a P2P streaming network. In this proposal, the provider decides a parent node for a new node which joins the P2P streaming network. First, the provider figures out candidate nodes which are close to the new node using the Round-Trip-Time (RTT) distance between the new one and others. Next, the provider checks the bandwidth between the new one and the parent candidates. The new node is connected to the parent node which is selected on the basis of the RTT distance and the bandwidth. After that, the bandwidth is adjusted between these nodes using OpenFlow meter table.

Othman et al. [6] proposed a method that the controller executes routing control. In this proposal, changing from the C/S model to the P2P model occurs depending on the server load. When changing to the P2P model, the server sends a request to redirect content requests to the controller. The redirection request includes the content IDs and the list of nodes which receive this content. This list contains the IP address of the node and the number of child nodes which can be connected to this node. When the controller receives the redirection request, the controller sends some necessary flows

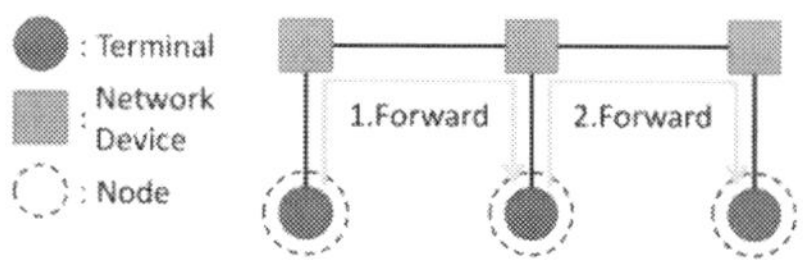

Figure 1. Content delivery of a traditional P2P network

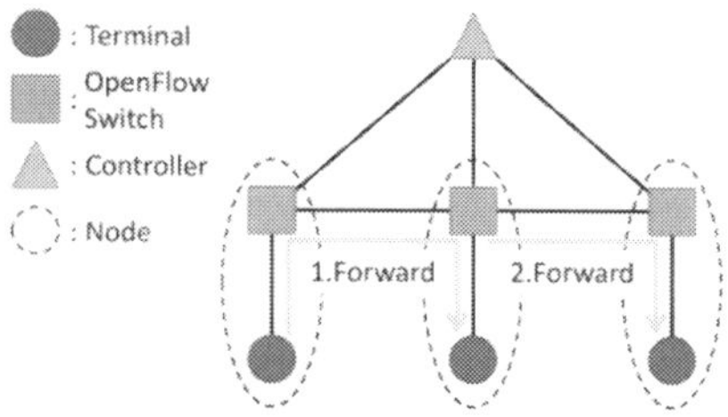

Figure 2. Content delivery of a P2P network using OpenFlow

to the OpenFlow switches. A content request is then redirected to a node which already has the content.

These proposals focus only on the situation when a node joins a P2P network. Additionally, some studies proposed reconfiguration of a P2P network dynamically. Akiyama et al. [7] applied the publish and subscribe (pub/sub) model to a P2P network. In the pub/sub model, a publisher sends a content to the middleware, and the content is categorized in some topic. Then the middleware sends the content to subscribers which are joined to the topic. In this proposal, the controller examines the physical topology using Link Layer Discovery Protocol (LLDP). The agent which runs on the node is migrated based on the physical topology and the topic name.

III. PROPOSED METHOD

This section introduces our proposal. Our proposal is based on the study by Ono et al. [1]. Ono et al. proposed a scheme to reconfigure a P2P streaming network dynamically. To implement this, each node monitors its neighbor nodes such as its parent and children. If the parent node can spare its capacity, a child node reconnects itself to the parent. Load balancing is achieved in this manner, and delay in content delivery is reduced. In this proposal, each node in a P2P streaming network performs data transfer and routing in an autonomous distributed manner. However, this kind of autonomous distributed manner is inefficient because each node performs a similar behavior and causes excessive control packets.

There are two kinds of streaming: on-demand and live delivery. In on-demand streaming, a content created in advance is delivered to clients when its server receives a content request. In live streaming, a content is delivered to clients in real time while recording and encoding. In traditional P2P live streaming, each leaf node which is joined to the P2P streaming network receives and sents the content so that all the nodes can decode and play the same content at the same time (Figure 1).

Since the same content is delivered at the same time, P2P live streaming has some resemblance with IP multicast by network devices (Figure 2). In this paper, a pair of a host and its corresponding switch is considered a "node."

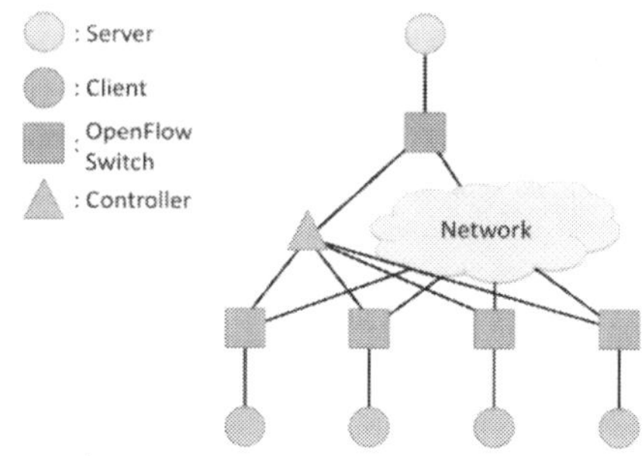

Figure 3. Proposal system overview

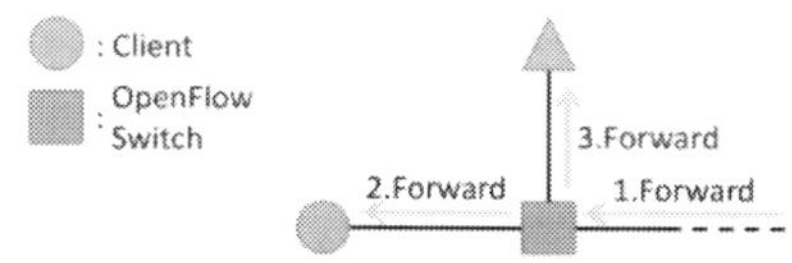

Figure 4. A content request is forwarded to the controller

Matching rule	
Destination IP address	Server's IP address
Action	
1. Forward to a server	
2. Forward to the controller	

Figure 5. The flow to forward a content request to the controller

In our proposal, the controller manages the route of the P2P streaming network. Our proposal comprises a server, clients, OpenFlow switches and the controller (Figure 3). The server forwards segments to clients according to a content request. The clients receive segments from a server. If a client has child nodes, the client forwards its segments to the children. The OpenFlow switch forwards a content request and segments according to the flows which are given from the controller. The controller sends flows so as to change the P2P streaming network. The procedure of the controller is described below.

A. *Management of nodes*

In our proposal, the controller manages nodes in the P2P streaming network in a centralized manner. To know a node which has joined or left from the P2P streaming network, a content request is forwarded to the controller (Figure 4). To forward to the controller, the flow which is shown in Figure 5 is given to an OpenFlow switch neighboring to the server. When the controller receives a content request, the controller reads the header of its packet to get the source IP address. After that, the controller updates the network topology information within it according to join or leave of the node of the IP address.

B. *Delivery of contents*

Segments which are forwarded from a parent node are copied in an OpenFlow switch. The segments are passed to the coupled host as well as transferred to its child nodes (Figure 6). To implement this, the flow which is shown in Figure 7 is kept in the OpenFlow switch. According to this flow, the client assumes that segments are forwarded from a server in spite that

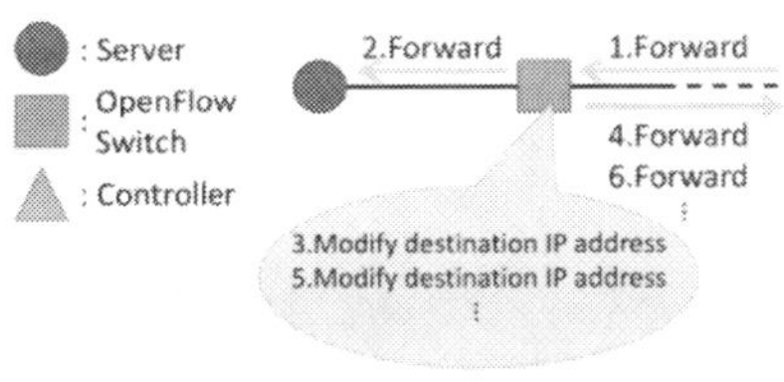

Figure 6. Delivery of segments

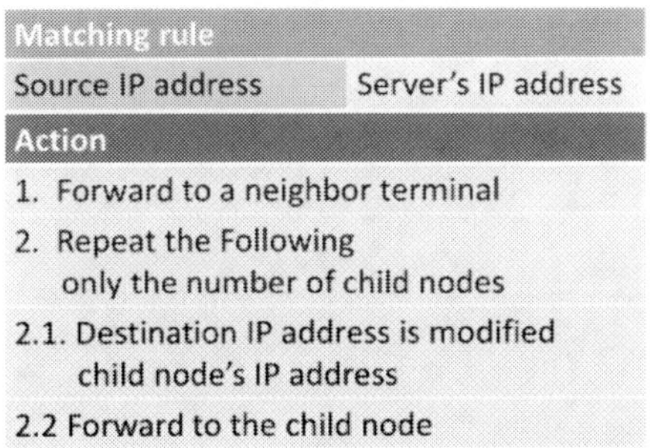

Figure 7. The flow to forward a content to child nodes

actually they are forwarded from the parent node. This delivery is similar to IP multicast using OpenFlow [8][9], however IP addresses are not necessary unlike IP multicast. Accordingly, the packet which is copied by this flow is forwarded on a network similar to ordinary packets.

C. *Reconstruction of a P2P stereaming network*

The controller must select a parent node of a new node which has joined the P2P streaming network. Similarly, the controller must select a parent node of nodes which were child nodes of a leaving node. A parent node is determined following the below procedure.

1) Select candidate nodes which is located at the lowest depth from the server among nodes which can spare their capasities.
2) Select a parent node which has the smallest number of child nodes out of the candidates.

Following these steps, a joining node or child nodes of a leaving node select a parent node to reconstruct a balanced P2P streaming network. However, the P2P streaming network may be unbalanced because this procedure does not consider descendant nodes of these nodes. Therefore, the controller checks the P2P streaming network topology regularly. If the P2P streaming network is unbalanced, an unbalanced node selects a parent node again using the above procedure. After that, the P2P streaming network is reconfigured to be balanced it. An unbalanced node is determined using (1).

In our proposal, the maximum number of child nodes which can be connected to a node is fixed to a constant (c). The total number of clients (n_{max}) which can be connected in the depth d is shown below when the server's depth is 0.

$$n_{max} = \sum_{i=1}^{d} c^i = \frac{c(c^d - 1)}{c - 1}$$

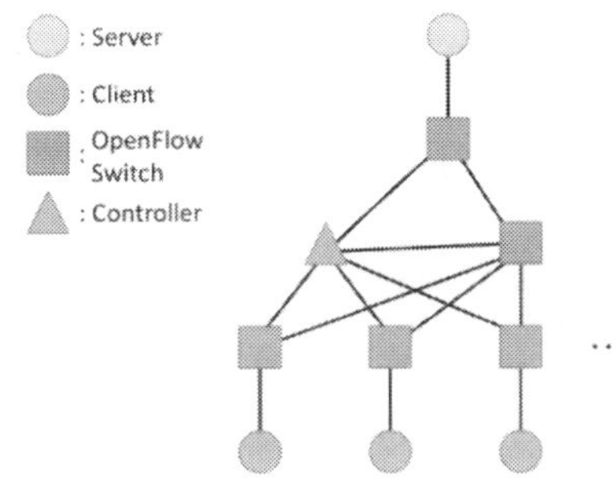

Figure 8. A virtual network used in the experiment

TABLE I. The parameters used in the experiment

Parameter	Value
The number of child nodes which are connected the node	2
The number of segments to be sent	10 packets per second
Check interval for the network topology	every 2 seconds
Interval for statistics of OpenFlow switches	every 1 second

Therefore, if the number of joining clients to the P2P streaming network is n, the optimal value of the depth of the P2P network is shown below.

$$\begin{aligned} n &\leq n_{max} \\ \frac{\ln(nc - n + c)}{\ln c} - 1 &\leq d \end{aligned} \qquad (1)$$

The optimal value is the minimum value of d which satisfies (1). If all the unbalanced nodes select a parent node again at once, the P2P streaming network changes drastically. As a result, the loss or the duplication of segments may occur. Furthermore, the reconfiguration does not complete by the time of the next check because processing time of the controller is increased. From the above, the depth of nodes which select a new parent node are restricted to $d_{min} + 1$.

The controller must send flows, which are shown in Figure 7, to the OpenFlow switches when the P2P streaming network topology is changed. In our proposal, segments that are forwarded from a parent node is considered equivalent to the ones forwarded from a server. Accordingly, if a parent node which is connected to the node is changed, the node does not have any influence. However, if child nodes which are connected to the node are changed, the node must send segments to these new nodes. The controller must send the flow to these nodes' switch to forward segments to child nodes. From the above, the OpenFlow switches which must update the flow are the old parent node and the new parent node.

IV. Evaluation

A simulator was made for experiments in order to confirm the effectiveness of our proposal.

A. *Simulator Design*

The simulator was implemented in Trema which is one of the OpenFlow frameworks. The experiment was performed using a virtual network on Trema. A virtual network is composed of star topology (Figure 8). The controller detects links between OpenFlow switches using LLDP in order to forward packets. Links between an OpenFlow switch and a leaf are detected using Packet-In messages. Packets are forwarded using Dijkstra's algorithm. The parameters used in

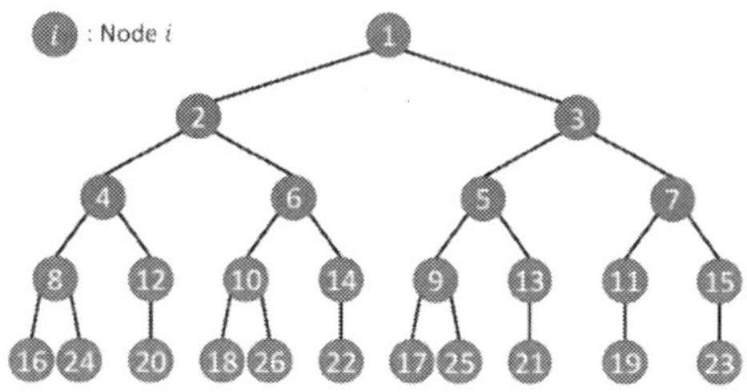

Figure 9. The P2P streaming network topology before nodes join

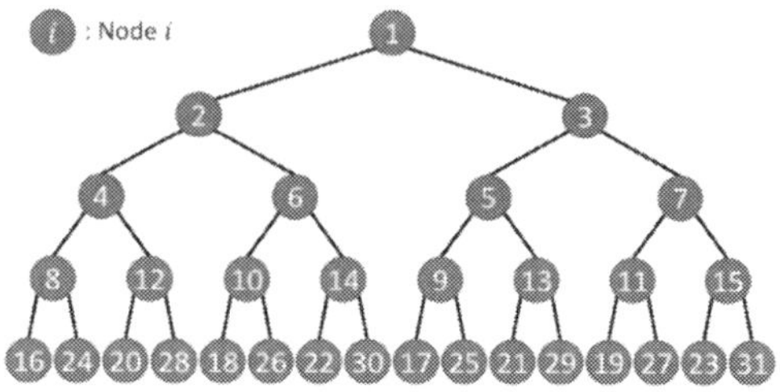

Figure 10. The balanced P2P streaming network topology

the experiment are shown in Table I. The controller knows a set of Server's IP address and an OpenFlow ID which neighbors the server in advance. A server forwards segments to the OpenFlow switch. The OpenFlow switch forwards segments according to the flow shown Figure 7. The experiment was performed as described below under these conditions.

- Join of nodes
  We examined the P2P streaming network topology when nodes join the network. Furthermore, we examined whether each client receives all the segments or not.
- Withdrawal of a node
  We examined the P2P streaming network topology when nodes left the P2P streaming network. Then, we examined the number of nodes which changed its parent node and flows which are forwarded to an OpenFlow switch from the controller. Furthermore, we examined whether each client receives all the segments or not.
- Comparison of the P2P model and the C/S model
  If the number of child nodes which are connected to a node is unlimited, our proposal constructs a network similar to the C/S model. Accordingly, we compared with the C/S model along with the P2P model and examined each client whether to receive segments or not. And then, we compared the load of OpenFlow switches in the P2P model and the C/S model.

The amount of segments which are sent from a server and received by the clients was compared in order to confirm examine that each client receives all segments or not. The amount of segments which are sent or received is obtained using statistics per port of an OpenFlow switch. However, the amount of segments which are sent from the server and received by the clients are not equal when the node joins or leaves in the P2P streaming network. Accordingly, we calculated the amount of segments per second and compared their values. The load of an OpenFlow switch is the sum of the number of packets which are sent from its switch and received by the switch.

B. *Results and Considerations*

- Joining of nodes

A node joined in the P2P streaming network which already includes a server and 25 clients (Figure 9) every 10 seconds. 5 new nodes joined the network in total. As a result, a P2P streaming network is reconfigured to be balanced (Figure 10).

Figure 11 compares the amount of segments which are sent from the server and an average of the amount of segments

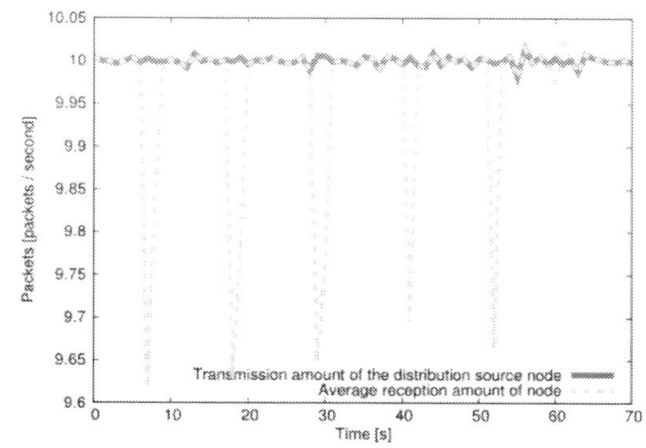

Figure 11. Comparison of the amount of segments which are sent from the server and received by the clients

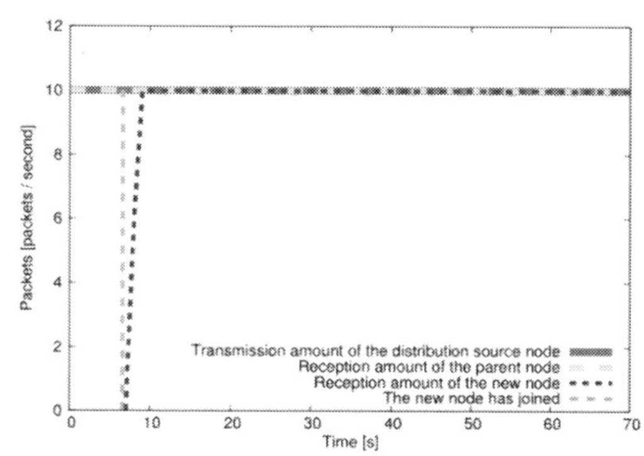

Figure 12. Comparison of the amount of segments which are sent from the server and received by the new node and its parent node

which are received by the clients when 5 nodes join the P2P streaming network. These values are equal in general. However, it is not equal occasionally due to delay such as to modify the flow and forward segments before a joining node begins to receive segments (Figure 12). The amount of segments which are received by its parent node is equal to the amount of segments which are sent from the server. Accordingly, a joining node causes the delay before receiving segments when it joins the P2P streaming network. However, other nodes do not suffer from this.

- Leaving of a node

A node whose depth from a server is 1 is left from the network which has the server and 30 clients (Figure 10). The unbalanced P2P streaming network topology is changed immediately after a node left (Figure 13). Its topology is reconfigured to be balanced by repeating the reconfiguration

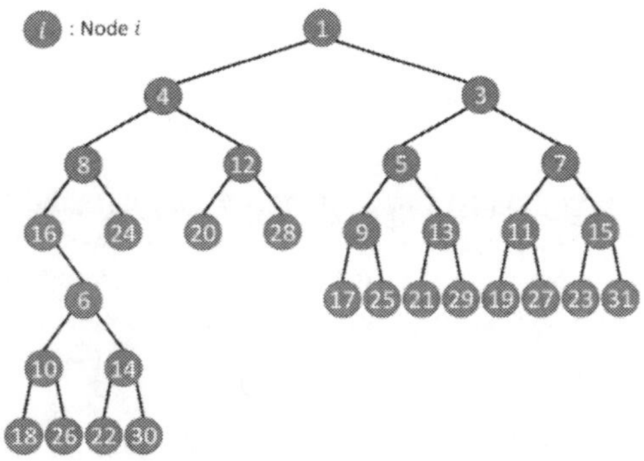

Figure 13. The P2P streaming network which is roconfigured immediately after a node left.

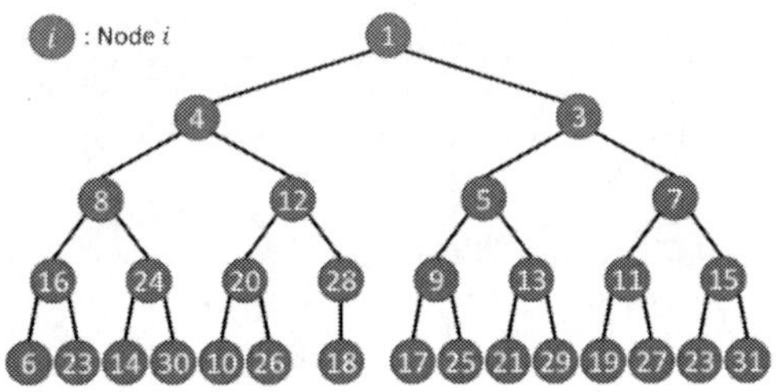

Figure 14. The balanced P2P streaming network after reconfiguration

TABLE II. Difference of the process according to the depth from a server

The depth from a server	1	2	3	4
The number of reconstruction	3	2	1	1
The number of nodes which reselect a parent node	8	4	2	0
The number of flows which are modified	12	6	3	1

procedure (Figure 14). Similar experiments were conducted repeatedly where a node in a different depth left. Then we examined the number of reconfiguration to make the P2P streaming network balanced, the number of nodes which reselect parent nodes and modified flows in the OpenFlow switches (Table II). If a node whose depth is d_n left, these values are as follows. $d = d_{min} - d_n$, where d_{min} is calculated using (1). The number of reconfiguration is d. The number of nodes which reselect parent nodes is c^d, where c is the number of child nodes which are connected to the nodes. Then, the number of flows which are modified in an OpenFlow switch is $c^d + c^{d+1}$.

Figure 15 compares the amount of segments which are sent from the server and an average of the amount of segments which are received by the clients when a node left from the P2P streaming network. These values are equal. Accordingly, other nodes do not suffer from any influence by a leaving node and reconfiguration of the P2P streaming network.

- Comparison of the P2P model and the C/S model

We performed similar experiment which the node joins or leaves to change the number of child nodes is unlimited. Figure 16 compares the amount of segments which are sent from the server and an average of the amount of segments which are received by the clients when 5 nodes join the P2P streaming network. If these values are not equal, a joining node causes delay as mentioned above. Figure 17 compares the amount of segments which are sent from the server and an average of the

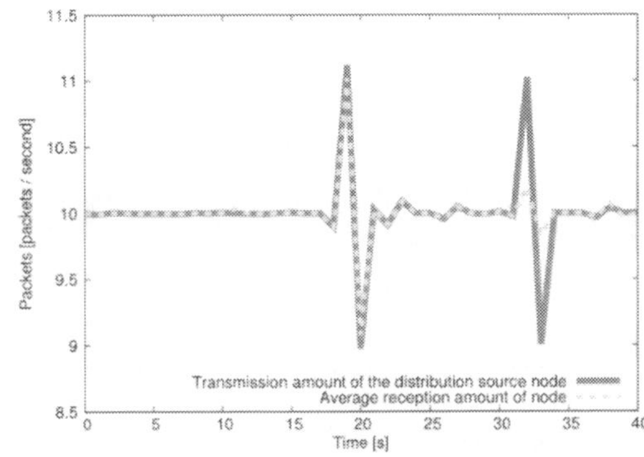

Figure 15. Comparison of the amount of segments which are sent from the server and received by the clients

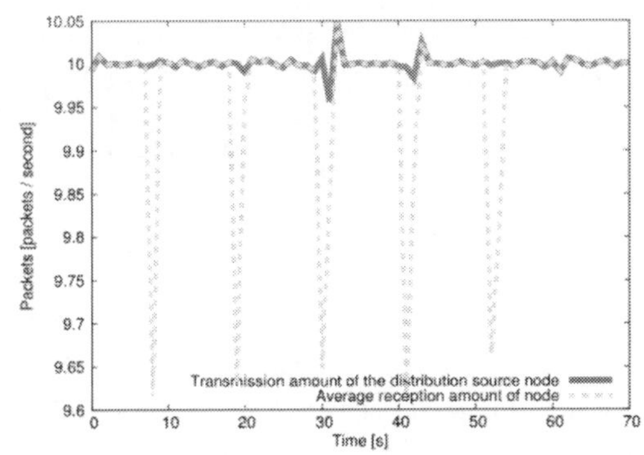

Figure 16. Comparison of the amount of segments which are sent from the server and received by the clients when 5 nodes join

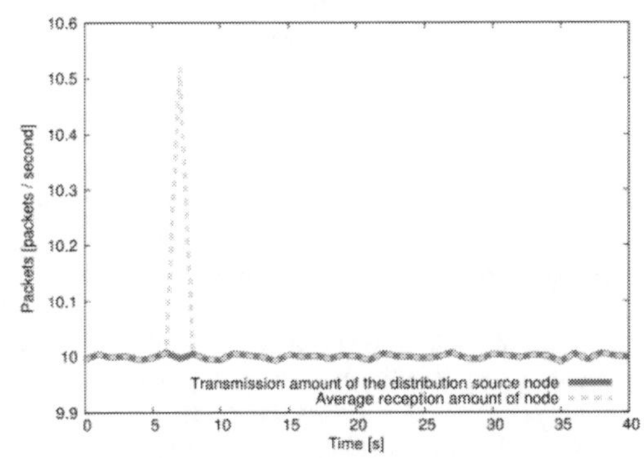

Figure 17. Comparisone of the amount of segments which are sent from the server and received by the clients when a node leaves

amount of segments which are received by the clients when a node leaves from the P2P streaming network. If the amount of the segments which are received by the clients is more than the amount of segments which are sent from the server, the leaving node receives segments after it left from the P2P streaming network. From the above, our proposal system would be able to perform also as the C/S model.

Figure 18 compares the P2P model and the C/S model when 5 nodes join. Similarly, Figure 19 compares the P2P model and the C/S model when a node leave. In the C/S model, the load of the OpneFlow switch which is next to the server is increased or decreased according to the number of clients.

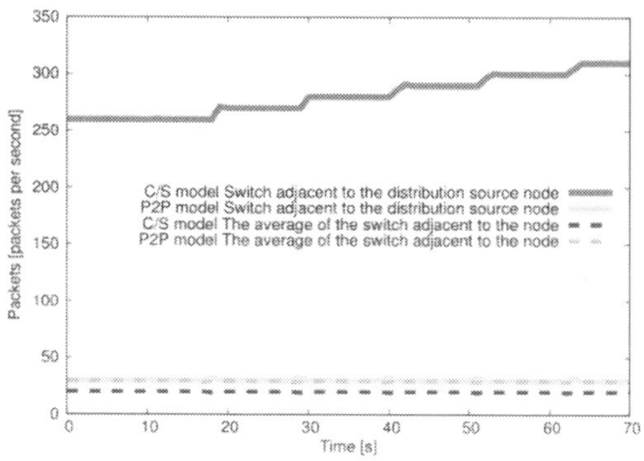

Figure 18. Comparison of the load of swithes when 5 nodes join

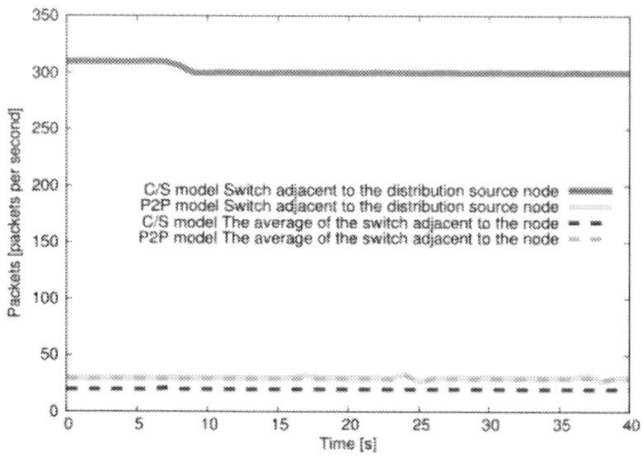

Figure 19. Comparison of the load of swithes when a node leave

On the other hand, in P2P model, the load of the OpneFlow switch which is next to the server is constant. Moreover, we can claim that the P2P model realized load balancing because the loads of all the OpenFlow switches are equal.

V. Conclusion and Future Work

In this paper, we proposed a method which the controller controls routing of the P2P streaming network. In our proposal, the controller reconfigures the P2P streaming network topology when a node joins or leaves. The proposal uses OpenFlow, and can reconfigure more flexibly and dynamically than the implementation which does not use OpenFlow. We conducted experiments using Trema in order to confirm the effectiveness of our proposal. As a result, a node causes delay before receiving segments. However, the node receives all segments.

The disadvantages of our proposal are as below. First, the wrong P2P streaming network topology may be configured due to complex control packets. Next, if OpenFlow switches and non-OpenFlow switches are mixed, the node which has a non-OpenFlow switch should be a leaf node. We will solve these disadvantages.

At last, we describe future works.

- In this paper, we performed experiments using test packets of Trema instead of segments. Therefore, we need to confirm the behavior of the server, clients and OpenFlow switches when segments are forwarded using streaming protocol, such as HTTP Live Streaming [11].
- In OpenFlow, network devices are controlled by the controller in a centralized manner. However, it is difficult to apply OpenFlow to a large network such as the Internet currently. Accordingly, if OpenFlow is applied to the P2P streaming network, the following methods may be needed. First, a virtual switch would be prepared on each host which joins the P2P streaming network. Next, an overlay network is configured using these switches. Lastly, the controller controls these virtual switches.

References

[1] K. Ono, A. Zhygmanovskyi, N. Matsumoto, and N. Yoshida, "Resilient Live-Streaming with Dynamic Reconfiguration of P2P Networks," EMERGING 2014, The Sixth International Conference on Emerging Network Intelligence, 2014, pp. 6–11.

[2] S. Jain, et al., "B4: Experience with a globally-deployed software defined WAN," ACM SIGCOMM Comp. Comm. Review. Vol. 43. No. 4. ACM, 2013, pp. 3–14.

[3] B. A. A Nunes, M. Mendonca, X. Nguyenm, K. Obraczka, and T. Turletti, "A survey of software-defined networking: Past, present, and future of programmable networks," Comm. Surveys & Tutorials, IEEE, 16.3, 2014, pp. 1617–1634.

[4] N. McKeown et al.,"OpenFlow: Enabling Innovation in Campus Networks," ACM SIGCOMM Comp. Comm. Review 38.2 pp. 69-74, 2008.

[5] I. Trajikovska, P. Aeschimann, C. Marti, T. M. Bohnert, and J. Salvachtia, "SDN enabled QoS provision for online streaming services in residential ISP networks," Proc. Consumer Electronics-Taiwan IEEE Int. Conf., 2014, pp. 33–34.

[6] O. M. M. Othman and K. Okamura, "On Demand Content Anycasting to Enhance Content Server Using P2P Network," IEICE TRANS. on Info. and Sys., 2012, pp. 514–522.

[7] T. Akiyama, K. Iida, J. Zhang, and Y. Shiraishi, "Proposal for a New Generation SDN-Aware Pub/Sub Environment," Proc. 13th Int. Conf. on Net., 2014, pp. 210–214.

[8] T. Akiyama, Y. Kawai, Y. Teranishi, R. Bannno, and K. Iida, "SAPS: Software Defined Network Aware Pub/Sub – A Design of the Hybrid Architecture Utilizing Distributed and Centralized Multicast," Proc. Comp. Software and App. Conf. on IEEE 39th Annual, 2015, pp. 361–366.

[9] Y. Nakagawa, K. Hyoudou, and T. Shimizu, "A management method of IP multicast in overlay networks using openflow." Proc. 1st workshop on Hot topics in software defined networks, ACM, 2012, pp. 91–96.

[10] Trema, http://trema.github.io/trema/ [retrieved: March, 2016]

[11] HTTP Live Streaming, https://developer.apple.com/streaming/ [retrieved: March, 2016]

Name-Based Dynamic Routing in Ad-Hoc Networks

Hayato Suzuki, Noriko Matsumoto, Norihiko Yoshida
Graduate School of Science and Engineering
Saitama University
Saitama, Japan
Emails: {suzuki, noriko, yoshida}@ss.ics.saitama-u.ac.jp

Abstract—**The ad-hoc network technology is an indispensable infrastructure for the digital society, and an IP-based routing scheme for ad-hoc networks is important to integrate with the Internet. Ad-hoc networks can work in the same routing scheme as the Internet using AutoIP and mDNS. However, they cause excessive power consumption and delay before establishing communication. In order to address these issues, we propose a new method of name-based dynamic routing based on Intentional Naming System (INS) and InterPlanetary Network (IPN.) In this paper, we show that our routing scheme is feasible through some simulation experiments.**

Keywords—ad-hoc networks; routing; naming

I. Introduction

Wireless mobile communication devices, such as laptops or smartphones, are increasingly used in every day communication. Recently, ad-hoc networks, which are composed of such devices, called nodes, have attracted increased attention [1]. In ad-hoc networks, communication between nodes is realized by multihop message forwarding, so that it does not require any infrastructure such as base stations or access points. For this reason, ad-hoc communication is used in various fields. The most important feature of ad-hoc networks is their dynamic topology. Most nodes have mobility and a possibility of disconnection because of their battery shortage, so the network topology changes continuously. Therefore, ad-hoc networks have problems in routing schemes and power consumption.

Ad-hoc networks can work in the same routing scheme as the Internet using AutoIP and multicast DNS (mDNS) [2]. AutoIP assigns an IP address to a node automatically, and mDNS realizes name resolution without Domain Name System (DNS). Using AutoIP, each node obtains an IP address when joining the ad-hoc network. Using mDNS, when each node communicates with each other, it requests name resolution to all nodes in the network as follows:

1) A node sends a request packet containing a name to be resolved to all the other nodes in the network.
2) The destination node sends back its IP address to the requesting node, when it receives the packet whose name matches its own.
3) The requesting node communicates with the destination node using the IP address obtained in 2.

However, this method causes some problems:

- Increase of traffic in the network,
- Delay before establishing communication,
- Excessive power consumption.

These problems are caused by the routing scheme that many packets are exchanged among the requesting node and the other nodes.

In order to address these issues, we propose a new scheme, name-based dynamic routing. Our proposal applies Intentional Naming System (INS), which was proposed for the Internet, and realizes routing without resolving a name of a node to its IP address. Additionally, in order to realize the dynamically adaptive routing corresponding to the change of network topology, we use the step-by-step routing scheme proposed in InterPlanetary Network (IPN). It does not require any name resolution. Our proposal aims at realizing reduction of traffic load and suppression of power consumption, as well as avoidance of delay before establishing communication.

Over time, there have been various naming schemes proposed for Wireless Sensor Networks (WSNs,) Delay Tolerant Networks (DTNs,) and so on. For example, Amoretti et al. [3] proposed a method based on tree-structured networks for WSNs. Bovet et al. [4] proposed a name resolution method for networks in smart buildings. Schildt et al. [5] proposed a name-based routing method based on Chord [6] for DTNs. Our routing scheme focuses on small ad-hoc networks, and this is a preliminary study to realize a routing scheme which replaces AutoIP and mDNS in a dynamic manner.

We built a simulator which makes virtual ad-hoc networks on a single computer, and we verified the effectiveness of our proposal through some experiments. The results confirmed that our name-based dynamic routing could work on ad-hoc networks, and our routing scheme reduced power consumption and delay.

This paper is organized as follows: we summarize some related works in Section 2. In Section 3, we describe our proposed method. Subsequently, we evaluate our method through some simulation experiments in Section 4. Finally, Section 5 contains some concluding remarks and future work.

II. Related Work

In this section, we summarize some related works: INS and the routing scheme in IPN.

A. INS

INS is a resource discovery and service location system for dynamic and mobile networks of devices and computers [7]. Communication between nodes in INS is realized using a name of service without performing name resolution.

INS realizes routing without name resolution by introducing nodes called Intentional Name Resolvers (INRs) in a

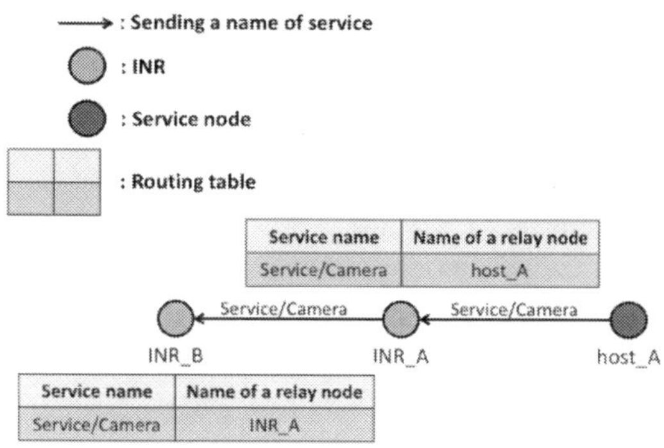

Figure 1. Registration of service.

network. INRs manage a routing table in which the following contents are kept.

- The name of service (called service name)
- The name of a relay node

In this manner, INS realizes suppression of traffic on a network and reduction of delay before establishing communication. This is because there is no need of resolving names by communicating with name resolution nodes such as DNS.

INS is implemented in two processes called registration of service and searching of service. The registration of service means that INRs update their routing tables, and the searching of service means that any nodes searches a node which provides service.

Here we describe registration of service. The following operation is repeatedly performed (Figure 1).

1) Any node which provides service (called a service node) sends a service name to a near INR.
2) Upon receiving the above message, the INR writes the service name and a name of a relay node in its routing table.
3) The INR transfers the name information to neighboring INRs.

In this manner, the INRs manage routing information for reaching any node which provides service.

Next, we describe searching of service. Communicating between a requesting node and a service node is realized by the request node simply sending a service name to any INR. Searching of service has a variety of features, as follows, that are different from the ones for the Internet.

- No node must convert a name of a destination node to an IP address.
- Relay nodes do not tell location information of the service node to the requesting node.

In this manner, INS eliminates the use of IP addresses.

B. Routing scheme in IPN

IPN aimed at implementing reliable communication between a node on a planet and a node on another planet through satellites. The issue was that it takes an enormous amount of time to perform communication, and the destination node often moves elsewhere during communication. Moreover, delay before establishing communication causes communication failure. Therefore, a step-by-step routing scheme using a hierarchical naming was introduced in order to address the issue [8].

TABLE I. Example of a routing table managed by each node.

Name of a destination node	Name of a relay node
Earth, host_A	host_A
Earth, host_B	host_B
Mars	host_C

A hierarchical name is assigned to each node and the name is a combination of two names as follows.

- *Region* : the name of a range in which node exists.
- *Region-specific-part* : the name which has been given to a node from the beginning.

For example, the name "Earth, host_A" is assigned to the node if the node has the name "host_A" and is placed on the Earth.

Now we describe the step-by-step routing scheme. Each node has a routing table as shown in Table I. First, a node sends a request packet toward a destination node. When a relay node receives the packet, the node checks the *region* of the destination node. On this step, there can be two scenarios: one is the case in which the *region* of the destination node is the same as the *region* where the requesting node is placed, and the other is the case in which the *region* of the destination node is different from the *region* where the requesting node is placed.

1) The first case: The node checks the *region-specific-part* of the destination node, and sends the packet to a relay node.

2) The second case: The node checks only the *region* of the destination node and sends the packet to a relay node. If the packet reaches the *region* where the destination node is placed, the node that received the packet checks the *region-specific-part* of the destination node, and sends the packet to a relay node.

In this way, each node sends a packet to a relay node closer to a destination node gradually. The routing scheme in IPN overcomes failures in the communication in an ever-changing and unreliable network.

III. PROPOSED METHOD

As described in Section I, this study introduces INS-based name-based dynamic routing, and also IPN-based step-by-step name-based routing to ad-hoc networks. More specifically, we perform registration of service and searching of service similar to INS, and step-by-step routing similar to IPN. This is to handle dynamic changes of a network topology and to improve communication availability.

However, it is difficult to apply the INS scheme to ad-hoc networks as they are. Most nodes in ad-hoc networks have mobility, so it is difficult to arrange stable nodes to behave as INRs. Therefore, it is necessary to select nodes to manage a routing table in place of INRs. Moreover, it is necessary to configure *regions* on a network and each node must belong to any *region*. Below is our proposal to address the above two issues.

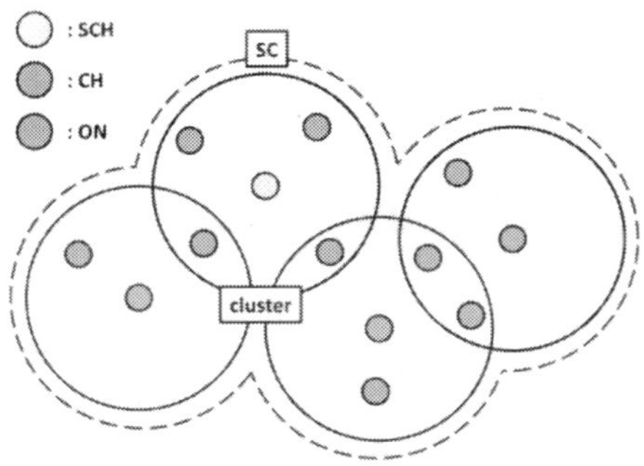

Figure 2. Example of a SC and a cluster.

TABLE II. Example of a routing table managed by each CH.

Name of a destination node	Name of a relay node
SC_A/Cluster_A/host_A	host_A
SC_A/Cluster_A/host_B	host_B
SC_A/Cluster_B	host_C
SC_B	host_D

A. Selection of nodes which manage a routing table in place of INRs

We configure clusters and super-clusters (SCs), which are aggregations of some clusters shown in Figure 2. Cluster-Heads (CHs) and SC-Heads (SCHs) manage routing tables respectively: a CH is a representative of a cluster, and an SCH is a representative of an SC. Routing information as below is written in a routing table. Example of a routing table is shown in Table II.

1) Information on a relay node to reach another cluster or another SC
2) Information on a relay node to reach another node belonging to the same cluster

B. Setting of regions

The name of each *region* is the name of a cluster or an SC. The name of each node is concatenation of "the name of its SC, the name of its cluster, and the name of itself".

C. Participation in a region

Participation of each node except for SCHs in any *regions* is realized with the following procedure (Figure 3).

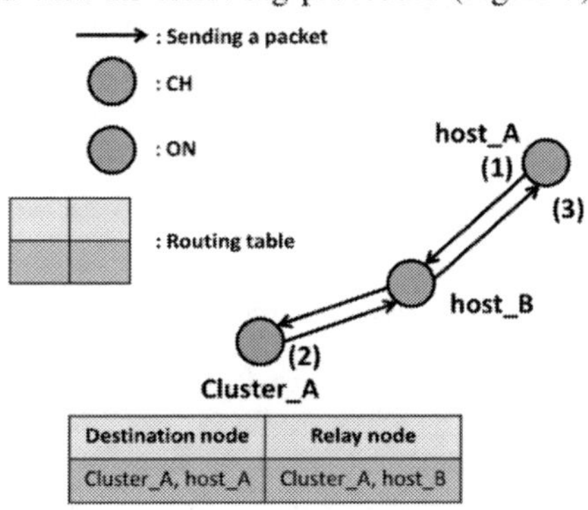

Figure 3. Participation in a *region* and creation of a routing table.

1) A node sends a packet to neighboring nodes when the node joins the network.
2) When a CH or an SCH receives the packet, it replies with a packet to the request node and updates its routing table.
3) The requesting node joins the *region* when the node receives the reply packet, and the node is named based on the name of the *region* where the node joins.

D. Searching a node

When a node communicates with a destination node, the node sends a packet called query packet to its CH or SCH. The CH or SCH which receives the query packet checks its routing table and transfers the packet to a relay node.

Something to be investigated is that the difference of contents in the routing tables affects the searching cost. Therefore, we consider four candidates based on the difference of contents and compare the four. After the comparative experiments, we will recommend one approach which achieves the best result.

E. Four candidates

We describe contents written in the routing table in detail, and four method candidates searching a node.

1) First approach: This is the simplest approach which does not consider congestion. This approach is designed so that routing information in the table is minimal.

In particular, SCHs manage two pieces of routing information: one is information on a relay node to reach each cluster in the same SC, and the other is information on a relay node to reach other SCs. CHs manage routing information on a relay node to reach a SCH of the SC it belongs. Nodes except for the CHs and SCHs, which are called ordinary nodes (ONs,)

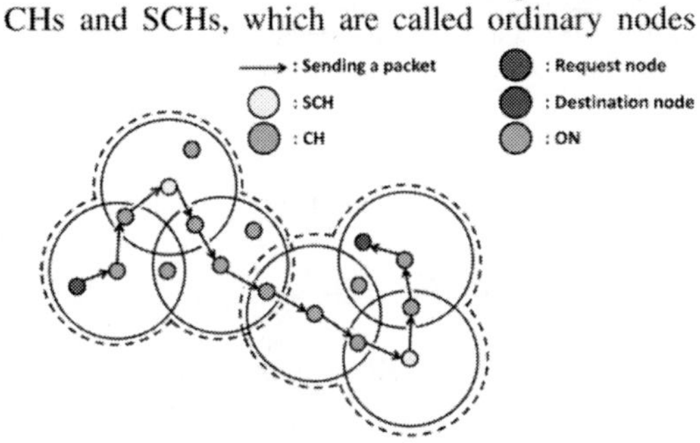

Figure 4. A communication path in the first approach.

Require: ON, CH, SCH, DEST
while DEST does not receive the packet **do**
  if ON receives the packet **then**
    ON sends the packet to CH or SCH
  else if CH receives the packet **then**
    if DEST belongs to the CH's cluster **then**
      CH sends the packet to DEST
    else
      CH sends the packet to the relay node to reach SCH
    end if
  else if SCH receives the packet **then**
    SCH sends the packet to the relay node to reach DEST
  end if
end while

Figure 5. Pseudo code of the first approach

have routing information to reach the CH of the cluster they belong.

In this approach, searching a node is performed as shown in Figure 4 and 5. Communication between SCs or clusters is realized via SCHs.

2) Second approach: This is an approach which aims at suppressing congestion of the network, although it increases load of the CHs. The amount of routing information in the table is larger than the one in the first approach. In particular, the CHs manage routing information on a relay node to reach each cluster in its SC in addition to the CHs' in the first approach.

In this approach, searching a node is performed as shown in Figure 6 and 7. Communication between clusters in the same SC is realized without the SCHs.

3) Third approach: This is an approach which aims an suppressing congestion of the network by removing distinction between SCHs and CHs. In particular, CHs manage routing information on a relay node to reach each SC in addition to CHs' in the second approach. Therefore, routing information managed by SCHs and CHs are the same.

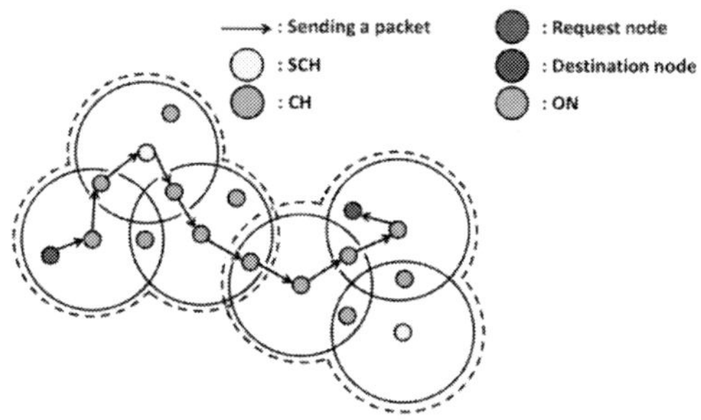

Figure 6. A communication path in the second approach.

```
Require: ON, CH, SCH, DEST
  while DEST does not receive the packet do
    if ON receives the packet then
      ON sends the packet to CH or SCH
    else if CH receives the packet then
      if DEST belongs to the CH's cluster then
        CH sends the packet to DEST
      else if DEST and CH belong to same SC then
        CH sends the packet to the relay node to reach DEST
      else
        CH sends the packet to the relay node to reach SCH
      end if
    else if SCH receives the packet then
      SCH sends the packet to the relay node to reach DEST
    end if
  end while
```

Figure 7. Pseudo code of the second approach

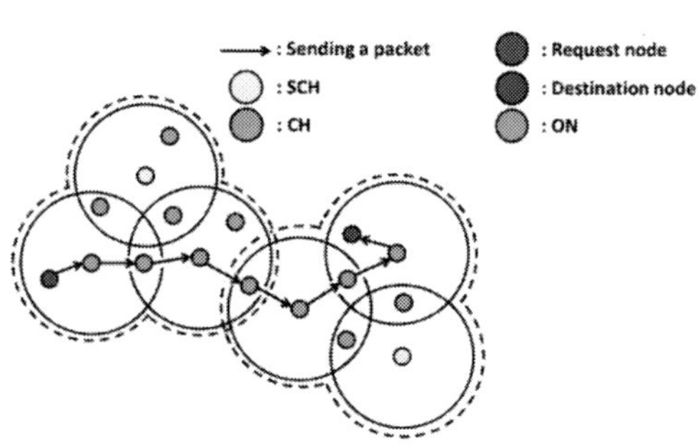

Figure 8. A communication path in the third approach.

```
Require: ON, CH, SCH, DEST
  while DEST does not receive the packet do
    if ON receives the packet then
      ON sends the packet to CH or SCH
    else if CH or SCH receives the packet then
      if DEST and the CH (SCH) belong to the same cluster then
        CH (SCH) sends the packet to DEST
      else
        CH (SCH) sends the packet to the relay node to reach DEST
      end if
    end if
  end while
```

Figure 9. Pseudo code of the third approach

In this approach, searching a node is performed as shown in Figure 8 and 9. Communication between SCs is realized without SCHs.

4) Fourth approach: This is an approach which aims at suppressing congestion of the network by adding routing information managed by ONs.

In ad-hoc networks, broadcast communication is performed when a node communicates to any node. In short, each node sends a packet to all nodes which exist in its wireless communication range and all nodes except for a relay node discard the packet. Therefore, ONs can obtain routing information towards neighboring ONs by these packets.

In this approach, searching a node is performed as shown in Figure 10 and 11. Communication between a node and a

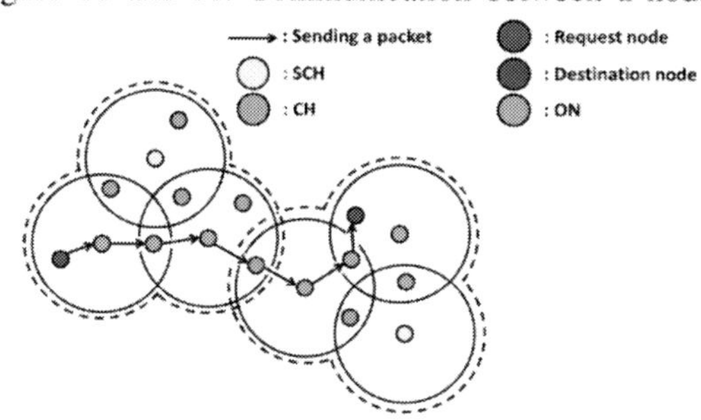

Figure 10. A communication path in the fourth approach.

```
Require: ON, CH, SCH, DEST
  while DEST does not receive the packet do
    if ON receives the packet then
      if ON has a routing information to reach DEST then
        ON sends the packet to DEST
      else
        ON sends the packet to CH or SCH
      end if
    else if CH or SCH receives the packet then
      if DEST and the CH (SCH) belong to the same cluster then
        CH (SCH) sends the packet to DEST
      else
        CH (SCH) sends the packet to the relay node to reach DEST
      end if
    end if
  end while
```

Figure 11. Pseudo code of the fourth approach

destination node is realized without the CH.

F. Loop elimination

Our routing scheme takes measures to loop of packets. Each packet has a unique identifier (ID), and if a node receives the packet with the same ID twice, the node discards the second one.

IV. EVALUATION

We implemented a simulator in Java and built a virtual ad-hoc network on a single computer. In simulation-based experiments, we examined and compared the effectiveness of the four method candidates and mDNS.

- The average number of packets which each node processes
- The average number of hops
- The success rate of searching

The environment of the simulation is shown in Table III.

In mDNS, the following operation is repeatedly performed. When the simulator creates 300 query packets, the simulation is completed.

1) 50 query packets are created, and each packet is given to a node respectively.
2) Each node sends the query packet $P1$ toward a destination node.
3) When the destination node receives $P1$, the node replies the packet $R1$ to the request node.
4) When the request node receives $R1$, the node sends a packet $P2$ to the destination node again.
5) When the destination node receives $P2$, the node replies the packet $R2$ to the request node.
6) When all packets on the network are processed, each node moves elsewhere.

In the proposed method, the following operation is repeatedly performed in a single simulation. When the simulator creates 300 packets, the simulation is completed.

1) CHs and SCHs are selected at random out of nodes, and clusters and SCs are formed in the network. (This operation is performed only once in one simulation.)
2) 50 query packets are created, and each packet is given to a node respectively.
3) Each node sends the query packet $P1$ toward a destination node.
4) When the destination node receives $P1$, the node replies the packet $R1$ to the request node.
5) When all packets on the network are processed, each node moves elsewhere. (And CHs and SCHs send control messages to update their routing tables.)

TABLE III. Environment of the simulation

Parameter	Value
Number of nodes	500
Number of query packets	300
Time to live of a query packet	20
Communication range	150
Experimental area	1000*1000
Number of the simulation	10

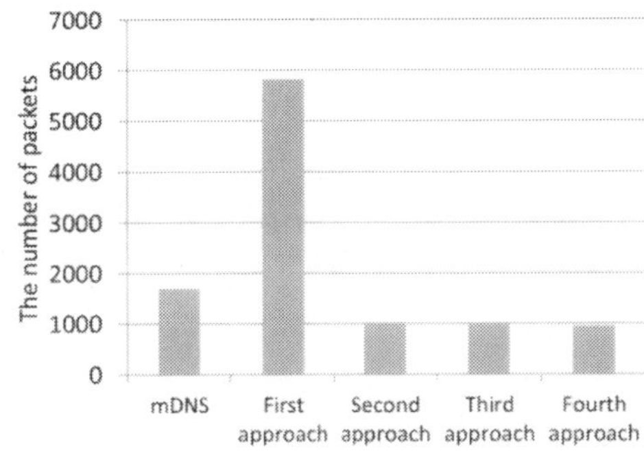

Figure 12. The the average number of packets which each node has processed.

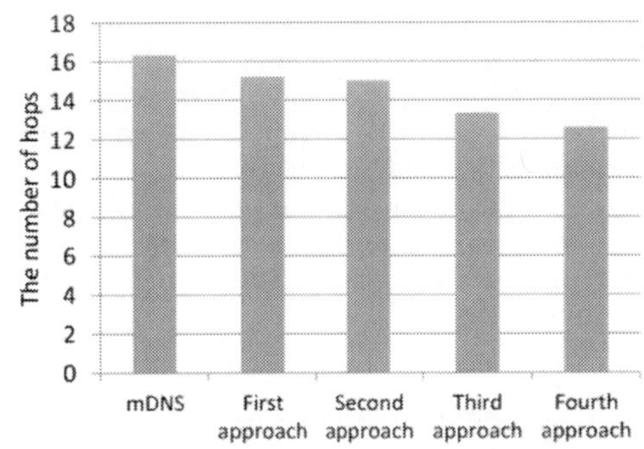

Figure 13. The average number of hops.

A. The average number of packets which each node processes

The result of the experiment is shown in Figure 12. The proposed approaches, except for the first approach, improved the number of packets compared to mDNS. In the first approach, each node must send a query packet to SCHs many times. We consider that the number of packets increases consequently. Therefore, the candidate approaches except for the first one will realize suppression of traffic in the network and power consumption.

B. The average of number of hops

The result of the experiment is shown in Figure 13. All the proposed method improved the number of hops compared to mDNS. In mDNS, each node must send a packet to a destination node twice. However, in the proposed method, each node must send a packet to a destination node only once. We consider that the number of hops decreases consequently. Therefore, all the proposed method will realize suppression of delay before establishing communication.

C. The success rate of searching

The success rate of searching is expressed in the following equation.

The success rate of searching $= \frac{NUM_{RP}}{NUM_{SP}} * 100$

NUM_{RP} represents the number of nodes which receive a packet from a destination node, and NUM_{SP} represents the number of nodes which sent a query packet. The result of the experiment is shown in Figure 14. The success rate of searching of the proposed methods is worse than mDNS. We consider that some clusters may be isolated to each other in the experiment.

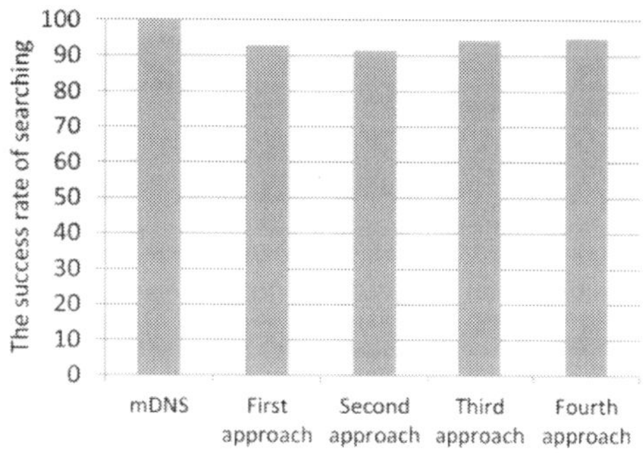

Figure 14. The success rate of searching.

V. CONCLUSION AND FUTURE WORK

Ad-hoc networks can use the same routing scheme as the Internet with such technologies as AutoIP and mDNS. However, using these technologies will cause delay before establishing communication and excessive power consumption. In this study, we aimed at introducing name-based dynamic routing based INS and IPN in order to address these issues. The result of the experiment proves that name-based dynamic routing can be realized on ad-hoc networks. It is also confirmed that our routing scheme, especially the fourth approach, can achieve the best result.

Issues to address in further studies are as follows.

1. Reselection of CHs and SCHs

CHs and SCHs consume more power than ONs because these nodes often become a relay node. Moreover, in a real world network, CHs or SCHs may be disconnected from the network due to movement or failure. Therefore, it is necessary to add a mechanism to reselect them to the proposed method.

2. Measures to duplication of a node name

In this study, we assume that each node is assigned a unique name. However, the name of any node may conflicte to each other in a real network. Therefore, it is necessary to take measures on duplication of the node name.

3. Selection of the routing scheme

In this study, it is revealed that the fourth approach is better than the other approaches. However, the size of a routing table managed by each node in the fourth approach is larger than the other's. The fourth approach can not be realized if the performance of each node on the network is poor. Therefore, it is necessary to select one of the four proposed approaches based on the performance of each node.

4. Application to Content Centric Networking

Recently, a content-oriented architecture has attracted increased attentions for a next-generation Internet [9]. Especially, Content Centric Networking (CCN) [10], which realizes routing using the name of contents only, is expected to solve some problems of the current Internet. We are now investigating relevance and applicability of our routing scheme to such architectures.

REFERENCES

[1] C. K. Toh, "Ad-hoc mobile wireless network —protocol and system—", Kyoritsu Publisher, 2003.

[2] Multicast DNS, http://www.multicastdns.org/, 2016.

[3] M. Amoretti, O. Alphand, G. Ferrari, F. Rousseau, and A. Duda, "DINAS: a DIstributed NAming Service for All-IP Wireless Sensor Networks", Proceedings IEEE Wireless Communications and Networking Conference, 2014, pp. 2781–2786.

[4] G. Bovet and J. Hennebert, "A Distributed Web-based Naming System for Smart Buildings", Proceedings 2014 IEEE 15th International Symposium on a WoWMoM, 2014, pp. 1–6.

[5] S. Schildt, W-B. Pottner, O. Ohneiser, and L. Wolf, "NASDI - Naming and Service Discovery for DTNs in Internet Backbones", Proceedings Mobilware 5th International Conference, 2012, pp. 108–121.

[6] I. Stoica, R. Morris, D. Liben-Nowell, D. R. Karger, M. F. Kaashoek, F. Dabek, and H. C. Balakrishnan, "Chord: A Scalable Peer-to-peer Lookup Service for Internet Applications", Proceedings of the 2001 Conference on Applications, Technologies, Architectures, and Protocols for Computer Communications, 2001, pp. 149–160.

[7] W. A. Winoto, E. Schwartz, H. Balakrishnan, and J. Lilley, "The design and implementation of an intentional naming system", 17th ACM Symposium on Operating Systems Principles, 1999, pp. 186–201.

[8] L. Clare and S. Burleigh, "Endpoint Naming for Space Delay / Disruption Tolerant Networking", Aerospace Conference, 2010, pp. 1–10.

[9] A. A. Barakabitze, T. Xiaoheng, and G. Tan, "A Survey on Naming, Name Resolution and Data Routing in Information Centric Networking (ICN)", International Journal of Advanced Research in Computer and Communication Engineering, 2014, pp. 8322–8330.

[10] V. Jacobson, D.K. Smetters, J.D. Thornton, M.F. Plasee, N. Briggs, and R. Braynard, "Networking named content", Proceedings of the 5th ACM Int. Conf. on Emerging Networking Experiments and Technologies, 2009, pp. 1–12.

An Approach to the Modeling of the P2P Streaming Network Based on Peers' Geolocation and Activity

Yuliya Gaidamaka, Ivan Vasiliev,
Konstantin Samouylov
Applied Probability and Informatics Department
Peoples' Friendship University of Russia
Moscow, Russia
E-mail: ygaidamaka@sci.pfu.edu.ru, iuvasiliev@gmail.com,
ksam@sci.pfu.edu.ru

Sergey Shorgin
Institute of Informatics Problems,
Federal Research Center
"Computer Science and Control"
of the Russian Academy of Sciences
Moscow, Russia
E-mail: sshorgin@ipiran.ru

Abstract— **In this paper, an approach to the simulation of peer-to-peer (P2P) live streaming network is presented. The simulation model considers peers' geolocation and their daily activity, time lags between the video server and a peer, lags between peers, collisions, and three types of selection strategies: neighbor selection strategy, peer selection strategy and chunk selection strategy. Geolocation is considered as distribution of users by time zones and the users' daily activity is defined as the distribution of the number of online users by the hour of the day. Initial data for the geolocation of users and their daily activity are taken from known Internet sources. The aim of this study is to show how the parameters of the geolocation and users' daily activity affect the performance of the network. To do this, we compare the download probability obtained analytically without geolocation and daily activity with the results of simulation. Preliminary numerical analysis carried out for the case of the Rarest First chunk selection strategy, shows difference in results of up to 30%.**

Keywords—P2P live streaming network; P2P tecnology; playback continuity; playback lags; positive analysis

I. INTRODUCTION

Peer-to-peer (P2P) technology is used by major service providers in the market of online TV, such as BBC iPlayer, Zattoo, PeerCast, Pulse, QQLive and many others [1][2]. A fairly complete overview on P2P technical aspects with an extensive list of references was done by Yue et al. [3]. One of the main advantages of P2P is high performance-cost ratio, that allows commercial companies to minimize the costs for technical equipment. Furthermore, P2P technology not only enables efficient use of network resources, but also reduces the load on the server that is the source of the video data. Thus, due to high load balancing, there is no need to install additional servers, as well as in the growth of network bandwidth to handle a large number of users. Other advantages of P2P technology are scalability and high network robustness: it gives an opportunity to have a trouble-free operation of at least one video server to provide services for all users at the acceptable level of Quality of Experience (QoE).

However, P2P networks also have disadvantages. The main shortcomings include insufficient level of security, relatively long start-up latency and data transmission delay, inter-peer playback lag, playback discontinuity. While information security is not required, the goal is to minimize the transmission delay, and hence lack of data on the network. To solve the optimization problem for these performance measures, mathematical models and simulators should be developed. Known mathematical and simulation models for streaming P2P-network pay much attention to investigation of the buffering mechanism [11][12][13][14][15][16] and usually take into account lags [7][10]. A lag means the delay of data transmission from the server to the user, as well as the data transmission delays between peers (inter-peer playback lag). These models allow to carry out a qualitative analysis of the key performance measures of video streaming P2P networks - the probability of playback continuity, that is the probability of watching video with no pauses, and the probability of chunk availability. In previous works [8][9][10] these models allowed to formulate and to obtain the solution of the optimization problems in a choice of the selection strategies [13][14] that are used in a network.

Each of the models in the aforementioned sources reflects one or more features of the analyzed network and enables to estimate and optimize the corresponding network parameters and strategies. For example, the problem is to estimate which chunk selection strategy is better: Rarest First, where a peer downloads the rarest chunk in the network, or Greedy, where a peer downloads the most popular chunk in the network, or Mixed strategy that combines these two strategies. Previously, [8][9][10] we build a stand-alone analytical model to select the optimal strategy. Having analyzed results, we have come to the conclusion that the Rarest First strategy is better if we want to increase probability of playback continuity, and the Greedy chunk selection strategy will most likely be used if we want to reduce the startup latency. Finally, it is better to use Mixture strategy in real networks, where both quality parameters, playback continuity and startup latency, are important to the users. Using a particular model, one can only examine how the behavior of peers in the network influence its target characteristics, but cannot evaluate what we get in real life when we measure these characteristics in a commercial P2P network. In order to get closer to reality and assess the adequacy of the individual models, to give at least the recommendations against some of the problems before they occur in a real P2P networks, we propose a new model that can help to avoid troubleshooting. The presented model takes into account the geographical location of each peer, remoteness of peers from the server and from each other and their daily activity. In contrast to recent results (see, i.e. [9][10]), in this paper, the problem is solved taking into account the distribution of users across time zones.

Previously, we have studied various models of streaming P2P networks that have focused on the study of the optimal downloading strategy with the criterion of maximizing the probability of playback continuity of the video stream [9][10]. Then, the model was modified to take into account the users' behavior by introducing the probability of arrival of new users, as well as the probability of their leaving the network. [10][12]. The negative effect of peers churns on playback continuity was observed and investigated. The analytical model [8][9] also gives the correct understanding of lags' impact on the network performance. Usually, it is believed that the lag affects only the shift of the data location in the buffers of different users. We have shown that there is at least one more important aspect of lags. It is that the remote user is unable to receive a chunk within a number of time slots and thus play the video stream continuously. Due to the problem complexity, each main feature of the P2P network was analyzed in the known models separately. In this study, we present an approach to simulation that allows to combine in a single model the basic aspects of functioning of the streaming P2P-networks.

This paper is organized as follows. In Section II, a simulation model of video data distribution in a P2P live streaming network with buffering mechanism, geolocation and daily peers' activity is proposed. Also, the detailed algorithm of chunk exchange between buffers of peers in P2P live streaming network is determined and the main performance measures are defined. In Section III, the numerical analysis and case study is performed. The conclusion of this paper is presented in Section IV.

II. SIMULATION MODEL

In this section, a simulation model of video data distribution in a P2P live streaming network with buffering mechanism is proposed. A previously developed model [12] was improved by taking in consideration buffer selection strategies [13][14], peers' geolocation [15] and activity [16]. In contrast to the previous model, in this paper, besides chunk selection strategy, two more strategies were considered - neighbor selection strategy and peer selection strategy. The choice of strategies has a significant effect on the P2P-network performance measures, including the probability of playback continuity; the probability of chunk availability; the probability of chunk selection, and also the probability of collision – a situation when a peer cannot download a chunk because the target peer does not have enough capacity for uploading. There are various definitions of collision in the P2P network. In the present model, it is considered that, in the case of collisions, the peer that requested the chunk will not receive it in the current time slot.

We consider the basic model of a P2P network with N users and a single server, transmitting only one video stream, which we developed in [12]. The process of video stream playback is divided into time slots, the length of each time slot corresponding to the playback time of one chunk. Each user has a buffer designed to accommodate $M+1$ chunks, where the buffer positions are numbered from 0 to M: 0-position is to store the freshest chunk just received from the server, the other m -positions, $m = 1,\dots,M-1$, are to store chunks, already received during the past time slots or that will be downloaded in the coming time slots. The buffer M-position is to store the oldest chunk that will be moved out from the buffer for playback during the next time slot. In Figure 1, a model of peer's buffer is illustrated. Thus, a state of n-th user is represented in the form of a vector $\boldsymbol{x}(n) = (x(n,0), x(n,1),\dots, x(n,M))$ where $x(n,m) = 1$ if the n-th peer has a chunk at the buffer's position m, and $x(n,m) = 0$ otherwise.

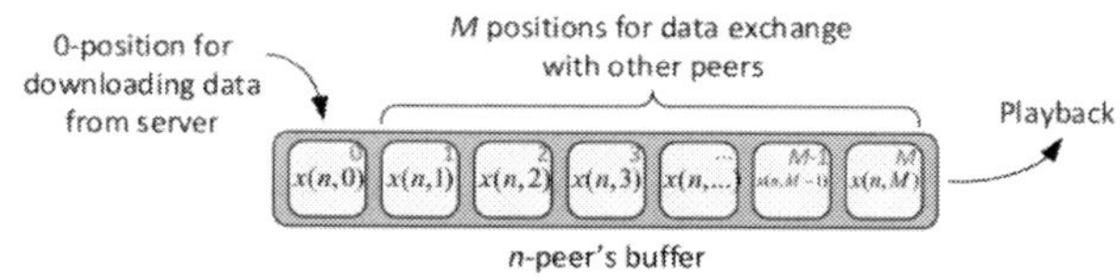

Figure 1. Model of n-th peer's buffer

Initially, a set of original parameters for each of N users is determined. They are upload U and download D rates, value of a lag LAG, and a set of neighbors **B** – the users from whom downloading is acceptable. A lag is the number of time slots between sending and receiving a chunk, thus, lag reflects the quantitative characteristics of a chunk delay. The algorithm works in such a way that, within a group, the user selects a neighbor to download data from using the criterion of minimum lag between the neighbors, regardless of their time zones distribution. Here is a simple example. Suppose that Peer 1 is in Poland and its neighbor, Peer 2, is located in Moscow, i.e. they are from different time zones. Suppose that Peer 3 is located in Angola, in the same time zone as Peer 1, and they are also neighbors. In this example, Peer 1 selects Peer 2 because they have the smallest lag, although Peer 2 is located in a different time zone. The set of neighbors for each user is formed according to the neighbor selection strategy depending on upload and download rates and lags. The neighbor selection is one of the target function parameters for optimization problems.

The algorithm of peers' actions at each time slot is described below according to the protocol of data distribution in P2P live streaming networks.

1) At the beginning of each time slot, the chunk at the M-position of the buffer is going to be played if it is present. Video data in the buffers shifts one position towards the end of the buffer. 0-position is nulled.
2) The server randomly chooses a peer and loads the newest chunk to 0-position of its buffer.
3) Each peer that was not chosen by the server selects a target peer from the set of neighbors to download a chunk during the current time slot. Target peer's selection is carried out in accordance to the peer selection strategy.

4) If collision takes place, the peer gets nothing during the current time slot. Otherwise, it selects a chunk to download according to the chunk selection strategy. If there is an available chunk to download, the loading starts. Otherwise, the peer gets no chunks during the current time slot.

It should be noticed that, in a real network, each peer is able to join the video stream and to disjoin it at any time slot of modelling and at any step of the algorithm, but we specify it by saying that the peers join or disjoin immediately after the first step of the algorithm.

The first difference from the previous model [12] is that in the presented model three strategies were considered: neighbor selection strategy, peer selection strategy, and chunk selection strategy. The second difference is that the presented model takes into account peers' geolocation [15] and twenty-four hours peers' activity [16].

The number of peers in the network is not constant. Every peer stays online a random amount of time each day, with the average value of $0<HO<86\,400=24h*60min*60s$:
$HoursOnline(n) \sim P(HO),\ n=1,\dots,N.$
Here, 86 400 is the number of time slots when modelling one astronomical day with one second as one time slot: $24h\times60min\times60s=86\,400$ time slots.

Let us introduce the parameter of users' activity, which reflects the behavior of peers in the streaming network:
$UserActivity(n) \sim RAND(1..UA),\ n=1,\dots,N;\ UA>1,$
where UA is the maximal number of peers joining the network within a day.

This parameter shows how often a peer joins the network, disjoins from it and switches channels. Here $UserActivity(n) = 1$ means that within a day n-th peer once came to a network and was online during the random time $HoursOnline(n)$ without switching to other channels. $UserActivity(n) = i, 1 \le i \le UA$, means that the n-th peer joined the network i times per day including switching channels, and each session lasted exactly $HoursOnline(n)/i$ time slots. Thus, e.g. if $UserActivity(n) = 100$ and $HoursOnline(n) = 15\,000$ the n-th peer per day during 15 000 time slots (seconds) carries out 100 sessions of 150 time slots each.

Figure 2 presents the distribution of the number of online peers versus the time of the day [15]. Here, the number of users of the mobile applications is depicted by the solid line. The dashed line represents the number of Internet users while the dotted line shows the number of TV watchers. To simplify the modeling process in this research, we investigate the influence of TV watchers' behavior only. The graph shows that the peak of the online users is between 6 p.m. and 12 a.m. while the minimum number of TV watchers is from 2 a.m. to 7 a.m.

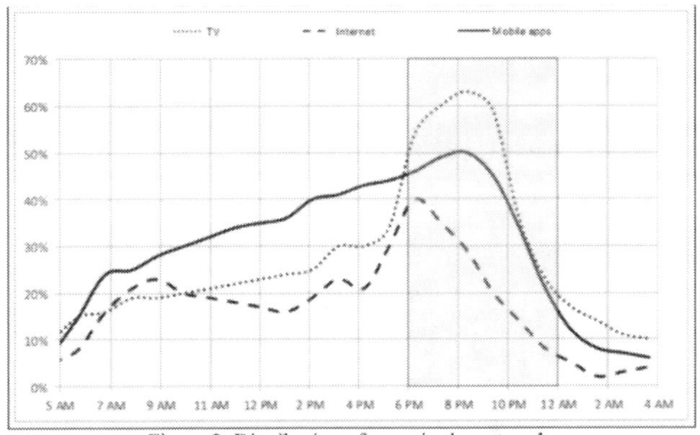

Figure 2. Distribution of users in the network

In accordance with the distribution in Figure 2, parameters $UserActivity = (UserActivity(n)), n = 1,\dots,N$, and $HoursOnline = (HoursOnline(n)), n = 1,\dots,N$, correspond to randomly generated intervals when peers are online. Let $TimeOnline = (TimeOnline(n,t)), n = 1,\dots,N;\ t = 1,\dots,T$, be a binary matrix of the $N \times T$ size, where T is the number of time slots in the simulation. The matrix indicates time slots when peers are online: $TimeOnline(n,t) = 1$ if the n-th peer at the t-th time slot is online, and $TimeOnline(n,t) = 0$ otherwise. Thus, if $TimeOnline(n,t) = 1$ and $TimeOnline(n,t+1) = 0$, then the n-th peer left the network at the $(t+1)$-th time slot, and $TimeOnline(n,t) = 0$ and $TimeOnline(n,t+1) = 1$ say that the n-th peer joined the network at the $(t+1)-th$ time slot.

Peers churns significantly influence the key performance measures. So, when a new peer joins the network it still has no data for exchange with other peers, but it uses other peers' resources to download content. Similarly, when a peer disjoins the network, it stops to participate in distribution of already downloaded video chunks. For a proper peers churns simulation, it is important to take into account the distribution of users by time zones. In this paper, the total of N peers in the network are divided in a random way across time zones according to the distribution shown in Figure 3 [16]. One can see that the majority of the users is located in -5, +1, and +8 time zones, which include the USA, Canada, Europe, and China - the most populated and technologically developed regions. In the model, splitting peers across time zones allows to reduce the probability of the global splashes corresponding to mass connections and disconnections of users.

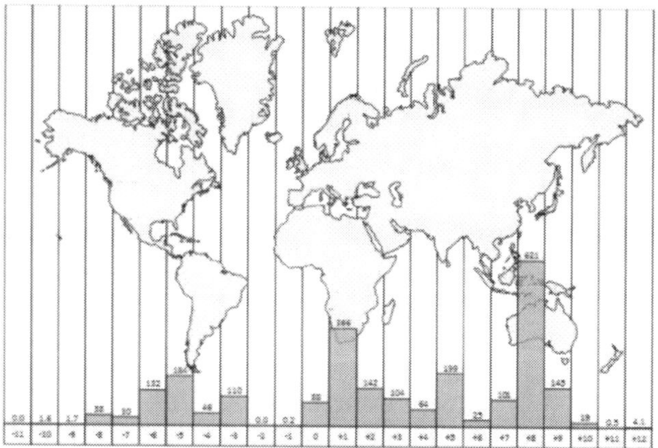

Figure 3. Distribution of users across the time zones

III. NUMERICAL ANALYSIS

In this paper, the aim of numerical analysis is to compare results of the models that do not consider distribution of users across time zones (we call it the basic model, [8][9][10]) to the results which are obtained by means of the model described above. We analyzed the network with $N = 300$ users and the size of the users' buffer $M = 40$. The time of modeling is $T = 1\,000\,000$ time slots, which corresponds to about 12 days. The basic model assumes values of lags equal to 0, 10, 20 between groups of neighbors. The Rarest First (RF) has been chosen as a chunk selection strategy, and neighbors, as well as the target user, were selected randomly.

As seen in Figures 4 and 5, the results of the simulation with splitting users across time zones (dashed line) qualitatively repeat the results of the basic model. The nature of the behavior of curves, including flexes in points of $m = 10$ and $m = 20$ is described in [9][10]. The probability of playback continuity for the model with time zones is much lower because the delivery of chunks takes, on average, more than one time slot. Note that, in Figure 4, value $p(40)$ corresponds to the probability of playback continuity. Numerical analysis shows that the basic model gives a very rough upper bound of the performance measures compared to the model with splitting users across time zones. On the other hand, the simulation model shows unsatisfactory (less than 70%) value of the probability of playback continuity. This means that it is necessary to use some other combinations of selection strategies, which will be the subject of further study. It is also necessary to explore a new way of peer's communication to improve the playback continuity, which is a key performance of the network.

IV. CONCLUSION AND FUTURE WORKS

We try to construct a model of a P2P streaming network, which is the most approximate to the reality. Preliminary numerical analysis showed that more research is necessary to find the optimal strategies; buyout will improve the quality of service parameters of streaming P2P-network. To do this, it is necessary to formulate the appropriate optimization problems, to find ways to solve them, even if numerical, and conduct computer experiments using the simulator described above. It is already clear that it is necessary to modify the strategies used in streaming P2P-network.

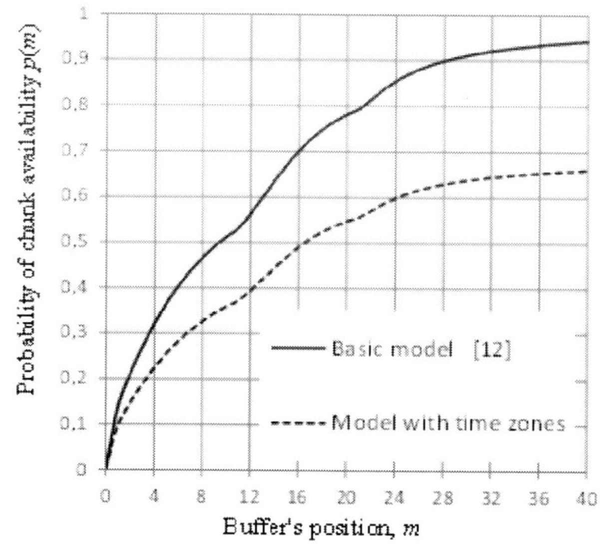

Figure 4. Probability of chunk availability at the buffer's positions. Value $p(40)$ corresponds to the probability of playback continuity.

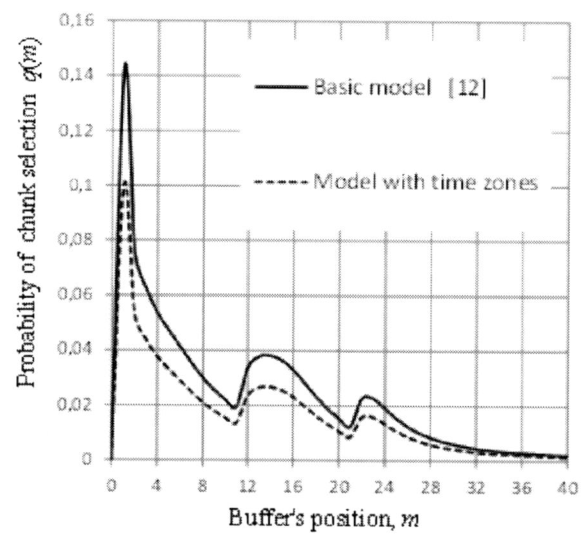

Figure 5. Probability of chunk selection to download at the buffer positions.

ACKNOWLEDGMENT

The reported study was partially supported by the RFBR, research project No. 14-07-00090.

REFERENCES

[1] X. Shen, H. Yu, J. Buford, and M. Akon, "Handbook of Peer-to-Peer Networking. Springer," pp. 1421, 2010.

[2] S.M. Thampi "A Review on P2P Video Streaming," arXiv preprint arXiv:1304.1235, 2013.

[3] G. Yue, N. Wei, J. Liu, X. Xiong, and L. Xie, "Survey on Scheduling Technologies of P2P Media Streaming," Journal of Networks, Vol. 6, No. 8, pp. 1129-1136, August 2011.

[4] F. Baccelli, F. Mathieu, and I. Norros, "Performance of P2P networks with spatial interactions of peers. Networks and Telecommunications Networks, Systems and Services, Distributed Computing," Equipes-Projets GANG, TREC, Centre de recherche INRIA Paris, Rapport de recherche, n°7713, pp. 1-23, August 2011.

[5] L. Ying, R Srikant, and S Shakkottai, "The Asymptotic Behavior of Minimum Buffer Size Requirements in Large P2P Streaming Networks", Information Theory and Applications Workshop (ITA), pp. 1-6, 2010.

[6] Y. Zhou, M. Dah, Chiu, and J. C. S. Lui, "A Simple Model for Analyzing P2P Streaming Protocols," Proc. of IEEE Int. Conf. IN Network Protocols (ICNP 2007), pp. 226-235, Oct. 19, 2007.

[7] Y. Zhao and H. Shen, "A simple analysis on P2P streaming with peer playback lags," Proc. of the 3rd IEEE Int. Conf. on Communication Software and Networks (ICCSN 2011), Xi'an, China, pp. 396-400, May 2011.

[8] A. Adamu, Yu. Gaidamaka, and A. Samuylov, "Discrete Markov Chain Model for Analyzing Probability Measures of P2P Streaming Network," Lecture Notes in Computer Science. Germany, Heidelberg: Springer. Vol. 6869, pp. 428-439, 2011.

[9] Yu. Gaidamaka and A. Samuylov, "Analytical Modeling of Playback Continuity in P2P Streaming Network with Latest First Download Strategy", Lecture Notes in Computer Science, Germany, Heidelberg, Springer, Vol. 8121, pp. 363-370, 2013.

[10] Yu. Gaidamaka, I. Vasiliev, A. Samuylov, K. Samouylov, and S. Shorgin. "Simulation of Buffering Mechanism for Peer-to-Peer Live Streaming Network with Collisions and Playback Lags", Proc. of the 13th Int. Conf. on Networks (ICN), Nice, France, pp. 86-91, 2014.

[11] N. Sluijs, T. Wauters, C. Develder, F. Turck, P. Demeester, B. Dhoedt, "Using topology information for quality-aware Peer-to-peer multy layer video streaming," Int. J. Commun. System, Published online:, DOI: 10.1002/dac.2919, January 2015.

[12] Z. Li, M.A. Kaafar, K. Salamatian, G. Xie "User Behavior Characterization of a Large-Scale Mobile live Streaming System," WWW 2015 Companion, Florence, Italy. ACM 978-1-4503-3473-0/15/05, May 2015.

[13] B. Fan, D. Andersen, M. Kaminsky, and K. Papagiannaki, "Balancing Throughput, Robustness, and In-Order Delivery in P2P VoD," In Proc. ACM CoNEXT, Dec. 2010.

[14] P. Romero, M.E. Bertinat, D. Padula, P. Rodr´ıguez-Bocca, and F.R. Amoza, "A cooperative model for multi-class peer-to-peer streaming networks," Proc. of the 1st Int. Conf. on Operations Research and Enterprise Systems (ICORES), pp. 274-282, 2012.

[15] How many internet users are there in your time zone, http://www.slideshare.net/pingdom/how-many-internet-users-are-there-in-your-time-zone [retrieved April 2016].

[16] F. Alan, "Study shows that in-app advertising is more effective than television or internet ads," http://www.phonearena.com/news/Study-shows-that-in-app-advertising-is-more-effective-than-television-or-internet-ads_id22556, [retrieved April 2016].

A Syntethic Measurement for Political Engagement of Spending:

Pilot study to measure performance of local government using Open Government Data

Lorenzo Gabrielli*§, Davide Guido†, Fosca Giannotti* and Luca Bastiani‡
*National Council of Research - ISTI
Knowledge Discovery and Data Mining Laboratory, Pisa, Italy
Email: {name.surname}@isti.cnr.it
† University of Pavia
Department of Public Health, Pavia, Italy
Email: davide.guido@unipv.it
‡National Council of Research - IFC
Epidemiology Section, Pisa, Italy
Email: luca.bastiani@ifc.cnr.it
§University of Pisa
Department of Information Engineering, Pisa, Italy
Email: lorenzo.gabrielli@for.unipi.it

***Abstract*—Can we predict the outcome of future elections? Many politicians wonder if they will be re-elected and often they rely on polls conducted on a small sample of the population. In this work, we propose a data-driven approach that, given the past expenditure of city mayors, considers what are the most important aspects that determine the re-election. Our empirical results show the emergence of a particular expenditure threshold: mayors who invest in current and capital expenditure over such threshold during the mandate are more likely to be re-elected, while those who invest differently are more likely not to be re-elected. The impact of this research is to provide a new analytical tool that objectively shows to a public administrator if his actions will lead to the re-election.**

***Keywords*–Open Data; eDemocracy; eGovernment; Citizen-Government eModels, Data Mining, Administrative elections.**

I. Introduction

The evaluation of the performance of public administration is a complex problem, for which the presence of Big Data and Open Data opens new scenarios. There are several works that, thanks to the digital traces left by all of us, studied the preferences of citizens in different economic and social areas [1] [2]. But, in the context of Public Administration, a new element to take into consideration is Open Data, in particular the data curated and made accessible by public administration. New data sources, in the field of political science, open up new scenarios for those who want to study the effectiveness of public administration in a data-driven approach.

As an alternative to the traditional surveys, several researchers have recently begun the use of social media such as Twitter to study the sentiment of voters before the election [3] [4]. On this aspect, other experiences led conflicting results, since users who use Twitter were not considered a representative sample [5]. The main limitation of this approach is that it is not applicable to small and medium realities. It is relatively easy to collect information on the voters' opinions about a national politician by means of social networks, but it is more difficult to do the same for all the mayors of each municipality.

In recent years, many governments began issuing the data as Open Data in order to ensure greater transparency of public administration. With this new data source, is possible to have the detailed expenditure of any public institution, in particular of Italian municipalities. In this paper, we propose a methodology that, using Open Data, produces a score and shows the trend of the expenditure managed by the re-elected and the not re-elected majors. To the best of our knowledge, there are no works that discuss this type of problem in a data-driven perspective, for administrative realities of small or medium size. This article is organized as follows: Section II describes the data used for the experiment, Section III introduces the analytical framework, Section IV is about the results obtained, Section V shows the main limitations of the approach and, Section VI details the impact of the research and the future works.

II. Materials

The experimental dataset results from the processing of three different sources. (1) The dataset regarding the number of residents and size of Italian municipalities, that is provided by Italian Statistics Bureau (ISTAT) and is updated to the 2011 census. (2) The dataset on the expenditure of Italian local authorities that is provided by the Italian government [1]. Available expenditure of Italian municipalities for the years 2013, 2014 and 2015 (only first semester). (3) The dataset containing the election results of about 600 municipalities that voted in June 2015 plus the results of the previous consultations held in March 2010. The dataset is provided by the Ministry of Interior [2].

About the second dataset, the expenditure items are organized in a hierarchical manner, with the lower level having 248 items of expenditure. There are levels of intermediate aggregation respectively of 77, 34 and 4 families. In this phase of the study, the maximum aggregation level was used; the four families of expenditure (our endogenous variable) are (i) current expenses, (ii) cost of services for third parties, (iii)

[1] soldipubblici.gov.it

[2] storico.elezioni.interno.it

capital expenditures, (iv) expenses for loans repayment. (i) Current expenditure covers all public expenditure necessary to the ordinary activities of the state structure (eg. staff, purchase of consumer goods). (ii) Expenses for services concerning transactions carried out on behalf of third parties as the institution acts as withholding agent. (iii) The capital expenditures are the ones in which the State aims to play an active policy in the economy (eg. buying movable and immovable assets, shareholdings). (iv) The costs of repayment loans consists of repayments of loans and cash advances. In our model, all the values of the costs are expressed on a monthly average basis, and are scaled to the number of residents of each municipality. For space reasons we only show the distribution of value for the period before election (Figure 1). The distribution in the other years shows a similar trend.

The third dataset allows to understand if a mayor or a coalition government was reconfirmed. For about 350 municipalities only, it is possible to understand if the mayor (or party) is re-elected and only 70 of these have more than 15,000 inhabitants. There are two criteria for determining whether a mayor or a party won the election, namely: (i) checking the name of the former mayor and the new one or (ii) analyzing the political area of the previous and new mayor, inferred from the name of the political party that won the elections. As mentioned above, only for 350 municipalities out of 600 it is possible to infer if a mayor was re-elected as if (i) it was not valid, (ii) had indicated a general civil list. In the municipal elections, especially in small ones, it is common that all candidates use civic lists without party symbols. For this reason, the mayor of the municipality always belongs to a civil list, preventing to understand whether this list belongs to a party of the left, right or center wing. For these 350 municipalities, in 45% of cases, the mayor or the coalition is reconfirmed, while in the remaining 55%, it is substituted.

III. Methods

The idea underlying our approach is that a single-factor model, synthetizing a set of families of expenditure, could facilitate the understanding of the expenses role to explain the political success.

Firstly, we used exploratory factor analysis (EFA) to investigate the expenditure factor structure [8]. Then, we used confirmatory factor analysis (CFA) to validate the factor structure provided by EFA. For each statistical unit (municipalities), we computed a synthetic score of"political engagement of spending" for each year using CFA [6].

Finally, were performed analysis of variance for repeated measures (ANOVA-Rm) for a single factor (time) stratified for the binary political success indicator, and t-tests to compare the "political engagement of spending" and the detached families of expenditure with a binary political success indicator (mayor re-elected or not) over time. At the end, for the year preceding the elections, we validated the "political engagement of spending" using Receiver Operating Characteristic (ROC) curve analysis. All statistical analyses were performed using R software (version 3.0.2 for Windows) [7].

A. *Confirmatory Factor Analysis*

A Confirmatory Factor Analysis (CFA) via Structural Equation Modeling (SEM) was performed to confirm the presence of a latent variable (factor) underlying the spending policies. The items (endogenous variables) are ($v1$) current expenses, ($v2$) cost of services for third parties, ($v3$) capital expenditures, ($v4$) expenses for loans repayment. The factor has been interpreted as "political engagement of spending". The coefficients linking the factor with items by linear equations are called "factor loadings".

The goodness of fit was evaluated with two indexes: (i) Standardized Root Mean Square Residual (SRMR); (ii) Root Mean Square Error of Approximation (RMSEA). In general, a model is considered to show good fit when the SRMR and RMSEA are not higher than 0.10. In addition, further CFA indexes as *gamma* for unidimensionality (acceptable if > 0.2) and the *general validity coefficient* (acceptable if > 0.8) verify the adequacy of single-factor measurement model. Finally, *the standardized factor loadings* (item-factor correlations) (acceptable if > 0.4) proved high-quality specific factor validity for each item.

Hence, the score validation (only for score of 2015) was performed by ROC analysis to evaluate the effectiveness of the (factor) score in distinguishing if the mayor was re-elected or not. Overall, the predictive performance was measured by the area under the curve (AUC): ROC curves with AUC of 0.5 indicating no predictive diagnosis versus AUC of 1.0 indicating perfect ones. Only the score of 2015 was validated because 2015 is the year before the elections, and expenses are directly related to the election campaign.

B. *Analysis of variance and independent t-tests*

The analysis of variance for repeated measures (ANOVA-Rm) is a useful multivariate method to evaluate changes of a continuous variable in relation to a categorical one, over the time. In this case, it was performed to assess the change of the score (obtained via CFA-SEM) over time, i.e., from 2013 to 2015, in relation to binary political success indicator (mayor confirmed or not).

Independent t-test is a useful statistical test to verify if the means of continuous variable across 2 independent groups are significantly different. It was performed to verify the differences of the mean of the score for each year, i.e., the differences of the families expenditure means between the 2 groups over the year.

IV. Case study: Italian Administrative elections

The starting assumption is that it is possible to synthesize all expenditure in a single factor. The factor analysis (EFA) confirming the one-dimensionality of the concept underlying the costs taken into account, i.e. eigenvalue > 1 and Horn's parallel analysis identified one factor.

We apply the CFA-SEM model on the dataset regarding the administrative election held in Italy in June 2015. Our aim is to shows that families of expenditure contribute with different weights in the construction of the factor "political engagement of spending". Although standardized factor loadings of all the variables of the model are acceptable, the most important variable is the current expenditure, followed by capital expenditure, expenses for services for third parties and refund loans. This rank is the same for the three years.

Figure 2 shows the triples of the standardized factor loadings for the three years of analysis. The high-quality specific factors are those higher than 0.4. For example, regarding

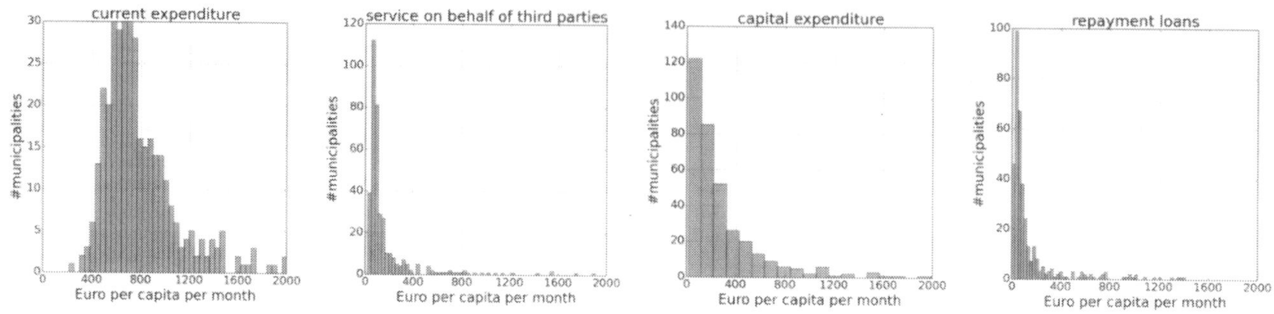

Figure 1. : Distribution of families expenditure per month per capita (2015)

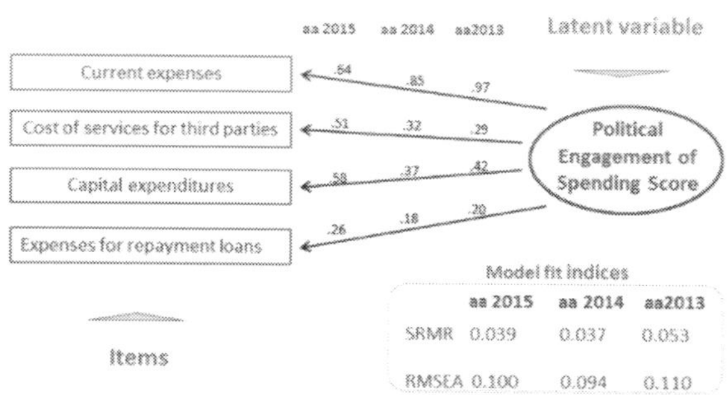

Figure 2. : Standardized factor loadings and goodness of fit indexes for 2013, 2014, 2015 models. The goodness of fit indexes (SMSR, RMSEA) of the "political engagement of spending" are acceptable for each year because they are less than 0.10

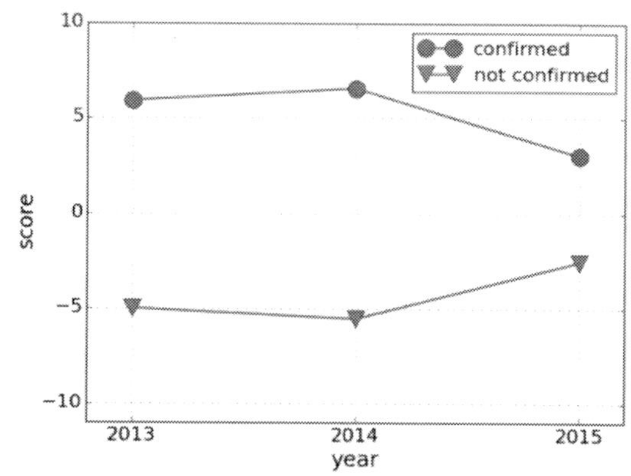

Figure 3. Plot of means of cPE score over 3 years. The relevance of this plot is confirmed by the ANOVA test that observes that within each group trends of the measure cPE are very similar. Instead comparing the cPE in each year between the two groups (green vs. red) with independent t-student, the differences are significantly different for each year (2013 $p = 0.019$; 2014 $p = 0.012$; 2015 $p = 0.007$).

current expenditure (the most important variable), values are respectively 0.97, 0.85, 0.64 for the years 2013, 2014, 2015. The goodness of fit (SMSR, RMSEA) of the "political engagement of spending" for each year is acceptable because it is lower of 0.10. Finally, we compute CFA indexes to measure internal validity of the model; *gamma* is higher than 0.2 (0.33) and *general validity coefficient* is higher than 0.8 (0.8). Thereby, we obtained a validated synthetic continuous score of "political engagement of spending" (centered factor score) (cPE) that we analyzed.

Figure 3 shows the trend of the means of score stratified for the binary political success indicator, divided into mayor confirmed or not confirmed. With the aim of assessing the trend of spending for mayors confirmed and unconfirmed, the analysis of variance (ANOVA) for repeated measures was performed. ANOVA did not show significant differences ($p > 0.05$) of cPE within the trend of the same group (2013 vs. 2014, 2014 vs. 2015). Comparing instead the cPE (in each year) between the two groups with independent t-tests (adjusted by Bonferroni method for multiple comparisons), the differences are significant for each couple of years (2013 vs. 2013, 2014 vs. 2014, 2015 vs. 2015).

Finally, Figure 4 shows the evaluation of individual families of expenditure during the three years with independent t-tests. In the trend of three years, confirmed mayors spent more in current expenditure ($p < 0.05$) and, in 2015, they also invest more in capital expenditures ($p < 0.05$).

Thanks to parameter estimates extracted from the CFA-SEM model 2015 (factor loadings and residual variance) an equation was defined (1) to compute the (rescaled) "political engagement of spending" score (rPE) of each municipality:

$$rPE = 0.0276*v1+0.0139*v2+0.0078*v3+0.0155*v4 \quad (1)$$

Then, to validate rPE and determine its cutoff to predict the election result, ROC curve analysis was performed. The optimal cutoff for rPE is 2.19, the AUC was 0.62 indicating an acceptable predictive accuracy. The sensibility was 0.649 and the specificity was 0.591. It is worth to remark this is just a preliminary result and further validation steps are needed, such as cross validation with one-leave-out methodologies and/or stratifying the datasets over a different dimension/wealth of Local Governments.

The remarkable result of our work is that city administration can use per capita expenditures sustained in the period before the elections, in order to understand, using (1), if the investment is similar of the mayors who were re-elected in the past.

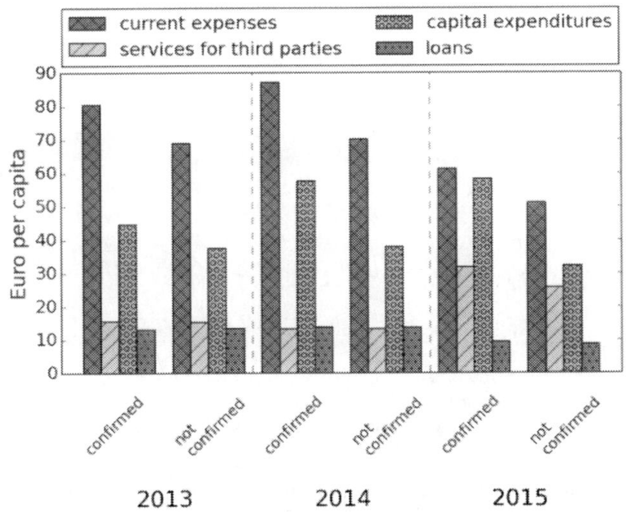

Figure 4. : Evaluation of individual families of expenditure during the three years with independent t-student. In the trend of three years, confirmed mayors spent more in current expenditure (2013 $p = 0.02$; 2014 $p = 0.010$; 2015 $p = 0.013$) and in 2015 also invest more in capital expenditures ($p = 0.025$).

V. Limitations

The main limitation of this approach is the difficulty of collecting the election results of the previous years. This limitation is overcome by the fact that, starting from 2014 the Ministry of Interior has provided an open data service, so, hopefully, in the future there will be more data available. In addition, the model can be specialized considering the political party affiliation of the mayor. At the moment, the Open Data website [3] does not provide the income of the municipalities, i.e., the taxes paid by citizens; with this information, the model could be further enriched.

VI. Learned lesson and next steps

Our work shows how Open Data of the public administration can be used to anticipate the judgment that citizens will express in the next election. The contributions of this study are: (i) provided different weights for the families of expenditure through the CFA-SEM model, (ii) build a synthetic measurement of expenditure called "political engagement of spending" score, validated using the election results, (iii) estimate a score cutoff to predict if an administration will be, more probably, confirmed or not.

The CFA-SEM model shows different weights (standardized factor loadings) among items of expenditure for the administrations confirmed or not confirmed. In the six months before the election the weight of current expenditure and capital expenditure is higher in municipalities that will be confirmed. This trend was detected in relation to binary political success indicator both overall, considering the score of "political engagement of spending" (Figure 3), and by comparing the detach averages of the municipal expenses in the various years. In addition, our framework provides an indication of the critical thresholds of individual cost items, on which one needs to take action in order to improve the overall score (Figure 4).

This result is of great impact, because a single administrator, by entering into a formula (1) expenditure per capita in four families can measure the "likelihood" of his reelection. Thinking in monetary terms, the threshold values that indicate a higher likelihood of re-election could be about $100 Euro$ per month per capita. This suggests that does not pay to invest only in the last six months. The rank of expenditure, per capita per month, is: current expense, i.e., the provision of main services to citizens ($45 Euro$), the second is cost of services for third parties ($27 Euro$), $12 Euro$ for expenditures capital and $6 Euro$ for repayment loans. Details will be further investigated with more complete data.

In the future, we plan to repeat the analysis by considering a greater level of detail of spending that compose each of the four families utilized. In addition, the experimental dataset will be enriched with the morphological and productive datasets (wealth, well-being, etc.) of the area, the seasonal trends of expenditure and income, the political party and subjective variables, such as the self-perception of the citizen on the effectiveness and efficiency of their own mayor.

VII. Acknowledgments

Thanks to the technicians of the Ministry of Interior for providing data of the past elections. Thanks to Pierpaolo Galleni, Fabio Coppede' and Francesca Pratesi for their hints in the preparation of work. This work is partially supported by the European Community's H2020 Program under the scheme 'INFRAIA-1-2014-2015: Research Infrastructures', grant agreement #654024 'SoBigData: Social Mining & Big Data Ecosystem'. (http://www.sobigdata.eu).

References

[1] Pennacchioli D, Coscia M, Rinzivillo S, Giannotti F, Pedreschi D. The retail market as a complex system. EPJ Data Science. 2014

[2] Rinzivillo S., Gabrielli L., Nanni M., Pappalardo L., Pedreschi D. and Giannotti F. The Purpose of Motion: Learning Activities from Individual Mobility Networks. In: DSAA 2014

[3] Bermingham, Adam and Smeaton, Alan F. (2011) On using Twitter to monitor political sentiment and predict election results. In: Sentiment Analysis where AI meets Psychology (SAAIP) Workshop at the International Joint Conference for Natural Language Processing (IJCNLP), 13th November 2011, Chiang Mai, Thailand..

[4] Murphy Choy, Michelle L. F. Cheong, Ma Nang Laik, Koo Ping Shung: US Presidential Election 2012 Prediction using Census Corrected Twitter Model. CoRR abs/1211.0938

[5] Alexander Furnas . You Can't Use Twitter to Predict Election Results. The Atlantic. 2012

[6] Kline RB. Principles and practice of structural equation modeling, vol. 156; 2011.

[7] Development Core Team (2012) A language and environment for statistical computing. R Foundation for Statistical Computing,Vienna.

[8] Horn JL. A rationale and a test for the number of factors in factor analysis. Psychometrika 1965;30:179185.

[3] soldipubblici.gov.it

Privacy Preserving Reconstruction-based Techniques and Randomisation-based Methods for Calculating Surveys' Statistics and Participants Sampling in Deliberative Consultations

Piotr Andruszkiewicz

Institute of Computer Science
Warsaw University of Technology
Warsaw, Poland
Email: P.Andruszkiewicz@ii.pw.edu.pl

Abstract—**In deliberative consultations, the most important are the opinions of residents that want to discuss an important issue. In order to encourage them to participate in such consultations, besides the Internet platform that facilitates the whole process of consultations, privacy preserving techniques should be employed. In this paper, we propose a framework for privacy incorporation in deliberative consultation that will improve eGovernment services provided for digital society. We present the solution for reconstruction-based privacy preserving technique and randomisation-based methods. The proposed framework enables a scientist to prepare a list of candidates and calculate statistics over privacy preserved survey data in deliberative consultations.**

Keywords–Privacy Preserving; Reconstruction-based techniques; Randomisation-based methods; deliberative consultations.

I. Introduction

In deliberative consultations [1], residents discuss issues important for them. An example could be a deliberative consultation run by a local government in order to find and understand opinions of residents about the desired place of building a new elementary school.

In the era of digital society, organizers provide Internet portals that facilitate the process of gathering opinions of residents. As a starting point, residents provide their characteristics in order to be invited to a deliberative consultation that is of their interest. Moreover, one of the most important methods of gathering data during consultations is providing electronic surveys, especially Internet surveys. Residents may give their opinions through the surveys.

In order to encourage candidates to provide their characteristics, participate in a survey and provide true opinions, privacy should be preserved. To this end, several techniques for incorporating privacy in data mining can be employed. These methods are also helpful in statistical tasks, e.g., mean calculation, that are often used in analysis of data collected in surveys. In [2] we performed the analysis of applicability in deliberative consultations of the following privacy preserving techniques: heuristic-based, reconstruction-based, and cryptography-based [3]. We showed that reconstruction-based privacy preserving technique is useful for deliberative consultations and can provide adequate level of privacy in order to encourage residents to participate in surveys which makes consultations valuable.

In this paper, we propose how to use reconstruction-based techniques and randomisation-based methods for deliberative consultations; namely, for calculating statistics over data colected by surveys and calculating a list of candidates for a deliberative consultation. In our solution we assume that data that was only distorted by means of randomistaion-based methods is collected and stored as a centralised database. The database describes candidates' characteristics and results of surveys.

The remainder of this paper is organized as follows: in Section II, we discuss works related to our task. Section III presents the privacy preserving data mining solutions important in the context of deliberative consultations. In Section IV we propose the solution for consultations with the usage of reconstruction-based technique. Finally, Section V summarises the conclusions of the study and outlines future avenues to explore.

II. Related Work

In this section, we present literature review of privacy preserving classification as it is the field closest to our task and we adopt some of the algorithms presented in literature in order to create a solution for the task in question.

Privacy preserving classification has been extensively discussed in literature [4]–[9].

The pioneer work in privacy preserving classification for centralised data was [10], where R. Agrawal and R. Srikant proposed how to build a decision tree over centralised data distorted with the randomisation-based method (except the target/class attribute) and then classify not distorted data with this decision tree. In this solution, they also presented the algorithm called AS (Agrawal-Srikant) for a probability distribution reconstruction for continuous attributes, which estimates an original probability distribution based on distorted samples (details about the algorithm AS can be found in Section III-B2).

Paper [11] extends the AS (Agrawal Srikant) algorithm and presents the EM (Expectation Maximisation) reconstruction algorithm, which does not take into account nominal attributes either (for details refer to Section III-B3).

Randomised Response technique for related-question model was presented in [12]. It allows creating a decision tree but only for nominal attributes. Randomised Response technique for unrelated-question model was discussed in [13], [14] and applied in building naïve Bayes classifier.

The solution we proposed in [15] differs from those above, because it enables a miner to classify centralised perturbed data containing simultaneously continuous and nominal attributes by means of randomisation-based methods to preserve privacy on an individual level. This approach uses the EM/AS (Expectation Maximisation/Agrawal Srikant) algorithm (described in details in Section III-B5) to reconstruct a probability distribution for nominal attributes and the ARVeSNA (Algorithm for Assigning Reconstructed Values to Samples for Nominal Attributes) algorithm (please refer to Section III-B7) for assigning reconstructed values to samples for this type of attributes to build a decision tree simultaneously with continuous attributes.

In [16], we proposed the EQ (the abbreviation comes from *system of EQuations*) algorithm (details can be found in Section III-B6) for reconstructing a probability distribution of nominal attributes. The algorithm achieves better results, especially for high level of privacy, i.e., low probability of retaining an original value of a nominal attribute.

Our work is different from the above mentioned proposals as it focuses on calculation of statistics based on privacy preserved centralised database and sampling participants for deliberative consultations. To this end we adopt algorithms developed for privacy preserving classification. We differ from Randomised Response technique for related-question and unrelated-question models because we assume that all surveys' participants answer the same questions.

III. Privacy Preserving Data Mining Preliminaries

A. Randomisation-based Methods

For detailed description of randomisation-based methods used in Privacy Preserving Data Mining please refer to [17].

B. Algorithms for Distribution Reconstruction and for Assigning Reconstructed Values to Samples

The algorithms for distribution reconstruction of both nominal and continuous attributes are described in this section. Moreover, the algorithms for assigning reconstructed values to samples for nominal and continuous attributes are presented. The definition of information loss in reconstruction is introduced, as well.

1) Information Loss: The lack of precision in the reconstruction of a probability distribution is called information loss. It is defined as follows [11]:

Definition Information loss $\mathcal{I}(f_X, \hat{f}_X)$ equals half of the expected value of L_1 norm between the original probability distribution f_X and its estimate $\hat{f}_X$.

$\mathcal{I}(f_X, \hat{f}_X) = \frac{1}{2}E[\int_{\Omega_X} \mid f_X - \hat{f}_X \mid]$

Information loss $\mathcal{I}(f_X, \hat{f}_X)$ lies between 0 and 1. $\mathcal{I}(f_X, \hat{f}_X) = 0$ means the perfect reconstruction, and $\mathcal{I}(f_X, \hat{f}_X) = 1$ implies that there is no overlap between the original distribution and its estimate.

2) AS Algorithm for Probability Distribution Reconstruction of Continuous Attributes: The algorithm AS for a probability density function reconstruction for continuous attributes distorted with the randomisation-based method was proposed in [10].

The algorithm solves the following problem:

Original values $x_1, x_2, ..., x_n$ of a one-dimensional distribution are the realisation of n independent random variables $X_1, X_2, ..., X_n$ with the same distribution as the variable X. To hide information, n independent random variables $Y_1, Y_2, ..., Y_n$ with the same distribution as the random variable Y have been used. Given $x_1 + y_1, x_2 + y_2, ..., x_n + y_n$ (y_i is the realisation of the random variable Y_i) and cumulative distribution function F_Y for the variable Y, a cumulative distribution function F_X for the random variable X is to be estimated.

The solution to the given problem is as follows:

Let w_i be the value of $X_i + Y_i$, thus $w_i = x_i + y_i$. The individual values x_i and y_i are not known, only their sums are revealed. Assuming that the probability density function f_X for variable X and f_Y for Y are known, Bayes rule [18] can be used to estimate the posterior (cumulative) distribution function F'_{X_1} for the variable X_1. The posterior distribution function F'_{X_1} can be written as follows:

$$F'_{X_1}(a) = \int_{-\infty}^{a} f_{X_1}(z|X_1 + Y_1 = w_1)dz, \quad (1)$$

where $F'_{X_1}(a)$ is the estimator of the posterior (cumulative) distribution function $F_{X_1}(a)$.

Using Bayes rule:

$$F'_{X_1}(a) = \int_{-\infty}^{a} \frac{f_{X_1+Y_1}(w_1|X_1 = z)f_{X_1}(z)}{f_{X_1+Y_1}(w_1)}dz. \quad (2)$$

After additional calculations [10] the posterior density function f'_X is obtained by differentiating F'_X:

$$f'_X(a) = \frac{1}{n}\sum_{i=1}^{n} \frac{f_Y(w_i - a)f_X(a)}{\int_{-\infty}^{\infty} f_Y(w_i - z)f_X(z)dz}. \quad (3)$$

Having a large number of samples, f'_X should correspond to the original probability density function f_X.

To estimate f'_X, the knowledge of f_Y and f_X is needed. f_Y is known, because the distorting distribution function is known for a miner. As the original probability density function f_X is unknown, a uniform distribution is assumed as an initial estimate of density function and then refined in an iterative way by applying (3). See Figure 1 for details.

Details about the calculation complexity reduction can be found in [10].

To stop an iterate reconstruction, three possible stopping criteria were proposed in [10].

The first criterion is met when the reconstructed distribution is statistically the same as the original distribution. To check the similarity of distributions, for instance, χ^2 measure (details about χ^2 can be found in [19]) can be used. This

f_X^0 := uniform distribution
$j := 0$ // iteration number
repeat
$f_X^{j+1}(a) = \frac{1}{n}\sum_{i=1}^{n} \frac{f_Y(w_i - a) f_X^j(a)}{\int_{-\infty}^{\infty} f_Y(w_i - z) f_X^j(z) dz}$
$j := j + 1$
until(stopping criterion met)

Figure 1. The AS algorithm.

$Pr(X = v_p)^0 := \frac{1}{k}, p = 1, ..., k$
$j := 0$ //iteration number
repeat
$Pr(X = v_p)^{j+1} = \frac{1}{n}\sum_{s=1}^{n} \frac{Pr(v_p \rightarrow X(s)) Pr^j(X = v_p)}{\sum_{t=1}^{k} Pr(v_t \rightarrow X(s)) Pr^j(X = v_t)}$
$j := j + 1$
until(stopping criterion met)

Figure 2. The EM/AS nominal attribute probability distribution reconstruction algorithm.

criterion could be used only for testing, because the original distribution is not known in practice.

The second solution is to compare the randomised current estimate of the original distribution with the distorted distribution used for the reconstruction and stop when these two distributions are statistically the same. This criterion assumes that the current estimate which is close enough to the original distribution should be the same after the distortion as the distorted distribution used for the reconstruction. As stated in [10], the difference between two distorted distributions is not a reliable indicator.

The last approach is to compare two consecutive estimates of the original distribution. When the difference is small enough, the process is completed. 1% of the threshold of χ^2 test was used in [10].

As stated in [11], the AS algorithm may not always converge and even it converges, there is no guarantee that it gives a reasonable estimate of the original distribution. There was no proof given for that statement and this issue was not mentioned in [10].

3) Algorithm EM for Probability Distribution Reconstruction of Continuous Attributes: The algorithm for a probability density function reconstruction for continuous attributes distorted by means of the the randomisation-based method was proposed in [11], as well. The algorithm was called EM by the authors. The problem to be solved is the same as for the AS algorithm.

The details about the EM algorithm and the proof that it converges can be found in [11]. The authors of the EM algorithm stated that it is theoretically the best algorithm and having a large set of distorted samples, the EM algorithm can reconstruct the original distribution with little or without information loss [11]. The definition of information loss can be found in Section III-B1.

4) Assigning Reconstructed Values to Samples for Continuous Attributes: The algorithm for assigning reconstructed values to samples for continuous attributes was presented in [10]. We describe this algorithm in this section.

Let $I_1, ..., I_m$ denote m intervals and $N(I_k)$ be the number of samples in I_k interval. Samples should be sorted in an ascending order and assigned to consecutive intervals as follows: $N(I_1)$ first samples are assigned to the first interval I_1, the next $N(I_2)$ samples to the second interval I_2, etc.

5) EM/AS Algorithm for Probability Distribution Reconstruction of Nominal Attributes: In [15], we proposed the EM/AS algorithm for reconstructing a probability distribution of a nominal attribute.

The EM/AS algorithm is based on two algorithms: AS proposed in [10] and its extension EM presented in [11]. Both algorithms reconstruct a probability distribution of continuous attributes.

To reconstruct probability distribution of a nominal attribute, both EM and AS algorithms were modified to obtain the EM/AS (Figure 2). The modifications of both algorithms (AS and EM) give the same result.

The algorithm solves the following problem: a nominal attribute X has the possible values $v_1, v_2, v_3, ..., v_k$ and n samples. Value for each sample is modified according to a probability $Pr(v_p \rightarrow v_r)$ (a probability that a value v_p will be changed to a value v_r). $X(s)$ means a value of an attribute X for a sample s. An original probability distribution of an attribute X should be reconstructed.

The algorithm starts with the uniform distribution and calculates the estimate of the probability distribution in every iteration.

Stopping criterion is the same as for the AS and EM algorithms (the algorithm is stopped when the difference between successive estimates of the original probability distribution becomes small, as little as 1% of the threshold of the χ^2 test).

6) EQ Algorithm for Probability Distribution Reconstruction of Nominal Attributes: In [16], we proposed the EQ algorithm, the name of the algorithm comes from the phrase *system of EQuations*, that reconstructs the probability distribution of nominal attributes and can be used instead of the EM/AS algorithm. The EQ algorithm outperforms the EM/AS, especially for high levels of privacy [16].

The problem to be solved is the same as for the EM/AS algorithm: there are a nominal attribute X with the possible values $v_1, v_2, v_3, ..., v_k$ and n samples. A value for each sample is modified according to a probability $Pr(v_p \rightarrow v_r)$ (a probability that a value v_p will be changed to a value v_r) and we want to reconstruct an original probability distribution of an attribute X.

Let us assume that there is an attribute *Colour* with 3 values: $v_1 = green$, $v_2 = blue$, and $v_3 = black$.

For the original value of the attribute, e.g., $green$, the probability $Pr(v_1 \rightarrow v_1)$ that the value will be the same after the modification is known, as well as the probability of changing the value from $green$ to $blue$ and from $green$ to $black$. Moreover, when the value of the attribute after the distortion is, e.g., $green$, the original value was one of the three possible values: $green$, $blue$, and $black$ and all the probabilities $Pr(v_1 \rightarrow v_1)$, $Pr(v_2 \rightarrow v_1)$, $Pr(v_3 \rightarrow v_1)$ how the value has become $green$ are known.

Let Z be the attribute after the modification with the possible values $v_1, v_2, v_3, ..., v_k$. In the example, the attribute

Z has 3 values: $green$, $blue$, and $black$ and the following equation can be written:

$$P(Z = green) = a_{1,1}P(X = green) + a_{1,2}P(X = blue) + a_{1,3}P(X = black),$$

where $a_{s,p} = Pr(v_p \rightarrow v_s)$. For colours $blue$ and $black$ the similar equations can be written:

$$P(Z = blue) = a_{2,1}P(X = green) + a_{2,2}P(X = blue) + a_{2,3}P(X = black)$$
$$P(Z = black) = a_{3,1}P(X = green) + a_{3,2}P(X = blue) + a_{3,3}P(X = black).$$

Now there are 3 equations and 3 unknown variables ($P(X = green)$, $P(X = blue)$, $P(X = black)$), thus the system of linear equations can be solved.

In general there is the following system of k equations:

$$P(Z = v_1) = a_{1,1}P(X = v_1) + a_{1,2}P(X = v_2) + \cdots + a_{1,k}P(X = v_k)$$
$$P(Z = v_2) = a_{2,1}P(X = v_1) + a_{2,2}P(X = v_2) + \cdots + a_{2,k}P(X = v_k)$$
$$\vdots$$
$$P(Z = v_k) = a_{k,1}P(X = v_1) + a_{k,2}P(X = v_2) + \cdots + a_{k,k}P(X = v_k)$$

with k unknown variables.

Let $\mathbf{X}$ be the column vector with elements $x_1, ..., x_k$, where $x_i = P(X = v_i)$ and $\mathbf{Z}$ be the column vector with elements $z_1, ..., z_k$, where $z_i = P(Z = v_i)$. Let $\mathbf{P}$ be the matrix of retaining/changing values of a nominal attribute. We can rewrite the system of equations in the matrix form as:

$$\mathbf{Z} = \mathbf{PX} \quad (4)$$

To find values of $P(X = v_i)$, $i = 1, \ldots, k$, we need to solve (4). We can solve it by left multiplying both sides by inverted $\mathbf{P}$, i.e., $\mathbf{P}^{-1}$ (only if inverted $\mathbf{P}$ exists).

Nonexistence of the inverted matrix is not troublesome because the number of values of a nominal attribute is known before collecting data starts and a non-singular matrix $\mathbf{P}$ can be chosen to guarantee the existence of inverted $\mathbf{P}$ matrix.

7) ARVeSNA Algorithm for Assigning Reconstructed Values to Samples for Nominal Attributes: We proposed the algorithm for assigning reconstructed values to samples for nominal attributes in [20] and describe this algorithm in this section.

Having reconstructed a probability distribution of a nominal attribute, reconstructed values can be assigned to samples.

The algorithm solves the following problem:

Since modified values of a nominal attribute are given, the probability distribution of a modified attribute (i.e., $P(Z = v_i)$, $i = 1, \ldots, k$) and the number of all samples n are known. The reconstructed probability distribution ($P(X = v_i)$, $i = 1, \ldots, k$) is estimated. The aim is to assign reconstructed values to samples taking into account the reconstructed probability distribution.

In order to solve this problem, the number of distorted samples ($n_Z(v_i)$) is counted separately for each value of an attribute and the number of original samples ($n_X(v_i) = P(X = v_i)n$) is estimated.

TABLE I. THE EXAMPLE OF THE ORIGINAL DATABASE.

Id	Salary	Age	Sex	Credits status	Children
1	1000	35	M	none	N
2	1500	37	F	overdue	Y
3	5000	41	M	present	N
4	3000	44	M	repaid	N
5	4200	50	F	repaid	N
6	2000	28	F	none	N
7	1000	30	M	none	Y

TABLE II. THE EXAMPLE OF THE DISTORTED DATABASE WITH UNIFORM DISTORTION DISTRIBUTION $\langle -500, 500 \rangle$ FOR SALARY, $\langle -10, 10 \rangle$ FOR AGE AND $p = 0.6$ FOR SEX AND CREDITS STATUS ATTRIBUTES.

Id	Salary	Age	Sex	Credits status	Children
1	1353.32	33.42	M	repaid	N
2	1611.83	40.64	M	overdue	Y
3	5428.27	51.27	M	present	N
4	2573.22	39.51	F	none	N
5	4145.89	42.67	M	repaid	N
6	2258.34	38.72	F	none	N
7	1054.03	36.65	M	overdue	Y

Then the difference, called $\delta(v_i)$, between $n_Z(v_i)$ and $n_X(v_i)$ is calculated. $\delta(v_i) > 0$ means that there are too many samples because there are more samples with distorted value of v_i than the reconstructed number of samples for the value v_i. A sample corresponding to a positive value of $\delta(v_i)$ is found and assigned with a reconstructed value v_j for which a value of $\delta(v_j)$ is negative and the reconstructed value v_j has the highest probability to be distorted to the value v_i. Values of corresponding $\delta(v_i)$ and $\delta(v_j)$ are updated and the process is continued until all values of $\delta(v_i)$, $i = 1, \ldots, k$ are zero.

Having completed the process, samples with the reconstructed values are assigned according to an original (reconstructed) probability distribution.

IV. CALCULATING SURVEYS' STATISTICS AND PARTICIPANTS SAMPLING

We define two tasks in deliberative consultations that involve calculations on data with preserved privacy by means of reconstruction-based techniques and randomisation-based methods; namely, calculating surveys' statistics and participants sampling.

A. Calculating Surveys' Statistics

In the task of calculating statistics from survey's data, we assume that there is a centralised database that is collected by means of electronic surveys. A participant provides an answer to each question in the survey. The answer is an attribute value. Thus, we can state that the database consists of: a definition of attributes and its values.

Each attribute describes possible answer's values for a survey's question. For example, an attribute that describes a question 'Do you have a car?' is a binary attribute with possible values: *yes* or *no*. The possible types of attributes are: binary, nominal, ordinal, and continuous.

Values of attributes are distorted answers provided by participants. Thus, if we have n participants and k questions, we have n values for each of k attributes. According to randomisation-based methods values of attributes are distorted at a client side; that is, participant's side, with one of the possible methods. For binary attributes we may use basic randomisation factor method or distortion with a matrix of retaining/changing values of a nominal attribute (for more details please refer to [2]). For ordinal attributes we may use a modified matrix of retaining/changing values of an attribute described in [21]. For continuous attributes the additive perturbation method [10], multiplicative perturbation [22], and the retention replacement perturbation [23] may be employed.

Tables I and II show the example databases that could be results of electronic survey after a deliberative consultation. Table I presents the original, not distorted, database that could be a real result of a survey if there is no privacy preserving methods applied. The example database that could be a result of a survey with privacy preserved by means of the randomisation-based method is shown in Table II. If we use the randomisation-based method in real applications, the original database (Table I) does not exist, only distorted values (Table II) are stored. *Id* attribute is not necessary and is shown to ease the process of comparing both databases.

In the aforementioned task, there is a table with distorted values, like in Table II and a scientist wants to calculate some statistics about participants of a survey. The statistics could be the number of participants that meet a specific condition which is based on gathered data, e.g., the number of participants that have children and are at least 30 years old. Another statistics to calculate is mean of some attribute for all participants or participants that meet a specific condition. For instance, mean salary for participants that have children and are at least 30 years old. Last but not least a scientist may want to see a distribution of an attribute for all participants or a group of participants.

1) Calculating Number of Participants that Meet Specific Condition: Fist we define a condition that a scientist may create in order to choose a group of participants. Let C be a condition that participants should meet. Let us assume that $c_1, c_2, ..., c_m$ are subconditions and form condition C, i.e., $C = c_1 \wedge c_2 \wedge ... \wedge c_m$. c_i condition is a condition that is based on one attribute. The possible types of this conditions are: $v_{a_j} > t$, $v_{a_j} \leq t, t_1 \leq v_{a_j} < t_2$ for continuous attributes, $v_{a_j} \in \{v_1, v_2, ..., v_l\}$ for binary, ordinal, and nominal attributes, where v_{a_j} is a value of attribute a_j, t is a known threshold, $v_1, v_2, ..., v_l$ are possible values of an attribute.

Let us consider that condition $C = c_1$ and c_1 is of a form $t_1 \leq v_{a_j} < t_2$ and is based on a continuous attribute. In this case we can choose intervals in a way that their end/begin in points t_1 and t_2 and apply AS or EM algorithm. Let us assume that we choose the following intervals: i_1 that starts in $-\infty$ and ends in t_1, i.e., $i_1 = (-\infty; t_1)$, $i_2 =< t_1; t_2)$, $i_3 =< t_2; \infty)$. The number of intervals need not to be limited to 3, however, it is important that they should be intervals that end/begin in t_1 and t_2.

The AS or EM algorithms estimate a distribution of values of attribute over intervals. The number of participants can be obtained by multiplying a probability for an interval by the number of participants. Thus the number of values that lie in each interval N_1, N_2, N_3 is known. If we assume that $t_1 < t_2$, then N_2 is the number of participants that meet condition C. Otherwise, $N_1 + N_3$ is the right number. For conditions of form $v_{a_j} > t$, $v_{a_j} \leq t$ the solution is analogous.

If c_1 is based on a nominal attribute with k possible values and is of form $v_{a_j} \in \{v_1, v_2, ..., v_l\}$ EM/AS or EQ algorithm can be employed. The output of the algorithm is the number of participants for each possible value of an attribute. As shown in the following equation, for condition $v_{a_j} \in \{v_1, v_2, ..., v_l\}$ we need to sum all numbers for values that are present in the condition; that is $v_{a_j} \in \{v_1, v_2, ..., v_l\}$.

$$N_{\{v_1,v_2,...,v_l\}} = \sum_{v_i \in \{v_1,v_2,...,v_l\}} N_{v_i} \tag{5}$$

where:

- $N_{\{v_1,v_2,...,v_l\}}$ is the estimated number of samples for which the original attribute has one of values in this set $\{v_1, v_2, ..., v_l\}$,
- N_{v_1} is the estimated number of samples for which the original attribute has a value v_1.

In order to calculate the number of participants that meet condition C with more than one subcondition, $C = c_1 \wedge c_2 \wedge ... \wedge c_m$, we need to calculate the number of participants in an iterative manner (see Figure 3). For the first subcondition we calculate the number of participants that meet subcondition c_1 as shown in this section. Then, we choose participants that meet this subcondition. For binary, nominal and ordinal attributes we can employ ARVeSNA algorithm (Section III-B7, [20]). For continuous attributes we can apply the algorithm described in Section III-B4 that sorts participants in the ascending order over a condition attribute. Then the algorithm assigns the estimated number of sorted participants to each interval. As a result, we obtain a set P_{c_1} of participants that meet a subcondition c_1. In the next iteration we start with P_{c_1} set of participants and apply a subcondition c_2. The result of this iteration is a set $P_{c_1 \wedge c_2}$ of participants that meet condition $c_1 \wedge c_2$. Then we proceed to the next iteration until $P_{c_1 \wedge c_2 \wedge ... \wedge c_m}$ is obtained and hence the number of participants that meet condition C. In the last iteration ARVeSNA or the algorithm for continuous attributes that chooses a subset of participants according to calculated distribution need not to be aplied because we need only the number of participants that meet condition C and the list of participants is not necessary.

As an example, we will analyse the calculation of the number of participants who meet the following conditions: females at most 30 years old.

Let us assume that the Table II contains the distorted results of a survey. We will use the algorithm presented in Figure 3. The first condition is *Sex* = F. In order to find the estimated number of objects that meet this condition we use EM/AS or EQ algorithm. Let us assume that the result of EM/AS or EQ algorithm is 3. Based on Table II without taking into account the distortion we would obtain the number 2. Then, by the means of ARVeSNA algorithm we assign participants to values of the attribute *Sex* in this case. Let us assume that the participants 2, 5 and 6 are assigned. The second condition is *Age* $\leq$ 30. The considered attribute is continuous thus we use EM or AS algorithm. It gives the number of participants at most 30 years old within participants 2, 5 and 6. The result is 1. If we used data from Table II directly without taking into

```
INPUT: m // number of subconditions
INPUT: C = c1 ∧ c2 ∧ ... ∧ cm // condition to be met
INPUT: P // set of participants
OUTPUT: P_{c1∧c2∧...∧cm} // set of participants that meet
                        // c1 ∧ c2 ∧ ... ∧ cm condition
OUTPUT: N_{c1∧c2∧...∧cm} // number of participants that meet
                        // c1 ∧ c2 ∧ ... ∧ cm condition

for i = 1 to m do
  if ci is based on continuous attribute then
    prepare intervals:
    i1 = (−∞; t1), i2 =< t1; t2), i3 =< t2; ∞)
    calculate distribution with AS or EM algorithm
    assign participants to intervals
    choose P_{c1∧...∧ci}
    calculate N_{c1∧...∧ci}
  elseif // binary, nominal, ordinal attributes
    calculate distribution with EM/AS or EQ algorithm
    assign participants to attribute values (ARVeSNA)
    choose P_{c1∧...∧ci}
    calculate N_{c1∧...∧ci}
  end
end
```

Figure 3. The list and the number of participants that meet a specific condition calculation algorithm.

account that values are distorted, we would conclude that there were no females at most 30 years old.

2) Mean Calculation: Considering the mean of continuous attributes and the additive perturbation the calculations are the same as for not distorted data if the distorting distribution with mean equal to 0 is used. The type of a distribution, e.g., uniform, normal, makes no difference. A distribution with mean equal to 0 does not statistically change the mean of attribute's values. The mean can be calculated for an arbitrary set of values of an attribute. Therefore, a scientist is able to calculate a mean if a group of participants is chosen. To this end, a scientist may use the algorithm presented in Figure 3 in order to find a set of participants that meet a specific condition and then calculate the mean.

B. Participants Sampling

In participants sampling, a scientist chooses a set of participants that take part in a deliberative consultation regarding participants' characteristics. Let us assume that all candidates provide information about them and the randomised-based method is applied, hence, only distorted data is stored. Table II may represent such characteristics provided by candidates. A scientist wants to find a condition that chooses a right group of people to be involved in a deliberative consultation. Hence, algorithm presented in Figure 3 can be used to perform this task, since it provides a number and a list of candidates that meet a specific condition.

If we assume that Table II represents characteristics of participants and we want to find the list of candidates for consultations that are females at most 30 years old, we may use the example from Section IV-A1 to illustrate participants samplig. However, in this case we need to perform the last step of ARVeSNA algorithm; that is, assign values of attribute *Age* to participants.

V. Conclusion and Future Work

In this work, we proposed a framework for reconstruction-based techniques and randomisation-based methods application in deliberative consultations. The solution for calculating statistics over privacy preserved survey data and candidates' characteristics has been presented. The proposed framework lets a scientist apply privacy preserving in real deliberative consultations.

In future work, we plan to investigate the possibility of k-anonymity application in a hybrid solution that combines aggregation, reconstruction-based technique and k-anonymity approach.

The incorporation of the presented framework in the system for deliberative consultations that is being under development is planned also.

Acknowledgment

This research has been supported by the National Centre for Research and Development under grant No SP/I/1/77065/10 and the Institute of Computer Science, Warsaw University of Technology under Grant No. II/2015/DS/1.

References

[1] J. Abelson et al., "Deliberations about deliberative methods: issues in the design and evaluation of public participation processes," Social science & medicine, vol. 57, no. 2, 2003, pp. 239–251.

[2] P. Andruszkiewicz, "Privacy preserving data mining for deliberative consultations," in (accepted for) Hybrid Artificial Intelligent Systems - 11th International Conference, HAIS 2016, Seville, Spain, April 18-20, 2016.

[3] V. S. Verykios et al., "State-of-the-art in privacy preserving data mining," SIGMOD Record, vol. 33, no. 1, 2004, pp. 50–57.

[4] L. Xiong, S. Chitti, and L. Liu, "Mining multiple private databases using a knn classifier," in SAC '07: Proceedings of the 2007 ACM symposium on Applied computing, 2007, pp. 435–440.

[5] M. R. Keyvanpour and S. S. Moradi, "A perturbation method based on singular value decomposition and feature selection for privacy preserving data mining," IJDWM, vol. 10, no. 1, 2014, pp. 55–76. [Online]. Available: http://dx.doi.org/10.4018/ijdwm.2014010104 [accessed: 2016-03-18]

[6] P. Andruszkiewicz, "Hierarchical combining of classifiers in privacy preserving data mining," in Hybrid Artificial Intelligence Systems - 9th International Conference, HAIS 2014, Salamanca, Spain, June 11-13, 2014. Proceedings, ser. Lecture Notes in Computer Science, M. M. Polycarpou, A. C. P. L. F. de Carvalho, J. Pan, M. Wozniak, H. Quintián, and E. Corchado, Eds., vol. 8480. Springer, 2014, pp. 573–584. [Online]. Available: http://dx.doi.org/10.1007/978-3-319-07617-1 [accessed: 2016-03-18]

[7] X. Li, Z. Yan, and P. Zhang, "A review on privacy-preserving data mining," in 14th IEEE International Conference on Computer and Information Technology, CIT 2014, Xi'an, China, September 11-13, 2014. IEEE, 2014, pp. 769–774. [Online]. Available: http://dx.doi.org/10.1109/CIT.2014.135 [accessed: 2016-03-18]

[8] P. Andruszkiewicz, "Frequent sets discovery in privacy preserving quantitative association rules mining," in Hybrid Artificial Intelligent Systems - 10th International Conference, HAIS 2015, Bilbao, Spain, June 22-24, 2015, Proceedings, ser. Lecture Notes in Computer Science, E. Onieva, I. Santos, E. Osaba, H. Quintián, and E. Corchado, Eds., vol. 9121. Springer, 2015, pp. 3–15. [Online]. Available: http://dx.doi.org/10.1007/978-3-319-19644-2 [accessed: 2016-03-18]

[9] J. Hamm, A. C. Champion, G. Chen, M. Belkin, and D. Xuan, "Crowd-ML: A privacy-preserving learning framework for a crowd of smart devices," CoRR, vol. abs/1501.02484, 2015. [Online]. Available: http://arxiv.org/abs/1501.02484 [accessed: 2016-03-18]

[10] R. Agrawal and R. Srikant, "Privacy-preserving data mining," in SIGMOD Conference, W. Chen, J. F. Naughton, and P. A. Bernstein, Eds. ACM, 2000, pp. 439–450.

[11] D. Agrawal and C. C. Aggarwal, "On the design and quantification of privacy preserving data mining algorithms," in PODS '01: Proceedings of the twentieth ACM SIGMOD-SIGACT-SIGART symposium on Principles of database systems, 2001, pp. 247–255.

[12] W. Du and Z. Zhan, "Using randomized response techniques for privacy-preserving data mining," in KDD, 2003, pp. 505–510.

[13] J. Z. Zhan and S. Matwin, "Privacy-preserving data mining in electronic surveys," in ICEB, J. Chen, Ed. Academic Publishers/World Publishing Corporation, 2004, pp. 1179–1185.

[14] ——, "Privacy-preserving data mining in electronic surveys," I. J. Network Security, vol. 4, no. 3, 2007, pp. 318–327.

[15] P. Andruszkiewicz, "Privacy preserving classification for continuous and nominal attributes," in Proceedings of the 16th International Conference on Intelligent Information Systems, 2008.

[16] ——, "Probability distribution reconstruction for nominal attributes in privacy preserving classification," in ICHIT '08: Proceedings of the 2008 International Conference on Convergence and Hybrid Information Technology. Washington, DC, USA: IEEE Computer Society, 2008, pp. 494–500.

[17] C. C. Aggarwal, "Privacy-preserving data mining," in Data Mining. Springer International Publishing, 2015, pp. 663–693.

[18] M. Fisz, Probability Theory and Mathematical Statistics. New York: John Wiley and Sons, 1963. .

[19] L. M. Surhone, M. T. Timpledon, and S. F. Marseken, Pearson's Chi-Square Test. Beau Bassin: Betascript Publishers, 2010.

[20] P. Andruszkiewicz, "Privacy preserving data mining on the example of classification (in Polish)," Master's thesis, Warsaw University of Technology, 2005.

[21] ——, "Privacy preserving classification for ordered attributes," in Man-Machine Interactions, ser. Advances in Soft Computing, J. F. P. U. S. Krzysztof A. Cyran, Stanisaw Kozielski and A. Wakulicz-Deja, Eds., vol. 59/2009. Springer, 2009, pp. 353–360.

[22] J. J. Kim and W. E. Winkler, "Multiplicative noise for masking continuous data," Statistical Research Division, US Bureau of the Census, Washington D.C., Tech. Rep., 2003.

[23] R. Agrawal, R. Srikant, and D. Thomas, "Privacy preserving olap," in SIGMOD '05: Proceedings of the 2005 ACM SIGMOD international conference on Management of data. New York, NY, USA: ACM, 2005, pp. 251–262.

Social Networking: Cyber Communities and Security Issues

Shaftab Ahmed
Software Engineering Department
Bahria University, Islamabad, Pakistan
email Shaftab_2010@yahoo.com,

Abstract -- **The world is experiencing a smart change of life style as a result of a wide range of developments in the information and communication technology (ICT) sector. The computation and storage centers are vanishing in the cloud domain leaving human communication interface as the only requirement for using these resources. Evolving cyber communities (CC) are groups of users having common interest areas. Information sharing across such communities is easily possible which, leads to more complexity and vulnerabilities. The platform independent applications in service oriented architectures (SOA) over the web offer a variety of opportunities for users of all walks of life. They are able to create mashups integrating different applications and services to suit their requirements. Cloud service providers (CSP) extend the social network applications for information collection and conducting surveys for business and marketing strategies. Internet of things (IOT) is a concept to converge data, process and people to extend business applications in virtual domain. ICT applications over cloud architecture are ubiquitous and pervasive; developers are extending the concept to develop smart city and smart home architectures for the future. In this paper, we address the challenges offered by growing interest in social networking and ease of information availability for applications in virtual domain. Various new issues have to be carefully studied as the component of human interaction has to be controlled besides the information security to avoid miss use of information.**

Keywords—Service Oriented Architecture (SOA); Information and Communications Technology (ICT); Internet of Things (IOT); Cloud Service Provider (CSP); Cyber Communities (CC)

I. INTRODUCTION

Mobile communications, networking and Internet based solutions for virtualization and resource sharing have given birth to a new life style through social networking. The participation of humans of all ages, professions and interests has given rise to formation of cyber communities. Community is a group of users sharing common interest for example content creators, users, developers and service providers, etc. form communities spanning social networks [1]. Hence, a community in the ICT domain may be seen as interlinked web pages in the Internet cloud. Social networks like LinkedIn, Facebook, Tweeter, WhatsApp, etc. have assumed importance for sharing information in professional and social groups or communities. These communities are usually able to interact with each other hence, making bigger picture of social networking. Whereas it is an interesting phenomenon, it is often complicated and dangerous [2].

The cyber communities (CC) usually have no restriction on membership and cross community information sharing. Hence, explicit and implicit communities may be formed. The implicit communities are difficult to control and monitor for content distribution, etc. Some methods are available to ensure privacy of information between participants of the groups but it is not effective when a group member may provide information knowingly or unknowingly to others which, may eventually be compromised. The social network users need to be educated on the weaknesses of global phenomena of social networking. The user must understand that all information placed in a social network is vulnerable so it should be carefully selected before sharing [3]. As the members present them in virtual domain it is often difficult to differentiate genuine or fake information. Hence, making judgment for selecting a member in a community is usually difficult.

Cloud services virtualize the platform and infrastructure to be used by clients through software. It offers infrastructure as a service (Iaas), platform as a service (Paas) and software as a service (Saas). Lately a new term IT as a service (ITaas) has also been introduced. Cyber communities enlarge their scope through a marriage of cloud computing and social networking [4]. Social network users may access information available in the cloud through service oriented architecture [5]. ICT tools are often used to extract information from social networks and cyber communities related to market trends, evaluation of strategies to forecast and setting targets for future.

Human reliance on the information systems hosted on the web has led to development of community based computing infrastructure or Community Cyber Infrastructure (CCI) in which, the information discovery and extraction is performed through various ICT technologies. National Science Foundation (NSF) defines Cyber Infrastructure (CI) as integration of computing, data networks, digitally enabled sensors, observatories, experimental facilities and interoperable suit of software and middleware services [1][6]. Cyber enabled Discovery and Innovation (CDI) is an initiative of NSF to develop a new generation of computationally based discovery concepts and tools to deal with complex data rich interacting systems. The discovery of information may be from structured (conforming to a schema) or unstructured (not conforming to a schema) data sets.

In Section II, we review related work. In Section III, social networking, cyber community and supporting technologies are discussed. In Section IV, the security issues in cyber communities are highlighted. In Section V, research work initiated is presented. Finally, in Section VI, the paper is concluded with discussion on challenges and future trends.

II. RELATED WORK

Social networks are attacked in mainly of two ways. First, manipulating executable code to gain access or be able to install malicious software. Secondly, the human hackers exploit personal information gathered by peeking and poking the social network. Sometimes, a passive listener is installed to gather information useful to attack a social network [7].

The data posted on the social media is not limited to malicious software attacks; the cyber criminals may mine networks to obtain persisting useful information, and use it to steal intellectual property, highjack a website or compromise company profile. Often data remains available in various cache buffers even after a user has logged out; malicious users may get access of this data intelligently [8]. Most enterprises have adopted security and firewalling schemes to control and filter malicious activities. Social networks open a new window where employees of a company may un-intentionally expose useful information in public domain leading to exploitation or financial losses to the enterprise.

Social network users must bear in mind that information posted on a social network is no longer private. However secure the site may be yet the information can be easily leaked either by a member or through a loop hole in the security mechanism [9]. Some of the tactics used are as under:

Click-jacking:	Concealing hyperlinks beneath a visible link
Cross –Site Scripting:	Injecting client side script into web page
Doxing:	Publically releasing identity information and pictures, etc.
Pharming:	Redirecting to fraudulent sites to extract personal data
Phishing:	An email or other content often sent on behalf a known user containing a malicious link
Phreaking	Gaining unauthorized access to telecommunication device also call physical theft.
Spoofing:	A passive listener to gather information to be used for exploitation

Business communities are using social media to extract useful information for marketing strategies and human resource management. For example [10] Linked in is being used for hiring skilled manpower. Business to business communications has strengthened collaboration for increase in productivity of a company due to broader area of exposure. The developers and service providers offer large storage spaces over the cloud e.g., S3 of Amazon. According to a recent survey [11] the commercial enterprises are not comfortable with the virtualization of storage for confidential information; they would prefer to explicitly know the location / custody of confidential data. To build their confidence it is important to implement proactive security strategies, effective user policies and reinforcing methods to monitor and protect enterprise resources [10]. The employees often use social networks while at home or work place; it is recommended that regular training on security issues and company policies should form a part of the policy. The network at home is usually not adequately protected hence, important information may be compromised.

The social networks have a niche market in e-Healthcare, and education sectors because of direct human involvement. Developers are providing all time guidance and help to patients through social media; often warning messages and other useful information is provided to the community.

III. SOCIAL NETWORKING AND CYBER COMMUNITY AND SUPPORTING TECHNOLOGIES

Social networks virtualize the usage of resources through applications used to interact with them. A typical social network is based on layers of abstraction, shown in Figure 1 where the human interface for user registration is the highest layer; followed by service registration and discovery mechanisms setup by service provider. The services are virtualized through tools for query, access control, data management and visualization. Resource virtualization presents the physical hardware and networks in a cloud hiding all the complexities and offering a service oriented architecture. The social networks allow users to form communities which, may be overlapping in terms of interests and users. Various controls over such groups are also provided to share or present only the authorized information. Some of the enabling technologies have been shown in Figure 2.

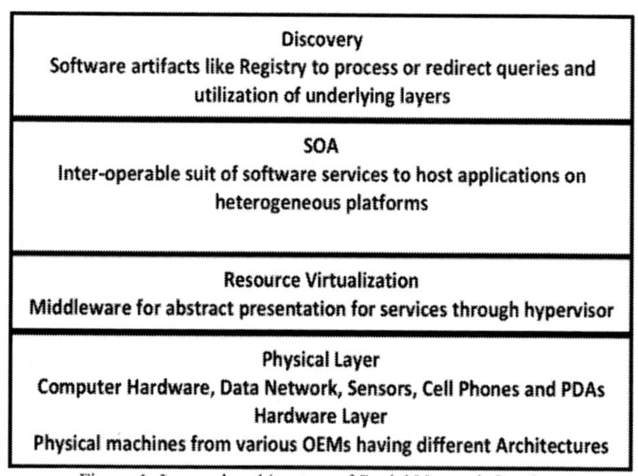

Figure 1. Layered architecture of Social Network Services

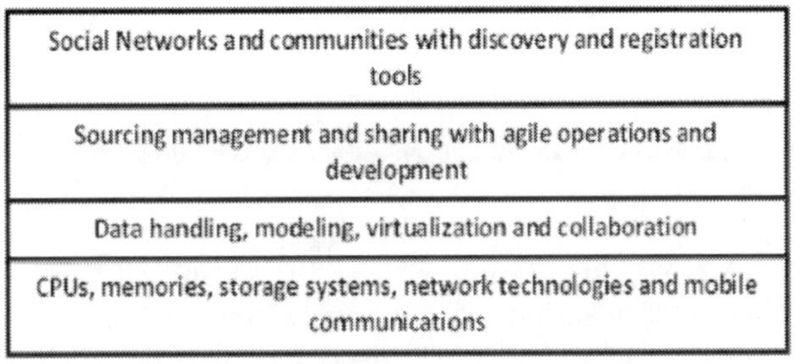

Figure 2. Enabling technologies for social networking

A. *Social networks implementation*

The growth of communities in social, healthacre, medicine and hundreds of others, has been possible as a result of developments of service oriented architecture (SOA) offered through web engineering and data communication networks. Service oriented architecture is used for abstration, low cohesive concepts for data mangement and presentation [5]. The services offered are recorded in a registry which, is looked up for selection. The discovery tools hosted by social networks facilitate selection of desred services. Web engineering is vital in abstracting the underlying network and communication systems. Hence, social network users may interact with virtual environments without being a computer literate. Lately cloud storage and archiving services are being offered by all the mobile commmuications companies used for availability on anywhere anytine basis through smart phones or PDAs.

B. *Cloud computing offered to social networks*

An emerging field in ICT domain is social networking conceived to exploit the ubiquitous nature of social networks and cloud services offered through various web sites. The users are able to share resources and use cloud services for creating mashups. A mashup application blends services for data, presentation and functionality. It also allows integration of different APIs in a single application. For example Facebook users can make applications hosted by a CSP like Amazon [12][13].

Volunteer computing is a distributed computing resource like SETI@Home, Storage@Home and Folding@Home. The experience of such sites can be used in social networks to provide enormous computing power and storage space through collaboration of IT communities [14]. Some examples of potential applications are:

- Document sharing by Google Docs and Zoho
- Pictures and video sharing by Piccasa and Flicker
- Location based services like Google Maps and Bingo Maps
- Context aware applications using mobile mashup services using memory enabled sensors, touch screen, cameras, GPS and accelerometer, etc.

C. *Social Networks and technology developments towards smart homes and smart cities*

The world is experiencing a fundamental change in social setup and lifestyles. The popularity of smart phones and all time Internet connectivity through wireless, Wi-Fi and WiMAX technologies has motivated technology developers to introduce a new concept of smart homes and smart cities. Some examples are smartcities of IBM [15], sustainable-cities of Siemens [16], citynext of Microsoft [17] and mycity of atos [18].

Smart cities require development of tools to address cross domain communication for information sharing and distributed computing. Such solutions have to cater for a variety of features and perspectives in modern society. The developers are in pursuit of tangible services and solutions for the social networks mostly ubiquitous and pervasive. Innovative solutions and new ideas are being matured to meet the requirements of smart homes especially for aging population [20].

Internet of Things (IOT) is a concept to converge data, processes, people, and business system providing an opportunity to extend business scenarios [21][22]. Cloud Service Providers are offering services to build and deploy smart city projects in real world to evaluate the potentials / weaknesses and devise methods to meet new challenges. For example Microsoft Azure services may be used to monitor assets for operational performance improvement and provision of innovative solutions through data analysis and business models [23]. Home care and e-Healthcare models are being rapidly developed to provide better quality of life, protection and health monitoring. The elder populations, patients getting prolonged medical treatment or requiring post-surgical monitoring are clients for smart homes and smart cities [24] [25]. A cyber-home connected to a service provider over the Cloud architecture is shown in Figure 3.

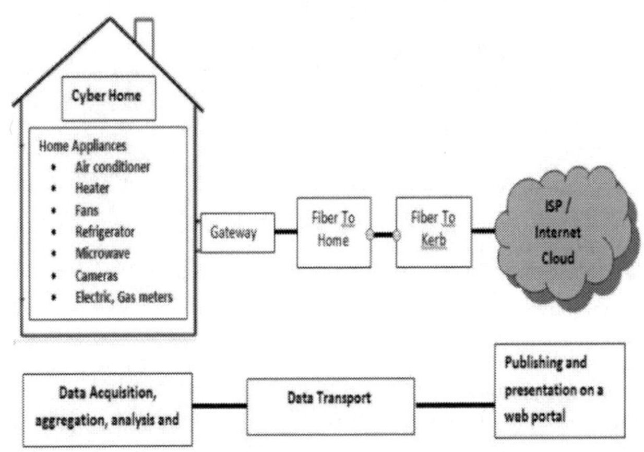

Figure 3. Smart applications in a cyber-home

Web Services	Information management, storage and presentation through APIs APIs support Chatting, Audio Visual communication Data recording				
Community Services	Education, Health, Traffic management, energy management, emergency and security				
Enabling Technologies	Social Networks, Cloud services, Mobility and Network Infrastructure				
Physical structure of a city	Communication • Roads • Airports • Railway Stations • Buses • Taxis etc	Residential • Homes • Shopping area • hospitals Community parks	Healthcare • Hospitals • Nursing homes • Pharmacies • Emergency	Utilities • Gas • Water • Electricity	Security • Police

Figure 4. IOT Smart city architecture

D. *Web and open access to learning and role of social networks*

Web 2.0 technologies promote effective use of collaborative network operation for information sharing and interactive learning [26]. The open access learning oportunities are available for integrated professional education. Open access helps break the barrier between instructor and student to promote academic learning. Shulman [27] states, "learning is useful when it is private and hidden; it is most powerful when it becomes public and commercial". Other scholars have emphacized the benifits of public learning and are of the view that, "open source" and "open access" software resources have been instrumental in generating useful academic activities and promoting innovative ideas [28].

ICT has experienced rapid development of open source tools including bulletin boards, courseware, portals and content mangement software for open access learning environments [29]. A number of institutions and research groups have used open sharing, mutual aid and knowledge disseminstion concepts to promote establishment of free e-learning resourses [30].

IV. Security Issues

A. *Cyber Domain of Social Networks*

The social networks are ubiquitous and pervasive; they have wide acceptability in communities shaped by human interest and social information interchange extending homes and offices into virtual domains. It has been observed that developers often use these networks for information gathering for their business and marketing applications. The information is live instead of old documented surveys so it is good for dynamic market engagement.

Hence, social networks strengthen connectivity, attract and engage customers to get inputs for devising strategies for the company. However social networks are easy targets for malicious activities. Often users expose themselves unnecessarily in social communities without releasing that their data or communication may be misused. Hence, it is extremely important to educate social network users about the risks and pitfalls that they have to watch out for fruitful experience and avoid embarrassment [31].

B. *School communitity concerns regarding networking*

Besides private, business and commercial organizations a large community affected by social networking is the students. Schools are integral part of society today; where besides academic activities, meetings and counseling sessions of teachers, parents and students are conducted to enhance academic performance and reduce discipline problems. The online environments are easily accessible to students of all levels; hence they are causing new problems in society and learning environments. While controlled online activities within a school may ensure safe usage to some extent; the students may use the networks from home or other places leading to serious problems.

It is necessary that school and community policy makers should realize the severity of problems associated with learning communities; where the students need parenting and guided use of information. It is necessary that comprehensive school wide and community wide policies should be made for collaborative management through training, sharing of information and introducing guidelines for safe schools and neighborhoods

C. *Limitations and vulnerabilities*

Social network users are inclined to have trust relationships and informal communications instead of well thought of and well-grounded business communication The sites encourage users to share personal information, photos and videos, opinions and comments or tagging which, is source of enjoyment. They are usually unaware that in spite of careful information sharing in restricted groups; the vulnerability of host site may compromise their information leading to misuse by cyber-criminal. Some of the scenarios are as under [32]:

i. A friendly looking website may incite a user to divulge his profile information and personal detail which, can be used by malware [7].
ii. The user may be fooled by a masquerading attack where he might engage with a cyber-criminal
iii. A community member may turn to be not trustworthy; he may expose the information unsafely
iv. The nonprofessional employees of a company are often unaware of the importance of exercising privacy in company details and secrets. If not properly trained they may help malware to break in the security barriers of the company. Some experts emphasize that periodic training and briefing is necessary for both professional and nonprofessional users. A professional user may forget that he is using the laptop of the company while at home; or visit a social network through his official mobile, etc.

v. Email spams are used for marketing of products and utilities; a user may be tempted to click a link, leading to malicious activity besides going to the website.

vi. Human resource managers are often using social networks to acquire profiles and professional detail of applicants. The negligence in maintaining this information may compromise the detail; for misuse by cyber-criminal.

vii. The website pages may have some security flaws which, may be identified by a hacker for misuse. Such incidents have been reported for Facebook and Tweeter where suitable measures were taken by them

D. Some of the concerns of using social networks:

The user experience with social networks has revealed many weak areas which, need to be addressed by the developers and managers of social networks. This is especially important in the evolving scenario of social network hosting in cloud domains. The iCloud, Google docs, etc. are a few of the important ones. They may have an overlap with social network activities.

A few weak areas to watch out are as under:

- No restriction on membership of social network
- No check on creating an official site hence, can be misused to create fake institutions
- Judgment of friend or foe in cyber network is difficult; users have to be educated on how to ascertain that he is communicating with a genuine member
- Cross community information sharing; either it should be restricted or sufficient controls and forensic data management should be enforced so that information may not land into irresponsible hands after legitimate usage
- Loss of control over information shared may lead to wrong reporting or making it controversial; hence, users in a community or an enterprise should be educated to avoid putting all information on the social site. An option to leave or migrate from the host site gracefully should be kept in mind
- Information sources like email, blogs, Twitter, Facebook and Myspace increase visibility in communities and widens the scope but overloads the educators and may be annoying in some cases.

E. Attack on host or computer network

Social networks weakness is not the only source of cyber attack [33]. The host network or service provider in virtual domain may also be hit by cyber-criminal compromising all the information of the clients maintaind on it. In such cases, the social services may suffer severely hence, the enterprises using social networks should have proactive strategies in place to handle such situations.

F. Recommendations and guidelines for secure use of social networks

Detailed study of social networking sites, discussion with user communities, entrepreneurs, students, scientists, researchers, medical professionals, etc. has revealed that the awareness of security threats is not adequate. We recommend that suitable measures should be adopted for their education as under:

- Self awareness of suitability of sharing information
- Avoid third party usage of account
- Treat everything is public; the world not only your closed community may be seeing the information shared
- Protect yourself protect others or the community by not allowing information to across to other communities without suitable authorization
- Campagn to educate social network users and administartors for rational usage and abiging by security policies.
- A regulatory framawork maintaining forensic data for social network is becoming important so that suitable measures can be taken to fix responsibility for unauthorized usage or informatin leak
- Stronger authentication and access control methods have to adopted to discourage BOTs by using captchas or other methods
- Provision of suitable tools to revoke user accounts as well as edit or remove profiles from the posts should be available
- The social networks should use filtering tools to establish legitimacy of information and forbidden content distribition

V. RESEARCH WORK

We have chosen e-healthcare, e-learning and business communities as domains of interest for research work. It is understandable that collection of useful social interaction data is instrumental for assessment and analysis. However, while using popular social networking sites, there are two issues i.e.

i) Non availability of data from popular sites
ii) Non serious activities are more common

Since we intend to focus on three domains (e-healthcare, e-learning and business), which require useful and extensive data, we will develop social networking facilities of our own. These sites will be available to the closed communities in the above said domains

The first two domains are human centric where sharing personal data and experiences securely is of prime importance. The third has a wide perspective where the market trends, user experiences etc., are used for making strategies to market products and human resource management etc.

In healthcare and patient handling / rehabilitation, the data collected from the patient history and interactive sessions will be used for treatment, rehabilitation, nutrition plans, etc. Learning communities have a wide perspective; however, we will focus on schools first. We aim to bring parents, teachers, students and policy makers together, through social network for learning, parenting, teaching and socialization. They may evolve strategies to be adopted for upbringing of children in highly volatile ICT induced information overload. Our forum will promote shared vision, communication without barriers and collaboration towards achieving common goals of education and integrated society.

For business community product marketing and human resource management have been identified. We intend to perform behavior analysis of social network users with respect to thoughts, daily routine, likes, dislikes etc. The data collected about market requirements, human consumption alongwith end user comments on social sites will be used to predict future trends and plan product marketing. Intelligent use of data available on other competitors / manufactures sites regarding their products and end user feedbacks will be used to derive competitive advantage.

For human resource management, the data will be collected through social networks and processed to help entrepreneurs in making strategies for carrier planning, hiring and granting relief or bonus for employees / shareholders. Managers may use the new applicant's data to prepare suitable probing questions before formally interviewing individuals.

While developing the above said model applications we will focus on vulnerabilities of the data collected and shared between communities. Suitable measures will be adopted, alongwith educating the users for safe usage of social networks through recommended policies, guidelines and safe practices for safe use of social networks.

VI. Conclusion and Discussion

Social networks are being used for business purposes for human resource management, marketing, forecasting etc. Trends indicate that the phenomena of increasing interest and usage of social networks in all walks of life will rapidly increase in future. It is important to avoid pitfalls and threats while reaping the benefits of social media. The business models need to be carefully developed through clearly articulated procedures, policies and role of users in various departments, guests and members from outside. It implies that clarity on what information can be posted on which, site and by who should be ensured. It is equally important to devise remedial strategies, in failures before engagement in social network.

The employees of a business enterprise are the weakest link which, is usually exploited by the cyber criminals. For example a careless download by an individual on his personal computer or mobile may be used to compromise important resources of an enterprise. Similarly an employee may innocently post information following a link helping malware to break the cyber defense of a company. It is recommended that companies using social networks should evolve a continuous training program for employees demonstrating threats and their impact. Furthermore, these sessions should include all the IT employees not just those who matter.

Social networking has significantly changed human life cycle, business models and the level of awareness / dependency in digital world today. It must be realized that opportunities offered by social networks should be tapped cautiously realizing risks and devising suitable strategies / counter measures for smooth running of an enterprise.

VII. References

[1] A. Elmagarmid, A. Samuel and M. Ouzzani," Community Cyber Infrastructure Enabled Discovery in Science and Engineering", RPI, Troy, NY, September 2007

[2] R. Kumar, P. Raghavan, S. Rajagopalan and A. Tomkins "Trawling the Web for emerging cyber-communities" 1999, pp 402-415, Published by Elsevier Science B.V. doi=10.1.1.387.3453

[3] S. A. de Chaves, C. B. Westphall, C. M. Westphall, and G. A. Gerônimo, "Customer Security Concerns in Cloud Computing" IARIA, 2001, pp. 7-11 ISBN 978-1-61208-113-7

[4] D. Fu, J. Zhu and G. Dasmalchi," IT as a service Cloud Computing" IBM Alliance at Cisco Systems Cisco Systems, IT Pro March/April 2009 Publ ished by the IEEE C omputer S ociet y, 1520-9202/09, 2009 IEEE, pp. 10-13

[5] L. Ngo, " Service-oriented architecture for home networks" TKK T-110.5190 Seminar on Internetworking 2007-3-4/5

[6] M. McDowell and D. Morda, " Socializing Securely: Using Social Networking Services", Carnegie Mellon University. Produced for US-CERT, a government organization 2007.

[7] S. Abraham and I. Chengalur, "An overview of social engineering malware: Trends, tactics, and implications" Technology in Society 32 2010, pp 183–196 doi:10.1016/j.techsoc.2010.07.001

[8] S. Singh , R. Bagga, D. Singh and T. Jangwal," Architecture of mobile application, security issues and services involved in mobile cloud computing environment", India International Journal of Computers and Electronics research, www.ijcer.org ISSN2278 August 2012, pp 58-67

[9] Mike Gotta, " Risks & Benefits of More Open Social Networking", Burton Group, http:// www.burtongroup.com

[10] F. Lin and C. hung, C. , "Developing and Evaluating the Social Network Analysis System for Virtual Teams in Cyber Communities" Proceedings of the 37th Hawaii International Conference on System Sciences – 2004

[11] A. L. Beberg and V. S. Pande2 ,"Storage@home: Petascale Distributed Storage" 1-4244-0910-1/07 2007 IEEE

[12] A. Mohaisen, H Tran, A. Chandra and Y. Kim, "Social Cloud: Using Social Networks for Building Distributed Computing Services" doi=10.1.1.232.1553

[13] K. Chard, S. Caton, O. Rana and K. Bubendorfer, "Social Cloud: Cloud Computing in Social Networks", DOI 10.1109/CLOUD.2010.28 IEEE Computer Society, 2010, pp 99-106

[14] S. S. Sivan and S. Durga, " A Survey on Accessing Cloud Services in Social Networks" International Journal of Advanced Research in

Computer Science and Software Engineering, Volume 4, Issue 1, ISSN: 2277 128X , January 2014, pp784-787

[15] http://www.ibm.com/smartercities

[16] www.siemens.com/sustainable-city

[17] http://www.microsoft.com/en-us/citynext

[18] http://www.oracle.com/us/industries/public-sector/national-local-government/city-platform/index.html

[19] http://atos.net/en-us/home/your-business/government-and-cities/mycity.html

[20] H. Chourabi et al," Understanding Smart Cities: An Integrative Framework" 45th Hawaii International Conference on System Sciences, 978-0-7695-4525-7/12 IEEE, 2012, pp 2289-2297, DOI 10.1109/HICSS.2012.615

[21] D. Evans, "The Internet of Things How the Next Evolution of the Internet Is Changing Everything" Cisco Internet Business Solutions Group (IBSG) 2011

[22] J. Gubbi, R. Buyya, S. Marusic and M Palaniswami, "Internet of Things (IoT): A vision, architectural elements, and future directions" Future Generation Computer Systems Volume 29, Issue 7, September 2013, pp-1645–1660, http://dx.doi.org/10.1016/j.future.2013.01.010

[23] C. Weinhardt, A. Anandasivam, B. Blau, and J. Stößer "Business models in the service world" IT Pro March/April 2009 Publ ished by the IEEE C omputer Societ y 1520-9202/09, 2009 IEEE, pp-28-33

[24] A. Venkatesh "Smart Home Concepts: Current Trends" CRITO, doi=10.1.1.125.8597

[25] M. Shanmugasundaram, G. Muthuselvi and S. Sundar, " Implementation of PIC16F877A Based Intelligent Smart Home System, ISSN : 0975-4024 Vol 5 No 2 Apr-May 2013, pp 1608-1624

[26] R. Guha and D. Al-Dabass, "Impact of Web 2.0 and Cloud Computing Platform on Software Engineering" International Symposium on Electronic System Design 2010,978-0-7695-4294-2/10 IEEE Computer Society, 2010, pp 213-218, DOI 10.1109/ISED.2010.48

[27] L. Shulman, "Taking learning seriously, Change: The magzine for Higher Learning", 31:4 March 2010, pp 10-17, DOI:10.1080/00091389909602695

[28] N. Jackson. "E-learning material and open access" 18th BILETA Conference: Controlling Information in the Online Environment, April 2003, QMW London, http://www.bileta.ac.uk/03papers/jackson.html

[29] K. Mentor,"Open source and open access: Alternatives to hidden learning environments", 20th annual conference on distance teachning and learning, http://UNWEX.edu/disted/conference, 2006

[30] J. Jiang "Web-Based Open Access for Wide Learning Platforms" 978-1-4244-4507-3/09, 2009 IEEE

[31] http://www.nsa.gov/snac, "Service Oriented Architecture Security Vulnerabilities Web Services" Systems and Network Analysis Center Information Assurance Directorate

[32] "Security: Protect Your Service-Oriented Architecture Network" Cisco Systems 2008, pp1-7.

[33] D. Sancho "Security Guide to social networks" white paper, Trend Micro

Online Intermediary Liability and Privatised Enforcement: the Content ID Case

Thomas Margoni
Faculty of Law
University of Stirling
Stirling, United Kingdom
Email: thomas.margoni@stir.ac.uk

Mark Perry
School of Law
University of New England
Armidale, NSW, Australia
Email: mark.perry@une.edu.au

Abstract—**Over the last two decades, the use of technologies to promulgate information at the click of a mouse has given rise to unprecedented access to information but has also facilitated the infringement of rights. There have been a number of responses by legislative bodies attempting to recover ground lost by rightsholders in this new environment. Some are reviewed in this paper. The problem facing legislators is that they wish to protect rightsholders without stifling the benefits of easy access to knowledge, information and data, hopefully maximising the advantages and societal benefits of improved accessibility. Content hosts, such as YouTube, suffer under a similar dichotomy but also face the prospect of litigation. Tools such as "Content ID" provide rightsholders with a means of combating potential infringements without litigation. However, as with legislation, it is not a panacea for reaching the balance between facilitating access and protecting rights. This paper illustrates these issues and underlines the importance of an approach that safeguards fundamental rights and freedoms and strikes a fair balance among the different rights involved. Technology can play a crucial role in this attempt.**

Keywords-web hosting services; rightsholders; safe harbour; comparative legislation; online intermediary liability.

I. INTRODUCTION

In the Internet ecosystem, hosting providers play a pivotal role: they supply the services and servers that users need to upload and hold the content that they have generated (User Generated Content, or UGC). There are many other kinds of hosting services, for example data warehousing, but herein we consider information sharing sites. UGC can take disparate forms, such as video, image, text, audio, and animation. Platforms that offer to store and make UGC available to the public have become the backbone of what is nowadays known as Web 2.0. Web 2.0 describes websites which employ technologies that "allow users to interact and collaborate with each other in a social media dialogue as creators of user-generated content in a virtual community, in contrast to Web sites where people are limited to the passive viewing of content. Examples of Web 2.0 include social networking sites, blogs, wikis, folksonomies, video sharing sites, hosted services, Web applications, and mashups [1].

Usually, hosting providers offer a comprehensive package of services to users. In addition to the possibility of uploading content to their servers, they may offer assistance in making content more accessible, appealing, and easier to consult and search. They may also help users develop better interfaces, in terms of look and feel, and content that complies with the web-site's technical requirements, for instance those regarding usability, file formats and meta-tags. In particular, hosting providers often offer services that allow the host and users to generate revenue from advertising. This is a very important aspect, as advertising is one of the main sources of income for hosting providers.

An issue arises with services that exceed the mere offer of hosting capacity. In particular, advertising services can be seen by Courts as non-neutral activities that have the potential to disqualify hosting providers from the "safe harbour" provisions created to exempt them from secondary liability. In this paper, the term secondary liability is used to refer to the possible liability of intermediaries, such as online service providers, for infringements committed by users of the service. This kind of liability is not harmonised at the international or European Union level. The result is a complex and often confusing landscape of different terminologies and rules [2].

This paper begins by exploring legislation that provides a limited "safe harbour" for service providers. It then examines the problems facing hosting services such as YouTube, and the Content ID system YouTube implemented in response to problems of potential liability.

II. LEGISLATIVE BACKGROUND

Hosting providers create the technical systems for users to upload content on the Internet. When a user uploads content that does not infringe another person's copyright, nor defames anyone, nor violates privacy or any other third party right, they perform a perfectly legitimate activity and should not, generally speaking, fear an injunction or claim for restitution. The same holds true for the intermediary, the hosting provider, which created the conditions for the upload of content. However, when a user uploads content that does infringe the copyright of a third party, or defames someone, or violates their privacy or another legal right, liability claims may not necessarily be limited to the person or entity that directly performed the uploading action. In many cases, under doctrines that vary significantly from jurisdiction to jurisdiction [3], the person or entity that has helped make the illegitimate act possible may be jointly liable for the wrongdoing.

Many countries have introduced specific safe harbour laws to exempt hosting providers from this secondary liability. The declared policy objective of this type of legislative provision is to favour the technological, economic and social function of digital intermediaries as long as they fulfil certain conditions. Early examples of these types of provision are in the EU E-Commerce Directive [8], US Digital Millennium Copyright Act [9], and Canadian Copyright Act [10].

A. The European approach

In Europe, Article 14 of Directive 2000/31/EC provides [emphasis added] [8]:

> 1. Where an information society service is provided that consists of the storage of information provided by a recipient of the service, Member States shall ensure that the service provider is not liable for the information stored at the request of a recipient of the service, on condition that:
>
> (a) the provider does not have actual knowledge of illegal activity or information and, as regards claims for damages, is not aware of facts or circumstances from which the illegal activity or information is apparent; or
>
> (b) the provider, upon obtaining such knowledge or awareness, acts expeditiously to remove or to disable access to the information.
>
> 2. Paragraph 1 **shall not apply when the recipient of the** service is acting under the **authority or the control** of the provider.
>
> 3. This Article shall not affect the possibility for a court or administrative authority, in accordance with Member States' legal systems, of requiring the service provider to terminate or prevent an infringement, nor does it affect the possibility for Member States of establishing procedures governing the removal or disabling of access to information.

Similar provisions are present in 17 USC 512 (created by the Digital Millennium Copyright Act Pub. L. 105-304 in 1998) and Sec. 31.1 of the Canadian Copyright Act 1985, as amended. It is important to note that while the E-Commerce Directive applies to all illegal content, the North American provisions are limited to copyright cases.

Unlike the aforementioned jurisdictions, Australia's legal framework has trended towards more control of Internet Service Providers (ISPs) (the legislation in Australia refers to "Carriage Service Providers") on many fronts [21]. However, rather than a direct set of provisions comparable to the "safe harbour" approach, there has been a blended legislative approach that allows ISPs to intervene when they wish.

B. The Australian approach

The Australian Copyright Act [20], which has been much amended to comply with the Word Trade Organization Agreement on Trade Related Aspects of Intellectual Property, United States–Australia Free Trade Agreement and subsequent international agreements, follows most copyright legislation worldwide. Nevertheless, much of the current legal and policy debate is a result of the findings of the High Court of Australia in Roadshow Films PTY Ltd & others v iiNet Ltd (2012) [22]. The action was brought with the assistance of the Australian Federation Against Copyright Theft (AFACT), along with a number of major studios and rights holders, including Roadshow Films. AFACT alleged that a large amount of copyright material had been downloaded by users of iiNet, and that iiNet authorised these infringements. AFACT employed an anti-piracy company, DtecNet Software (DtecNet software company was bought by MarkMonitor in 2010, and MarkMonitor itself was bought by Thompson Reuters in 2012). iiNet is a major player in the Australian internet provision market, with annual revenue exceeding one billion Australian dollars [25].

Upon appeal to the High Court of Australia, the question addressed was whether the term "authorise" could be applied to the activities of iiNet. That is, did iiNet's inaction with regard to putting users on notice of possible infringement amount to authorisation of infringement [23], that would then make the company liable. The court held that it did not, saying: "[An] ISP is not to be taken to have authorised primary infringement of a cinematograph film "merely because" it has provided facilities for making it available online to a user who is the primary infringer", and that an ISP is under no duty to continually monitor the activities of users. However, this case has been diluted by the current trends in Australian courts and legislation.

Recent amendments to the Copyright Act in Australia bring into light again the competing interests of users, hosts, rightsholders and policy makers. The new Section 115A is interesting in that it allows rightsholders, "on application by the owner of a copyright", [25] to seek an injunction to have a foreign website blocked from access, but allows the service provider, the intermediary, to not take part in the proceedings if they do not wish to (and in that case avoid costs). The injunction, if granted, requires the ISP (carriage service provider) to take reasonable steps to disable access to the online location [25]. This kind of legislation, and perhaps the whittling away of safe harbour protection, makes it more attractive for content hosts and service providers to make use of voluntary technologies to protect themselves. Whether this approach is respectful of users' fundamental rights, i.e. of their right to freely express themselves, is yet to be confirmed.

C. Evaluation of the current legislative trends

It is vital for hosting providers to meet the conditions required within their jurisdiction in order to enjoy the liability exemptions provided under so-called "safe harbour" provisions (or similar). In all cases, liability exemptions do not apply when the host provider partakes in activities that give them actual knowledge and control of the infringement [11]. Other conditions vary. For example, national courts in the EU have shown a tendency to exclude the applicability of Art. 14 E-Commerce Directive and apply their own traditional liability categories [3]. Therefore, it is of paramount importance for hosting providers to take the necessary steps to clearly remain within the boundaries established by the safe harbour or equivalent legislation to enjoy the relative immunity. At the same time, however, they have to maintain the services which, by making the hosting site more appealing, will attract more users and consequently more advertisement related revenue. All this needs to be done without displeasing rightsholders, which may, and usually do, threaten hosting providers and users with legal actions based on the infringement of their rights, most notably copyright [14].

For intermediaries, an option to ensure that their activity will not conduce to liability claims is to voluntarily enter in private agreements with rightsholders and users. Such agreements are a form of private enforcement that do not suffer the common problems of traditional, State-dominated regulatory interventions: slow, rigid, and lacking insights or participation by key stakeholders [11]. Accordingly, privatised enforcement measures can become particularly appealing to those operators that seek quick, flexible and reliable forms of enforcement. When these privatised measures prove of particular success and become employed by an entire sector they are usually referred to as forms of self-regulation [11]. However, privatised enforcement is not always quick, flexible, reliable or especially balanced towards all the subjects involved. From the below discussion it emerges that of the three categories of players involved in the typical scenario – rightsholders, intermediaries and consumers – the latter is the weakest party and often left in an even weaker position after negotiations.

III. Case Scenario: YouTube

YouTube, the video sharing website created in 2005 by three PayPal employees and owned by Google since 2006, provides a good illustration of the issues involved. Almost all the videos uploaded on YouTube are provided by users, even though some content is provided directly by rightsholders, such as CBS and the BBC. Any Internet user can watch the videos without authentication but only registered users can upload them. The maximum length of videos is 15 minutes. However, users with a good track record of compliance with the web-site rules and with an account verified by a mobile phone number may be allowed to upload longer videos. This limitation is not related to technical issues and at the beginning of YouTube's operations there was no time limit. It was noted, though, that most videos exceeding 15 minutes were infringements of copyright specific to TV shows and movies [13].

Videos can be watched on the YouTube website or embedded in different websites in such a way that users of an embedding website can watch the video without having to be redirected to the YouTube website. The video, nonetheless, is physically stored on YouTube servers and not on those of the embedding website. Downloads of videos are not usually offered as an option by YouTube but there are exceptions. There are also a number of third party applications that allow users to download videos from YouTube. It has been reported that in the past YouTube sent "cease and desist" letters to websites offering the possibility to download and separate the audio or video components, as this was in violation of YouTube's Terms of Service [13]. YouTube also implements a number of localised websites, that is to say websites that are exactly the same as the main one but translated into the local language and, frequently, adapted to meet the requirements of the local legal framework. YouTube usually redirects users to the localised version of the website on the basis of the IP address: this explains why, for instance, users from a given country trying to watch a video sometimes see the message "Video not available in your country" while users from a different country can still watch that same video.

IV. Voluntary Measures: the Content ID Tool

In spite of all the described efforts to limit the upload of videos infringing third parties' copyright, YouTube, together with its parent company Google, has increasingly been the object of rightsholders' claims. Rightsholders tend to perceive YouTube's business model as not completely fair, since most of the content, they claim, is uploaded by users without the authorisation of copyright owners. On different occasions, rightsholders have reported that the number of infringing videos available is in the order of hundreds of thousands, which have led to claims for billions of dollars in damages [14]. In addition to the delicate liability issue, Google's 'deep pockets' constitute a strong incentive for this type of litigation, an aspect that increases both the number of cases filed and the amount of damages sought [15]. Individual prosecutions take a lot of time and resources and, particularly in copyright infringement cases, the amount of damages that courts award does not always justify the investment. This is also true in countries where courts can award statutory damages, such as the United States, which in cases of wilful acts can reach the sum of US$150000 per infringement [16]. In Australia, the annual economic cost of piracy is around AUD$551 million [17]. While the punitive nature intrinsic in the award of particularly high damages is certainly perceived by convicted infringers, it does not represent a real restoration for rightsholders when compared to industry claims that attribute 'piracy' losses at billions of US dollars [14]. Additionally, many content and media corporations have gained awareness of the counterproductive consequences that a strategy of suing your own customers (actual or potential) triggers in public opinion. Whereas, on the other hand, to prosecute a big corporation allows copyright holders to try to recover damages in the claimed amounts of billions and to have a realistic expectation that the defendant, if convicted, is solvent for the entire amount. Furthermore, the public perception of lawsuits against and between corporations is much more neutral, compared to the case of a corporation suing an individual user.

In 2007, in order to further limit the amount of uploaded infringing content and consequently reduce its exposure to copyright infringement lawsuits, YouTube implemented the Content ID tool, a voluntary system that in the intention of the promoters could seriously limit – or even eliminate – the possibility to upload content previously identified as infringing.

At this point, a brief description of the tool is necessary. Rightsholders that meet certain criteria are eligible to take advantage of the tool and can file a request to YouTube to be admitted to the program. Once accepted into the program, rightsholders can submit their copyrighted material (any sort of audio visual material) to YouTube, which in turn will "scan" it and store the resulting ID into a database. YouTube quantifies over 25 million IDs stored in its database [19]. When a user uploads a new video on YouTube, the video is automatically checked against the ID content in the database and if a match is found, YouTube contacts the rightsholder.

At this point, YouTube (more properly Google) shows its deep understanding of Web 2.0 social and economic dynamics by offering rightsholders the possibility to take any of the following actions:

- Mute the audio that matches their music;
- Block a whole video from being viewed;
- Monetise the video by running ads against it;
- Track the video viewership statistics.

Interestingly, any of these actions can be country-specific, in light of the IP address identification mentioned before. Accordingly, rightsholders are able to determine in which countries they want the content to be blocked, or monetised, and in which the statistics of the video need to be analysed. The actions can also be device-specific, meaning that rightsholders can determine which action should apply depending on the type of device used (desktop, mobile, e-reader, embedding system) [11].

Nevertheless, not every rightsholder can participate in this scheme. To be approved, users "must own exclusive rights to a substantial body of original material that is frequently uploaded by the YouTube user community", a status currently recognised for about five thousand 'partners'. Under this condition, it seems clear that the Content ID scheme's main function is to accommodate the needs of big audio visual and media groups, and not those of small or individual rightsholders. The latter can – except in very special cases – rarely demonstrate ownership of rights "to a substantial body of original material that is frequently uploaded". After all, the Content ID tool has been in action since 2007, which is the year Viacom filed its multibillion dollar lawsuit [14].

V. ENFORCEMENT

Another critical element that emerged in the aftermath of the new tool is connected with the accuracy of the ID matching system. As Fred von Lohmann – at the time an attorney with the Electronic Frontier Foundation (EFF) – noted, the tool has been used by some of the groups admitted to the program to remove extremely large amounts of audio-visual content. Many of these removals were clear fair use cases, which led von Lohmann to describe the practice as "wholesale censorship" [27]. Other observers called this a "fair use massacre" and substantiated the accusation with a number of real cases [28]. The problem is recognized by a large cross-section of civil and academic society, and projects aimed to monitor the evolution of removal claims have blossomed. Indeed, fair use claims, together with other uses related to freedom of expression, cannot be properly evaluated by an automated process that merely identifies similarities in the object uploaded on the basis of a fingerprinting mechanism.

As a matter of fact, the hardship of determining when a use is legitimate is recognised by the law, which has created systems intended to balance conflicting claims and to give the party whose content was removed for alleged copyright infringement the possibility to reply. One such legal mechanism is the United States *Digital Millennium Copyright Act* notice and take-down procedure ('DMCA procedure'). Other jurisdictions offer similar solutions in their provisions regarding the removal and replacement of content, although often they do not reach the level of detail present in the US case [4]. The DMCA procedure is based on a highly regulated enumeration of the steps that a take-down procedure should follow offering alleged infringers the possibility to respond and establishing specific sanctions for rightsholders who file ilicit claims [5]. On the contrary, YouTube's Content ID system automatically scans in real time all content that is uploaded by usersr against the database of works owned by quaflifying rightsholders. No evaluation of possible fair use cases is at this point present or possible. If a match is found, the rightsholder is informed and can decide what to do with the content: block it in a variety of ways, monetize it or analyse viewership. Only at this point, the rightsholder has the possibility of determining whether the identified material could constitute a case of fair use. However, it seems quite apparent that a rightsholder is not the most neutral judge when he has to determine whether the unauthorised use of his own material by a third party (use that often criticise or mock the original work, such as in the case of parodies) constitutes fair use.

The user who uploaded the blocked content is left with two choices. The first is to take no action, in which case the content remains under the condition chosen by the rightsholder. Alternatively, the uploader of the blocked content can decide to take action and dispute the claim, alleging the reasons why he or she believes that the content was uploaded lawfully. If this happens, the rightsholder can release the claim or confirm it. In the latter case, the uploader can "appeal" a Content ID claim but only if they possess a pristine and verified account. At this point, the rightsholder may release the claim or take down the audio or video. The latter option, also known as a "copyright strike", leads to an immediate halt to the audio-visual content and causes the account of the uploading user to enter a state of "bad standing", with limited features. If three copyright strikes are received, the user's account is terminated. On the basis of the information available on the YouTube website, and of the data required to submit (or counter-notify) a copyright strike, it seems that the latter integrates a DMCA notification to all legal effects.

A last critical element is related to "contractual agreements" concluded by YouTube and rightsholders. These agreements eliminate the possibility for users to oppose a claim of copyright infringement filed through the Content ID scheme, or even through a formal notification scheme such as the DMCA notice and take-down procedure. YouTube informs users about "Videos removed or blocked due to YouTube's contractual obligations" and explains that:

> "YouTube enters into agreements with certain music copyright owners to allow use of their sound recordings and musical compositions.

> In exchange for this, some of these music copyright owners require us to handle videos containing their sound recordings and/or musical works in ways that differ from the usual processes on YouTube. Under these contracts, we may be required to remove specific videos from the site, block specific videos in certain territories, or **prevent specific videos from being reinstated after a counter notification. In some instances, this may mean the Content ID appeals and/or counter notification processes will not be available.** Your account will not be penalized at this time" [29].

In other words, users will be denied the possibility to have their content reinstated on YouTube if they file a Content ID claim or a DMCA counter-notification under the conditions established by 17 USC Sec. 512(g) [16].

The consequence of failing to comply with Sec. 512(g) is that the intermediary is not eligible for the liability exemption granted under the first part of the same provision. Therefore, YouTube, at least under US law, by refusing to reinstate the content under the aforementioned conditions, exposes itself to potential liability claims from all those users that have properly filed a counter-notification which did not cause the rightsholder to start a court action. This is the type of balance that the DMCA puts, at least apparently, in place. Intermediaries can be exempted from liability for the actions of their subscribers, however they need to follow certain procedures. One of these, meant to counter-balance the power attributed to rightsholders to take-down content, is the obligation to replace such content when certain conditions are met under the penalty of becoming liable towards users.

Nevertheless, YouTube limits the ability of its users to file such claims by establishing that the reinstatement of content is at the sole discretion of YouTube. In fact, the US version of YouTube's Terms of Service states:

> "If a counter-notice is received by the Copyright Agent, YouTube may send a copy of the counter-notice to the original complaining party informing that person that it may replace the removed Content or cease disabling it in 10 business days. Unless the copyright owner files an action seeking a court order against the Content provider, member or user, the removed Content **may be replaced**, or access to it restored, in 10 to 14 business days or more after receipt of the counter-notice, **at YouTube's sole discretion**" [29].

From this brief analysis it is possible to conclude that if the DMCA notice and take-down procedure is intended to balance the position of rightsholders and users in the quest for either fast removal or fast reinstatement, then YouTube's agreements with rightsholders clearly removes only one arm of this important balance, namely the one leading to the protection of users. This voluntary and contractual based approach allows YouTube and rightsholders to circumvent the legislative safeguards created to rebalance the positions of the parties involved in UGC activities and to help users – the traditionally weaker party – to express themselves freely through the content they upload.

Concluding, the voluntarily implemented Content ID scheme is clearly a way to meet the needs of the content industry which is interested in faster and automated procedures for the removal of copyright infringing content on YouTube. However, YouTube also hosts extremely large amounts of perfectly legitimate content, including items that copy or reproduce parts of protected works but which are nonetheless lawful (e.g. fair use). In all these caes, the Content ID scheme not only fails to improve an already critical situation but worsens the position of users who upload legitimate content.

VI. CONCLUSIONS

In the various dimensions of the intellectual property spectrum there has been a 'normalisation' of intellectual property rights through the adoption of international agreements that establish ever growing protections for rightsholders. There are also a growing number of instances that point away from this harmonisation of intellectual property rights. Indeed, there is a great number of changes facing technology mediated information sharing [26].

The hosts of information sharing servers around the world are coming under pressure to take greater control of their content, or at least responsibility for it. This trend is driven by rightsholders. Despite some international and jurisdictional efforts to mitigate liability through safe harbour provisions, it seems likely that the coming years will see the greater adoption of 'voluntary' controls, such as those seen in Content ID.

Future legislative interventions in this field should aim to strike a fair balance between fundamental rights, such as freedom of expression, the proprietary rights of rightsholders and the economic and technology interests of intermediaries. In order to reach this delicate balance, basic consumer protections cannot be contractually overridden.

Additionally, the application of better technologies for rights management, such as notices regarding where and how information can be used, would allow users to be better informed as to the provenance and uses to which they can put such materials.

VII. Acknowledgements

The authors thank their respective institutions for making available the facilities to contribute this paper. Thomas Margoni thanks the European Commission FP7 programme for providing the resources funding this research. Mark Perry thanks IBM for funding and K Lingard for research assistance.

References

[1] Web 2.0 site http://www.wikipedia.org/_Accessed 4th March 2016.

[2] L'Oréal SA, Lancôme parfums et beauté & Cie, Laboratoire Garnier & Cie, L'Oréal (UK) Limited v eBay International AG, eBay Europe SARL and eBay (UK) Limited (C-324/09) http://curia.europa.eu/juris/document/document.jsf?text=&docid=107261&pageIndex=0&doclang=EN&mode=lst&dir=&occ=first&part=1&cid=150764 Accessed 11th April 2016.

[3] C. Angelopulos, "Beyond the Safe Harbours: Harmonising Substantive Intermediary Liability for Copyright Infringement in Europe", Intellectual Property Quarterly, 2013-3, p. 253-274.

[4] J. Urban & L. Quilter, "Efficient Process or 'Chilling Effects'? Takedown Notices Under Section 512 of the Digital Millennium Copyright Act", Santa Clara Computer and High Technology Law Journal, Vol. 22, p. 621, 2006.

[5] W. Seltzer, "Free Speech Unmoored in Copyright's Safe Harbor: Chilling Effects of the DMCA on the First Amendment", Harvard Journal of Law & Technology, Vol. 24, p. 171, 2010.

[6] P. Savola, Blocking injunctions and website operators' liability for copyright infringement for user-generated links, (36)5 (2014) EIPR 279.

[7] B. van der Sloot, "Welcome to the Jungle: the Liability of Internet Intermediaries for Privacy Violations in Europe", 6 (2015) JIPITEC 211.

[8] Directive 2000/31/EC of the European Parliament and of the Council of 8 June 2000 on certain legal aspects of information society services, in particular electronic commerce, in the Internal Market [E-Commerce Directive].

[9] Digital Millennium Copyright Act, Public Law 105–304 Oct. 28, 1998 https://www.gpo.gov/fdsys/pkg/PLAW-105publ304/pdf/PLAW-105publ304.pdf Accessed 11th April 2016.

[10] [Canadian] Copyright Act, RSC 1985, c C-42 https://www.canlii.org/en/ca/laws/stat/rsc-1985-c-c-42/latest/rsc-1985-c-c-42.html

[11] C Angelopoulos et al, "Study of fundamental rights limitations for online enforcement through self-regulation", University of Amsterdam, 2016, forthcoming.

[12] YouTube Help "Uploading videos longer than 15 minutes" at https://support.google.com/youtube/answer/71673?hl=en and "Your 15 minutes of fame" at http://www.youtube.com/blog?entry=oorjVv_HDVs Accessed 4th March 2016.

[13] YouTube "Terms of Service" https://www.youtube.com/static?gl=AU&template=terms Accessed 5th March 2016.

[14] Viacom International, Inc. v. YouTube, Inc., No. 07 Civ. 2103 (S.D.N.Y.).

[15] T Margoni and M Perry "Deep Pockets, Packets, and Harbors" Ohio State Law Journal, v. 74 (6), p. 1195-1216 (2013) http://ssrn.com/abstract=2296216 Accessed 11th April 2016.

[16] 17 U.S. Code § 504 – 513 http://www.copyright.gov/title17/92chap5.html Accessed 11th April 2016.

[17] Ipsos MediaCT and Oxford Economics "Impact of motion picture piracy: Australia Report" at http://www.screenassociation.com.au/uploads/reports/IPSOS_Economic_Consequences_of_Movie_Piracy_-_Australia.pdf Accessed 4th March 2016.

[18] 2015 Special 301 Report United States Trade Representative https://ustr.gov/sites/default/files/2015-Special-301-Report-FINAL.pdf Accesdeepsed 11th April 2016.

[19] T Bartholomew "The Death of Fair Use in Cyberspace: YouTube and the Problem with Content ID" Duke Law & Technology Review Vol 13, No1, 66 (2015).

[20] Copyright Act 1965 (Commonwealth of Australia) https://www.legislation.gov.au/Details/C2016C00253 Accessed 10th April 2016.

[21] N Suzor, R Choi, and K Pappalard "Moments of flux in intermediary liability for copyright infringement" Chapter 6 in M Perry Intellectual Property Governance for the 21st Century: a Global Perspective, (in press Springer 2016).

[22] Roadshow Films Pty Ltd v iiNet Ltd [2012] HCA 16 (20 April 2012). Note, the High Court (HCA) is the highest court in the Australian legal system.

[23] Federal Court report, Roadshow Films Pty Ltd v iiNet Limited (No. 3) [2010] FCA 24 (4 February 2010).

[24] M Bingemann "NBN usage fee will burn consumers: iiNet", The Australian, 22 August 2014

[25] Section 115A, Copyright Act 1968 (Commonwealth of Australia).

[26] M Perry (ed) Changing Directions: Global Governance of Intellectual Property in the 21st Century (in press, Springer 2016) http://www.springer.com/de/book/9783319311760#aboutBook Accessed 4th March 2016.

[27] F von Lohmann, Testing YouTube's Audio Content ID System, April 29 2009, available at https://www.eff.org/deeplinks/2009/04/testing-youtubes-aud.

[28] C Mcsherby, The Fair Use Massacre Continues: Now Warner's Going After the Babies, March 12, 2009, available at https://www.eff.org/deeplinks/2009/03/fair-use-massacre-continues-now-warner-s-going-aft.

[29] YouTube Terms of Service, http://www.youtube.com/t/terms?gl=US_Accessed 11th April 2016.

Motivations and Risks of Social Media Crowdsourcing in War-torn Societies: Evidence from Syria

Khaled Saleh Al Omoush
Al-Zaytoonah University of Jordan
Amman-Jordan
e-mail: k.Alomoush@zuj.edu.jo

Saad Ghaleb Yassen
Al-Zaytoonah University of Jordan
Amman-Jordan
e-mail: Saad.yaseen@zuj.edu.jo

Abstract—**This research aims to investigate motivations of social media crowdsourcing, potential risks, as well as the determinants of continuity of participating in online crowdsourcing communities via social media during civil wars. Maslow's hierarchy of needs has been used for understanding motivations of social media crowdsourcing. The present research also investigates three major potential risks associated with social media crowdsourcing in civil war-torn societies, including direct personal threats, the penetration of terrorism ideology, and advocacy of hatred. The present study revealed that social media is not just a platform for social interaction or other traditional purposes that have been mentioned in the related literature. In the current Syrian crisis, social media crowdsourcing has been employed effectively in exchanging, disseminating, and sharing information, solutions, and advices to meet the basic Syrians' needs and how to deal with the different and complex features of the crisis.**

Keywords-social media crowdsourcing; motivation; risk; moral continuity of participation.

I. INTRODUCTION

The beginning of the 21st century has been marked by the repetitive occurrence of large-scale natural disasters and human-provoked emergencies, events commonly known as crises [1]. Civil wars and the spread of terrorism in different parts of the world are the most tragic human-provoked disasters causing catastrophic humanitarian crises, where civilians are paying the highest price. According to Global Peace Index (2015), Syria has been named as the most dangerous country in the world on international levels of peace and violence for the year 2015. An estimated hundreds of thousands of Syrian civilians were killed. The conflict has also contributed to expulsion and flight of millions of civilians from their homes into refugee camps.

With the absence of governmental institutions, millions of people are still steadfast in their country and struggling to survive using all means available. In such cases, citizens have only themselves to rely on, coping with unpredictable events, and encouraging each other to stay in their homes in spite of the risks. In such situations, the collaboration of citizens is becoming more and more indispensable, where citizens are moving from a reactive behavior to a proactive outlook characterized by free involvement and self-responsibility [2][3]. In such large-scale and long-term crises, one of the greatest challenges to those involved in crisis management efforts, including citizens, is to have efficient, stable, and accessible tele-communication platforms for reaching a large number of people on a limited amount of time and resources [2]-[4].

The effectiveness of social media tools, including Social Networking Sites (SNSs), image and video hosting sites, Wikis, and blogs, has been increasing in every area of human life in recent years [5]. In the past few years, the initial role of social media as a means to keep in touch with friends, family and colleagues has evolved and they are becoming a more important means of communication and collaboration during emergencies, disasters, and crises [6]. Events of the current civil wars are showing a new kind of powerful crisis community, which is made possible by new social media that supports crowdsourcing approaches.

More than five years ago, social media has represented the artery for feeding the peaceful revolutions aiming to change regimes that protested many Arab countries. Later on, it has played a role in civil war ignition as mobilizing tools on the basis of ethnic and religious identity behind one of the parties to the conflict. The most important good role that a social computing plays is enabling Syrian civilians to participate in the large-scale humanitarian crisis management that is sweeping across the country. Nowadays, Syrians are employing social media crowdsourcing effectively in exchanging, disseminating, and sharing information, solutions, and advices on how to deal with the different and complex features of the crisis.

The current Middle East crises constitute historical events for Information and Communication Technology (ICT) researchers to study the social media crowdsourcing in war-torn societies. Although there is an extensive interest in the role of social media in harassing crowdsourcing, little research exists on the role, uses and potential risks of social media crowdsourcing in war-torn societies. Therefore, the purpose of the present research is to investigate motivations of social media crowdsourcing, potential risks, and the determinants of continuity participating in the online crowdsourcing communities via social media during civil wars. The present study sheds light on the critical role of social media in providing the opportunity for society's members to participate in the crises management alleviating the hardship, miseries, and tribulations of civilians in War-torn Societies.

II. AN OVERVIEW OF SOCIAL MEDIA CROWDSOURCING

Crowdsourcing is basically used to describe the act of taking a task traditionally performed by a designated agent and outsourcing it to an undefined, generally large group of people in the form of an open call [7]. The real power and uniqueness of crowdsourcing lies in the active participation of intelligent humans in a task assigned to them changing the way of solving problems, producing knowledge, generating ideas, and making them actionable [8]. The philosophy of crowdsourcing is grounded in the concept that every member of crowd has knowledge that some other person will find to be valuable, where unique and different perspectives derived from a diverse community represents a very powerful machine for collaborative problem solving [7]. The literature (e.g. [7] - [10]) has emphasized the role of social computing in empowering the concept of crowdsourcing.

The effectiveness of social media tools, including SNSs, image and video hosting sites, Wikis, and blogs, has been increasing in every area of human life in recent years [5]. They have provided a fertile ground for collaborating, accessing and disseminating information, and sharing knowledge. There is a rapid growth of online social networks and an explosion in user-generated content published on the social platforms. Image and video hosting sites, such as YouTube and Flicker enable anyone to upload content such as videos or pictures to be shared with everyone or with a restrictive community of users. Blogging and micro-blogging media also represents a free platform to share facts, values, emotions, ideas, opinions, and expectations. Actually, social media is providing unprecedented levels of citizen engagement and participation in their local and wider communities, revolutionizing the way problems are addressed, and allowing all actors to monitor and act upon almost anything, anywhere, in real-time [11]. These tools have provided unprecedented opportunities to bring individuals and groups of people together constituting the crowdsourcing communities seeing beyond the self.

III. LITERATURE REVIEW

The review of literature indicates that crowdsourcing, as a new model to harnesses the creative solutions from the crowds, is receiving a growing attention. With the rapid development of social computing, and the increasing importance of social media in people life, social media crowdsourcing is gaining more and more attention from researchers in many fields. The unexpected flow and evolving nature of crises accompanied the revolutions that protested many countries did not provide the opportunity to study any aspect of the extensive adoption and contribution in social media crowdsourcing as a platform to participate in the crises management.

Crowdsourcing is an emerging field of study and still in its early stages. The adoption and use of social media crowdsourcing in crises management has not yet received much research attention. However, much of the previous research (e.g., [10][12]) has focused on developing different applications to involve the crowds in the crises management. Another line of research (e.g. [9][13]) has been dedicated to describe the usage patterns of social media crowdsourcing in the crises and disasters.

A considerable body of researches (e.g., [2][14]) were conducted to investigate the role of social media in the efforts of search, rescue, and emergency response. At a time that some crises, especially those arising out of civil wars, necessitate civilians' self-protection and resilience, it is worth mentioning that the majority of previous studies (e.g., [2][3][15]) have revolved around the existence of a wide range of authorities, such as police, fire, emergency medical and governmental authorities that can be relied upon to coordinate the efforts of crisis management.

The previous research (e.g., [12][15]) agreed that appraising the contribution of social media to crisis management depends on the nature of the crisis and risks that people face, as there is no one-size-fits-all approach. This agreement confirms the need to study the harnessing of social media crowdsourcing for long term crises; especially those accompany with armed conflicts in civil war-torn societies, where very little efforts have been made in this area.

Based on the previous literature review and following up on the Syrian crisis via social media, the present study has derived the constructs of research framework as shown in Table I.

TABLE I. THE CONSTRACTS OF THE FRAMEWORK

Constructs	Dimensions	References/ Evidences
Motivations	Survival	[17]-[20]
	Safety	[15] [21]
	Sense of Community	[22]-[26]
	Cognitive Motivation	[28]-[30]
	Self-actualization	[1] [4] [28]
Potential Risks	Direct Personal Threats	[4] [24] [32]
	The Penetration of Terrorism Ideology	[33]-[35]
	Advocacy of Hatred	[31] [34] [36]

IV. RESEARCH MODEL

In civil war-torn societies that witness blind deadliest terrorist attacks threatening the life and survival of civilians, it is axiomatic that people are suffering and struggling to secure their basic humanitarian needs and avoiding risks. However, one of the prominent ways to explain motives for using social media crowdsourcing in civil war-torn societies is through Maslow's need hierarchy theory. Maslow's hierarchy of needs has enjoyed widespread acceptance in the area of human motivation. According to Maslow's hierarchy of needs, all human beings endeavor to fulfil a hierarchy of five motivational needs consisting of physiological, safety, belongingness and love, esteem, and self-actualization. Following Maslow's logic, lower physiological and safety needs can come back into focus when facing complex crises, such as those arising out of civil wars, where the people can drop to a lower level that reflects needs of what was lost. Therefore, Maslow's hierarchy of motivational needs is an appropriate choice to explain motivations of creating and participating in social media crowdsourcing during the crises in war-torn societies. The research model (Fig. 1) proposes that, during large- scale and long-term crises, such as those arising out of civil wars, social media crowdsourcing are motivated by five humanitarian needs consisting of survival, safety, sense of community, cognitive motivations, and self-actualization.

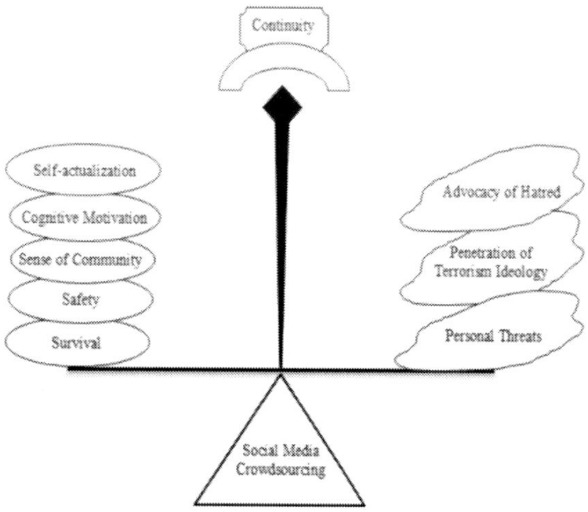

Figure 1. Motivations and risks of social media crowdsourcing in war-torn societieS

On the other hand, the present research proposes three major risks associated with social media crowdsourcing in civil war-torn societies that could threaten the participants and society as a whole. Furthermore, the research model suggests that participants continually negotiate and direct the tension between motivational needs and perceived risks to determine the continuity of participation value in social media crowdsourcing.

A. Motivations

Theories of motivation posit that an individual's behavior is driven by his needs that transformed into goal-directed actions to fulfill these needs through available means [16]. There are different motivational theories that have been used to investigate the motivational issues of crowdsourcing. Each motivational theory has its unique ways of motivating factors. For example, Self-determination theory (SDT) that has been developed by Deci and Ryan [16] distinguishes between intrinsic and extrinsic motivations. This theory represents a broad framework for the study of human motivations and explaining the reasons for online crowdsourcing. However, one of the lessons of the literatures is that there are no standard sets of motivations for adopting and using social media, where motivations vary across social media services, environments, situations, and cultures. In civil war-torn societies, people are forced to return to backwardness, disintegration, racism, absolutism eras, and early human communities' needs. On the other hand, using social media in general is mostly selective and motivated by self-awareness of the individual's own needs and his expectation of satisfying them by particular types of media that give a certain advantage above other already known alternatives. Therefore, for the purpose of the present research, Maslow's hierarchy of needs theory was adopted to clarify the needs that motivate people to engage in social media crowdsourcing in crises situations. Below, we discuss in more detail each dimension of these motivations.

Survival

Maslow considered survival needs as being the first and foremost of all needs through obtaining air, food, drinking water, shelter, warmth, sleep, clothing and others. It is ironic that people who are forced to return to backwardness, disintegration, racism, absolutism eras, and early human communities' needs are thankful for most advanced technologies in securing their basic needs to stay alive and continue their resilience. In Syria, conflicting parties are using siege and starvation as a weapon of civil war. Inhabitants of the besieged cities have inquired about Fatwas (religious edicts) allowing them to eat cats, dogs and donkeys to stave off hunger.

The tools of social media that are used by Syrians include countless examples of disseminating and exchanging information regarding food, drinking water, medical assistance, pharmaceuticals for chronic diseases sources, fuel sources, transportation services to areas where needed, and temporary shelters for Syrians who had lost their homes. The international humanitarian aid organizations mainly depend on the interaction with the crowd through social media in addressing the shortage of human needs and utilities and launching humanitarian aid appeals to help the affected areas. The best examples of these organizations are International Committee of the Red Cross in Syria [17]; and Syrian Arab Red Crescent [18]. Furthermore, SNSs have been employed effectively to help find and collect information about missing and abducted persons. For example, a lot of groups and pages have been initiated on Facebook by volunteers, such as community Organization in Damascus [19] and Missing *and* Martyrs [20].

Safety

Safety represents the second level of Maslow's hierarchy of needs. This motivation represents the needs for security and protection from harm which is psychologically perceived to threaten life and survival. In the context of civil wars, such needs include freedom from danger, absence of threat, and stability. Many emergencies require an early warning which reaches people as quickly as possible. More and more evidence shows that citizen-driven emergency response is a critical part of an effective response to major disasters and emergencies [15]. In war-torn societies, civilians are looking forward to having guidelines on how to act and what kind of actions are expected from them [21].

Experiences from the current Syrian crisis show that social media plays an important role in providing to the general public up-to-the-minute information about emergencies, risks, and how to respond. It represents a valuable channel for emergency services to send an alert and warning in real time and even to initiate actions. They are using it to raise awareness of the risks related to the geographical areas where the follower is located and provide recommendations if needed. Social media also used by crowd to send cautions, conduct situational wakefulness instantly, and to provide advice by posting information such as emergency phone numbers, location of hospitals requiring blood donations, evacuation routes.

Sense of Community

The sense of community concept refers to individuals' subjective feeling of attachment and belongingness to a bigger and stable structure which can be relied upon for a variety of purposes [22]. It meets the third level of Maslow's hierarchy of needs, which is fulfilling the need for belonging and love, including friends, a family, and a community. Social media and, more specifically, SNSs can help create a sense of community that gives individuals the feeling that they are not alone in the crisis and that there are others experiencing similar hardships and difficulties [6]. The tools of social media have provided unprecedented opportunities to bring Syrian individuals and groups together constituting a new kind of societies seeing beyond the self. They have provided a fertile ground for sharing the pain of victims.

Social media has provided an open arena to these communities to target specific groups and the wider public to deliver messages about conflict prevention and reduction, disarmament, and reconciliation. It has allowed the voices of ordinary citizens to be amplified communicating and submitting human rights abuses and war crimes committed by all parties in conflict, and calling to neutralize civilians and populated residential areas. Examples of these groups are Syrian Network for Human Rights [23] and Raqqa is Being Slaughtered Silently campaign [24]. Innovative initiatives have been taken place on SNSs to support dialogue for conflict reduction and peace efforts, such as pray for Syria [25] and the Permanent Campaign for Peace in Syria [26], and Peoples Commission for National Reconciliation [27].

Cognitive Motivation

According to Maslow [28], cognitive needs that include perceptual, intellectual, and learning capacities represent a set of adjustive tools, which have, among other functions, that of satisfaction of basic needs. These cognitive needs explain the motivational role of desire to know and understand, curiosity, learning, philosophizing, experimenting or, in other word, to see rather than to be blind [28]. Actually, the cognitive needs have been considered as a major motivation to use social media [29]-[30].

The platforms of social media have contributed widely to build, raise, and share Syrians' awareness about the essence of the crisis, threats and risk, and gaining a broader understanding of the situation as a whole. Furthermore, the growing phenomenon of citizens' journalism through social media has been a great value in providing the first-hand account of Syrian crisis events as they occur in the forms of images, video and audio messages, and information, thus contributing to the enhancement of the general public' situational awareness. In fact, in the Syrian case, it has been of great value for Syrians and the world to satisfy the need to have the latest and unique information available during crises raising the situation awareness at real-time.

Self-actualization

Maslow [28] believes that in the highest level of needs are self-actualization that leads to creativity and openness to experience. According to Maslow [28], self-actualization refers to individual's aspirations to achieve self-fulfillment, namely, to the tendency for him to become actualized in what he is potentially. This tendency describes a desire that could lead to realizing one's capabilities potential to the fullest [28]. The increased use of social media during a crisis can often involves the recording of the self and others at the scene of a crisis [4]. The great advantage of social media as a driver of creative innovations is that anyone can create a platform to voice their thoughts and set up his own online initiatives.

According to Manso and Manso [1], citizens prove to be highly proficuous in launching and contributing to online innovative initiatives during crises, such as websites, Facebook pages and groups, Wikis, hashtags and tweets created by volunteers to place them at the services of society. These initiatives are highlighting the importance of social media in catalyzing people to be ideal citizens, accept and express of their inner core or self, provide aid and information to others, support dialogue for conflict reduction and peace efforts satisfying their self-actualization needs. The most striking example of self-actualizing efforts in the Syrian civil war is the growing phenomenon of citizens' journalism through social media to communicate, track, and share factual information and hard facts in real time. Furthermore, millions of Syrians fled their country seeking beyond covering their basic humanitarian needs. Social media has driven the awareness to those outside the affected areas, generating volunteers and donors to enhance a community's resilience on the long run.

B. Potential Risks

When dealing with any form of outsourcing of tasks, including crowdsourcing, the risks are non-trivial especially for groups that are more distant geographically, culturally, and intellectually where many situations arise that cannot be foreseen [8]. According to Buecheler et al. [8], crowdsourcing is an extreme case of dealing with the unknown, where the individuals of the crowd are a priori unknown and contingency plans for unexpected behavior of this interacting mass cannot be fully prepared beforehand. The literature on crowdsourcing has raised different risk factors and sources. However, following up on the Syrian crisis, the present research identified three major potential risks that threaten social media crowdsourcing in civil war-torn societies. These are:

Direct Personal Threats

Social media aggregates vast volumes of personal and social information, such as information about the family, relationships, political views, social activities, and religion. Photos, video footage, message or status updates may contain a visual evidence of an individual being present and help identify his identity and disclosing of private and confidential personal details [4]. In civil war-torn societies, user's anonymity is important if content is to be generated and disseminated without fear of recrimination [31]. Being able to locate individuals in particular places can associate them with certain activities that can put citizen journalists and other individuals at risk [4][32]. For example, the use of social media during the Arab revolutions met with resistance whereby some government authorities used citizens' social media trails to identify, locate, and target online protestors [32]. In the periods of political unrest or civil wars, activists on social media are encountering a wide range of risks and threats, including, but not limited to, exposing the private information, online attacks, imprisonment, harassment, threats to relatives, torture, kidnapping, and death.

In the Syrian civil war, unfortunately, social media are used to identify and target the online antagonists and, in a lot of cases, anti-war activists. According to the website of "Raqqa is being slaughtered silently" (2015), the terrorist Daash (Arabic acronym for ISIS) has launched electronic cells to tail the online anti-activists and gather information leading to arrest and prosecute them. These cells launch fake websites and depictive pages and groups on SNSs opposed to ISIS, attracting and hunting the anti-activists within the city of Raqqa to reveal their true identities. Usually, such people are sentenced to death by beheading. In 30 October 2015, Raqqa is Being Slaughtered Silently campaign has announced that two activists of the group were found beheaded in the Turkish town of Urfa, in what is believed to be the terror group's first assassination out. The Syrian Observatory for Human Rights (2015) reported that Daash elements have executed a girl in Deir al-Zour because they found a conversation against via the application "WhatsApp" on her mobile phone with her brother and another relative. In many instances, the use of social media by members of the public can result in harm to specific individuals who were erroneously identified through vigilante justice and potential harm to responders, including members of the public, who may be operating in a crisis [4].

The Penetration of Terrorism Ideology

The spread of terrorist ideology and the ability of terrorists to penetrate the most fortified segments of societies represent one of the most complex risks facing not only the Middle East but also the entire world. Terrorism ideology can be thought of as the virus that is looking for hardware to settle in. Unfortunately, social media has provided a unique opportunity to disseminate the terrorist ideology across borders and recruit hundreds of thousands of fighters and sympathizers from around the world under cover of religion. It became one of the strategic factors driving the efforts of terrorist organizations for a wide range of purposes, including recruitment, radicalization, indoctrination, and incitement to terrorism [33]-[35].

One of the primary uses of the social media by terrorists is for the dissemination of propaganda to validate the terrorist cause in religious, political and ideological terms in the context of conspiracy theories [33]. For example, According to the Atlantic Website (2015), one of Daash's more successful ventures is an Arabic-language Twitter app called The Dawn of Glad Tidings, or just Dawn as a way to keep up on the latest news about the jihadi groups. The tweets include links, hashtags, and images, and the same content is also tweeted by the accounts of everyone else who has signed up for the app. Propaganda generally takes the form of multimedia communications providing ideological or practical instruction, explanations, justifications or promotion of terrorist activities. The visitors' number of Daash official Website has reached by October, 20015 to more than 3,425,032. Propaganda videos for Daash are disseminated on the Youtube, where users can view over 144,000 videos ranging from messages, interviews by prominent leaders and fighters to videos of beheadings and other terrorist operations using advanced cinematic techniques.

Social media represents an effective platform for the recruitment of minors, who comprise a high proportion of users in the Middle East. According to UN [34], terrorist organizations and their affiliates have employed social media effectively to target minors using a variety of tactics, such as mixing cartoons and children's stories, mixing blaring religious songs and terrorist operations, computer games with messages promoting the terrorism ideology. Moreover, several studies [33]-[35] have described the influential role of the social media in enhancing the likelihood of self-radicalization. Behr et al. [35] clarified the impact that watching terrorists' videos on a daily basis and having constant access to terrorists' online platforms have on the speed of self-radicalization without even socializing with radical groups.

Advocacy of Hatred

While hatred is found in almost all societies, including those where the risk of violence is limited, the concept of hate speech aims at isolating acts that have a significant probability of catalyzing violence by one group against another [36]. In this context, the purpose of hate speech is to intimidate, create a fear denigrate the dignity, humiliate, harass, and put antagonists under psychological and social pressures. Many of international civilian institutions as well as researchers have expressed their concern over the spread of hate speech in the social media [31][34][36]. Hatred represents the spirit of Middle East conflicts, especially the current civil wars. It is the dominant motivation for the continuation of destructive Syria's civil war. In the Syrian civil war, social media has become a platform for organized hate groups to recruit and organize attacks against their antagonists.

Syrian religious population is made up of many faiths and sects, including Sunni, Alawites, Shia, and Ismaili, as well as Christians. The Syrian population also has traditionally been composed of a rich diversity of ethnic communities, such as Arabs, Kurds, Armenians, Chaldeans, Assyrians, Turkmen, and Circassians.

Actually, many of Syrian antagonists are using social media to disseminate, incite, and justify all forms of hatred including aggressive nationalism, discrimination, ethnocentrism, and hostility. The online ruthless campaigns are targeting, particularly, families of minority communities to force them to leave their cities and towns in an attempt to change the demographic map of the Syrian society structure, carrying out widespread ethno-religious cleansing. Terrorist organizations are depending to a large extent on social media to stir up panic and hatred of other members' branches and religions to keep and maintain the sectarian clashes. The terrorist social media platforms have exploited, in the most horrendous manner imaginable, hatred against followers of other branches and religious communities to attract fighters and a popular incubator among the Syrians.

C. The Continuity of participation in Social Media Crowdsourcing

Many of previous studies (e.g., [37] [38]) confirmed that satisfaction of users' needs is the major driver to continue using social media through perceived usefulness and conformation of expectations. At the same time, prior studies (e.g. [37] [39]) revealed that perceived risks are a critical determinant to the decision of continue adopting and using social media. In essence, by engaging in social media crowdsourcing, the members decide to deal with various degrees of risk of the free actions of others.

The literature (e.g. [32][40]) reveals that participants continually negotiate and direct the tension between perceived risks and expected outcomes of using social media. A number of researchers (e.g. [39] [40]), agreed that because of the perceived risks, users may change their evaluation of participating in social media crowdsourcing over time. Therefore, the present research suggests that, in war-torn societies, civilians and activists are constantly evaluating the value of using social media and building their own perceptions towards the benefits and risks of participating in social media crowdsourcing. The consequences may affect their inner thoughts concerning the value of continuity of participation in such crowds.

V. CONCLUSION AND FUTURE WORK

Although there is an extensive and evolving interest in the social media crowdsourcing in the normal stable conditions, comparatively little research exists on harnessing social media crowdsourcing to participate in crises management in war-torn societies. The purpose of the present research was to investigate motivations of social media crowdsourcing in war-torn societies and potential risks as the determinants of continuity of participating in online crowdsourcing communities via social media during civil wars. The present study revealed that social media is not just a platform for social interaction or other traditional purposes that have been mentioned in the related literature. Maslow's hierarchy of needs has been used for understanding motivations of social media crowdsourcing. The present research also investigates three major potential risks associated with social media crowdsourcing in civil war-torn societies, including direct personal threats, the penetration of terrorism ideology, and advocacy of hatred.

There are some limitations which can serve as directions for future research. The research framework needs to be tested empirically. Furthermore, the present research did not address all possible motivations and risks that have been discussed in previous studies.

REFERENCES

[1] M. Manso and B. Manso, "The Role of Social Media in Crisis: A European Holistic Approach to the Adoption of Online and Mobile Communications in Crisis Response and Search and Rescue Efforts," Proceedings of the International Command and Control Research and Technology Symposium (ICCRTS), June 19 - 21, 2012, Fairfax, Virginia, USA, 2012, pp. 1–50.

[2] C.-M. Huang, E. Chan, and A. A. Hyder, "Web 2.0 and Internet Social Networking: A New tool for Disaster Management? Lessons from Taiwan," BMC Medical Informatics & Decision Making, 10(1), 2010, pp. 57–61.

[3] S. Wigley and W. Zhang, "A Study of PR Practitioners' Use of Social Media in Crisis Planning," Public Relations Journal, 5 (3), 2011, pp. 1–16.

[4] H. Watson, L. Baruh, R. Finn, and S. Scifo, "Citizen (In)security?: Social Media, Citizen Journalism and Crisis Response," Proceedings of the 11th International ISCRAM Conference –, May 2014, University Park, Pennsylvania, USA, S.R. Hiltz, M. Pfaff, L. Plotnick, and P. Shih, eds, 2014, pp. 294–298.

[5] A. Eksi, S. Çelikli, and G. Kıyan, "The Effects of Social Networking on Disaster Communication Used by the Emergency Medical and Rescue Staff," The Journal of Academic Emergency Medicine, 13 (2), 2014, pp. 58-61.

[6] K. Sedra, "The Role of Social Media & Networking in Post-Conflict Settings: Lessons-Learned from Egypt," Proceedings of the World Bank/TDRP – African Development Bank Conference, June 5-6, Tunis, 2013, pp. 1–12.

[7] J. Howe, "Crowdsourcing: Why the Power of the Crowd is Driving the Future of Business," New York, 2008. NY: Crown Business.

[8] T. Buecheler, J. Sieg, R. Füchslin,, and R. Pfeifer, "Crowdsourcing, Open Innovation and Collective Intelligence in the Scientific Method," Proceedings of the 12th International Conference on the Synthesis and Simulation of Living Systems, Odense, Denmark, 19 23 August, 2010, pp. 679-686.

[9] S. Vieweg, A.L. Hughes, K. Starbird, and L. Palen, "Microblogging during two Natural Hazards Events: What Twitter may Contribute to Situational Awareness," Proceedings of the SIGCHI Conference on Human Factors in Computing Systems (2010, April) ACM, 2010, pp. 1079–1088.

[10] J. Rogstadius, et al., "CrisisTracker: Crowdsourced Social Media Curation for Disaster Awareness, " IBM Journal of Research and Development, 57 (5), pp. 2013, 4:1–4:13.

[11] M. Boulos, et al., "Crowdsourcing, Citizen Sensing and Sensor Web Technologies for Public and Environmental Health Surveillance and Crisis Management," International Journal of Health Geographic, 10(1): 67, 2011, pp. 1-29.

[12] L. Sweta, "Early Warning Systems and Disaster Management using Mobile Crowdsourcing," International Journal of Science and Research, 3(4), 2014, pp. 356-365.

[13] K. Starbird, L. Palen, A. Hughes, and S. Vieweg, "Chatter on the Red: What Hazards Threat Reveals about the Social Life of Microblogged Information," Proceedings of the ACM Conference on Computer supported cooperative work, 2010, pp. 241-250.

[14] M. Latonero and I. Shklovski, "Emergency Management, Twitter, and Social Media Evangelism," International Journal of Information Systems for Crisis Response and Management, 3 (4), 2011, pp. 1–16.

[15] I. Kotsiopoulos, "Social Media in Crisis Management: Role, Potential and Risk," Proceedings of the 2014 IEEE/ACM 7th International Conference on Utility and Cloud Computing, 8-11 Dec, London, 2014, 681 – 686.

[16] R. M. Ryan and E. L. Deci, "Intrinsic and Extrinsic Motivations: Classic Definitions and New Directions," Contemporary Educational Psychology 25(1), 2000, pp. 54–67.

[17] https://ar-ar.facebook.com/ICRCsy [retrieved: March. 2016].

[18] https://www.facebook.com/SYRedCrescent [retrieved: March, 2016].

[19] https://www.facebook.com/missing.syria[retrieved: March. 2016].

[20] https://ar-ar.facebook.com/MissingAndMartyrs [retrieved: March, 2016].

[21] A. Flizikowski, W. Hołubowicz, A. Stachowicz, L. Hokkanen, T. Kurki, and N. Päivinen,"Social Media in Crisis Management the iSAR+ Project Survey" Proceedings of the 11th International ISCRAM Conference, University Park, Pennsylvania, USA, S.R. Hiltz, M.S. Pfaff, L. Plotnick, and P.C. Shih, eds, 2014, pp. 707-711.

[22] https://www.facebook.com/snhr [retrieved: March. 2016].

[23] https://ar-ar.facebook.com/vdcsv [retrieved: March. 2016].

[24] https://twitter.com/Raqqa_SL [retrieved: March, 2016].

[25] https://www.facebook.com/prayforpeaceSYRIA [retrieved: March, 2016].

[26] https://www.facebook.com/-\l‚no-ik-ℴiafl-efl-cd-ö Y'aYfl-WXYZ [\- 389850064469574-_/timeline/ [retrieved: March, 2016].

[27] https://www.facebook.com/PeoplesCommissionforNationalReconciliation [retrieved: March, 2016].

[28] A. Maslow, "A Theory of Human Motivation," Psychological Review, 50(4), 1943, pp. 370-396.

[29] Z. Tufekci, "Can You See Me Now? Audience and Disclosure Regulation in Online Social Network Sites," Bulletin of Science, Technology & Society 28 (1), 2008, pp. 20–36.

[30] J. Hart, C. Ridley, F. Taher, C. Sas, and A. Dix, "Exploring the Facebook Experience. A new Approach to Usability," Proceedings of the 5th Nordic Conference on Human-computer Interaction: Building Bridges, 18–22 October 2008, Lund, Sweden, 2008, pp. 471–474.

[31] A. Skuse and T. Brimacombe, "Social Networking, Social Media and Complex Emergencies," Australian Civil-Military Center,https://www.acmc.gov.au/wp-content/uploads/2014/09/Social-Media-and-Complex-Emergencies-Annotated Bibliography.pdf, 2014, pp. 1–76.

[32] E. Iskander, "Connecting the National and the Virtual: Can Facebook Activism Remain Relevant after Egypt's January 25 uprising?," International Journal of Communication, vol. 5, 2011, pp. 1225–37.

[33] A. Aly, "The Terrorists'Audience: A Model of Internet Radicalisation," Journal of Australian Professional Intelligence Officers, 17(1), 2009, pp. 3–19.

[34] United Nations Office on Drugs and Crimes, "The Use of the Internet for Terrorist Purposes," United Nations, New York, 2012,https://www.unodc.org/documents/frontpage/Use_of_Internet_for_Terrorist_Purposes.pdf, 2012, pp. 1–158.

[35] I. Behr, A. Reding, C. Edwards, and L. Gribbon, "Radicalisation in the Digital Era: The Use of the Internet in 15 Cases of Terrorism and Extremism," (RAND Research Reports, RR-453-RE), 2013, pp. 1–76.

[36] I. Gagliardone, D. Gal, T. Alves, and G. Martinez, "Countering Online Heat Speech," UNESCO, France, 2015, pp. 1–73.

[37] T. Hu and W. Kettinger, "Why People Continue to Use Social Networking Services: Developing a Comprehensive Model", Proceedings of the International Conference on Information Systems (ICIS), Paris, France, 14-17 December, 2008, pp. 1–11.

[38] Cao, H., et al., "Maslow's Hierarchy of Needs Analysis of Social Networking Services Continuance," Journal of Service Management, 24(2), 2013, pp. 170–190.

[39] F. Stutzman, R. Capra, and J. Thompson, "Factors Mediating Disclosure in Social Network Sites," Computers in Human Behavior, 27(1), 2010, pp. 590–598.

[40] K. Al Omoush, S. Yassen, M. Alma'aitah, "The Impact of Arab Cultural Values on Online Social Networking: The Case of Facebook," Computer in Human Behavior, 28(6), 2012, pp. 2387–2399.

Design and Evaluation of Place Oriented Radio by the Measurement of Cross-Cultural Understandings

Ayaka Ito
Graduate School of Media and Governance
Keio University
Fujisawa, Japan
e-mail: ayk@sfc.keio.ac.jp

Katsuhiko Ogawa
Faculty of Environment and Information Studies
Keio University
Fujisawa, Japan
e-mail: ogw@sfc.keio.ac.jp

Abstract— **The number of foreigners who visit Japan is increasing and it is important to build mutual understanding with people of different cultural backgrounds. In order to enhance foreigner's visits to Japan, we propose a place oriented Internet radio called Cross-Cultural Radio (CCR). Subsequently, a Cross-Cultural Understanding Scale (CCUS) was proposed and an evaluation experiment was conducted in Tokyo to measure the effectiveness of CCR. Our experimental results illustrate that CCR can be effective in certain aspects of cross-cultural understanding. This paper intends to explore the acculturation process amongst foreign visitors to Japan by analyzing the behavior of participants in the experiment.**

Keywords— ***place orientation; Internet radio; cross-cultural understanding; measurement; evaluation.***

I. INTRODUCTION

Because of the great diversity in the modern world and its continuous change, defining the term "culture" is an extremely tough activity. However, like Damasio [1], who claimed that "culture is a regulator of human life and identity", many scholars have attempted to conceptualize their understanding of culture. Nonetheless, several aspects of culture such as goods, feelings, actions and words can be very specific to a particular region. They are difficult to grasp from guidebooks or from just browsing the Internet, because, in many cases, these contents are provided based on visible (and generally superficial) information. It is quite easy to gain stereotypical ideas about Japan in front of the laptop but there will never be a better experience than direct interaction with local people. This is because they give foreigners real cultural ideas, and thus having a channel to boost this kind of communication is highly important.

For instance, a keyword which seems to be distinctive for the culture of Japan is "Kodawari", which is difficult to translate literally in English; yet "to be particular about a manner" would be the closest. Its meaning is not just to be particular, but to have a strong belief, or an excessive target on the action. Many craftsmen in Japan have "Kodawari" in what they create or how they are getting involved in the industry, and having strong pride in what they do and would never compromise their work is regarded as a virtue.

Another example of a keyword is "Omotenashi", a word that became slightly famous after the presentation to host the Olympics in 2020. "Omotenashi" means to treat anyone sincerely and warmheartedly, whether or not that person is a customer, a guest, a family member, or an acquaintance. The core of this concept is to express consideration and respect to others. This act would also require the person to understand the atmosphere, feel the mood and the invisible energy, which is wrapped around the occasion or person. Ultimately, it does not mean to entertain the person and achieve any kind of self-satisfaction, but to quickly perceive the person's needs, desires, overall mood, and entertain the person accordingly with a warm heart.

As the mobility of people has been rapidly improved and the number of foreigners who visit Japan is increasing [2], recognizing diversity to build cross-cultural understanding is becoming a crucial interest in the country. We have to be aware that all foreigners are unique individuals, and we should not generalize them by nationality, ethnic groups, and religion. Foreigners are visiting Japan for several purposes such as sightseeing, studying abroad or working. Likewise, depending on the length of time in Japan or their cultural background, the problem they encounter greatly varies, and there will never be a solution applicable for everyone. Especially, the problems which foreign visitors face are derived from not knowing Japanese cultural keywords exemplified previously (and there are countless of other words, not only "Kodawari" or "Omotenashi"), or it occurs when the meaning of keywords conflict with their cultural beliefs in various communicative settings. To propose a way to solve their problems individually, thus creating new media to provide foreigners opportunities to know Japanese culture at a deeper level is meaningful from a cross-cultural viewpoint. In other words, foreign visitors further understanding of Japanese culture will be achieved when they listen to local people's story in a particular place, or other foreigners opinion about the place they are visiting.

In terms of tourists revisiting places, previous literature has shown the effect of motivation and satisfaction is prominent according to Yoon [3] and Bramwell [4]. Alegre [5] and Ekinci et al. [6] also pointed out, the eagerness of tourists' visiting in relation to the characteristics of places.

In terms of information system, Masuda [7] and Takagi [8] suggested a recommender system for tourists, which provides customized tour information, depending on user's needs, including using smartphone applications. However, there is almost no research on using Internet radio specifically as a tool for building cross-cultural understanding in Japan.

In this paper, we propose a place-oriented Internet radio called CCR, which helps foreigners to recognize Japan from a cross-cultural perspective by providing place oriented content. In addition, we created an original criteria CCUS and conducted an evaluation experiment in Tokyo to measure the actual effectiveness of content and CCR itself.

The paper structure is explained as follows: first, Section II describes the design phase of CCR including its concept and system configuration. Secondly, detailed explanation of measurement CCUS is offered in Section III, including background research. Section IV gives a complete set of evaluation experiments conducted in Tokyo, and Section V digs the result into a further behavioral analysis. Lastly, the conclusion and future works are mentioned in Section VI.

II. Design of Cross-Cultural Radio

A. Concept

Previously referred related research, especially Masuda and Takagi's recommender system for tourists, are designed for the usage in a specific place. However, the information they provide to listeners only focuses on tourist's preference and does not include cultural perspectives of the host country, which promotes cross-cultural understandings amongst international listeners.

As for the type of information available, visual material such as detailed information on smartphone contributes to get a general idea about a place to a certain extent. Nevertheless, sound information is far superior to visual information in giving listeners flexibility, by allowing them to stretch their imagination about what they have heard. Furthermore, sound information can provide direct interaction connected to the place including local people's story or comments from other tourists. This also might be a trigger for international listeners to understand Japanese culture more.

For these reasons, this paper intends to propose a place oriented Internet radio called CCR as a new sound-focused media, by providing international listeners several types of content. The detailed concept is shown in Figure 1.

CCR works in three steps. First is content design for personalities. Second is listening process by various listeners such as international tourists, studying abroad students and multinational corporations employees who are not familiar with Japanese culture. Third is getting feedback plus revision of the content. To maximize the influence of contents, the preferred target of CCR is international visitors who are staying in Japan for a relatively long period of time, from a few months to years rather than just a couple of days, because, in general, understanding a certain culture often takes time and the experience they have in the host country is enriched in daily life settings.

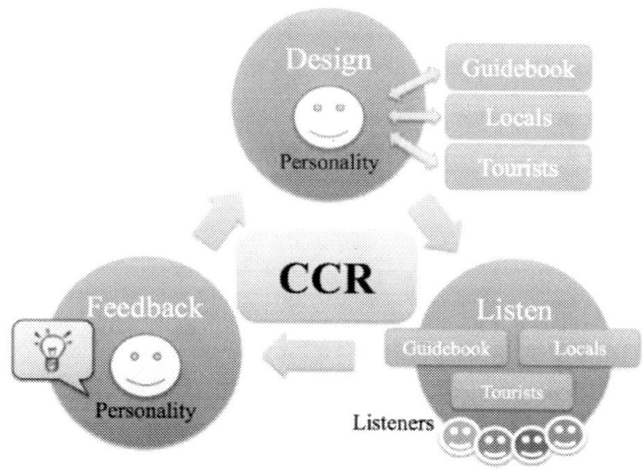

Figure 1. Concept of Cross-Cultural Radio "CCR"

Three types of content are available for international visitors: the guidebook (audio clips from the famous Lonely Planet guidebook), the locals (stories or tips from local people), and tourists (feedback from the listener to be shared with other tourists). As a first step of the cycle, this paper explicitly deals with the content Guidebook and Locals.

B. System

Previous research [9]~[12] shows that the acceptable duration of content should be around 1 minute to 1 and half minutes. Several companies deal with the production of audio guide players supporting the delivery of content as described above.

1) Selecting Location

As CCR is designed for international visitors for Japan. The selection of a place where the content is mapped is also important. In this research, Asakusa, one of the most famous and popular tourist spots in Tokyo, was chosen. The reason is that Asakusa has a rich cultural heritage such as Japanese traditional temples or shrines, as well as dining venues and souvenir shops that attract many international tourists. Besides, Asakusa is located in the heart of Tokyo and has great accessibility, which enables us to conduct fieldwork effortlessly.

2) Content "Guidebook"

For guidebook content, several tips of accommodation, introduction of restaurants and explanation of famous architecture were picked from Lonely Planet Tokyo [13] and recorded using voice synthesis software (Figure 2).

"Asakusa Engei-hall"
Have you ever seen standup comedy in your country? If you want to experience Japanese traditional comedy performance, here is the place. This is called Asakusa Engei-hall, provides humorous talking by classic rakugo speakers. The audience also enjoys stage arts unique to the theater, including the paper cutout and funny music played by carpenters tool.

Figure 2. Example of content Guidebook

3) Content "Locals"

For locals content, a couple of interviews with locals were conducted in Japanese and stories related to their daily lives in Asakusa were selected. Each story was translated into English and supplementary explanation about cultural activity was added if needed (Figure 3).

"Future of Asakusa"
(After the local's interview in Japanese) Before World War 2, Asakusa has been one of the most energetic, cutting edge cities in Japan. But unfortunately nowadays it's taken over by other big cities like Roppongi or Shinjuku. She feels to revitalize Asakusa as a vivid city, collaboration with local community is important, not only bringing lots of tourists from outside. Using social networking service can be one of them; so young generation helps older shop owners to introduce these up-to-date technologies into traditional Japanese shops.

Figure 3. Example of content Locals

4) Mapping content into CCR

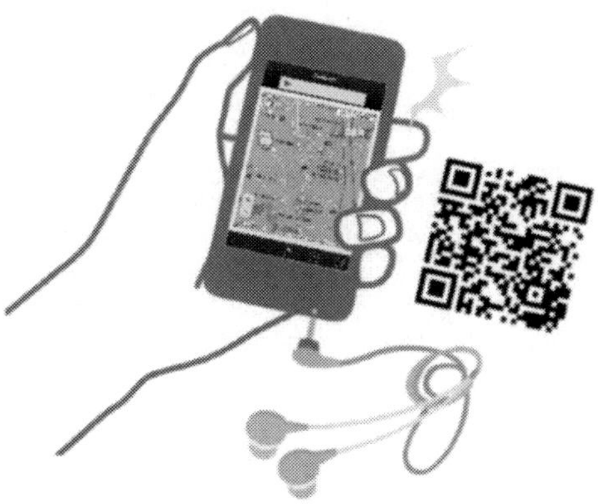

Figure 4. CCR can be accessed through a QR code

The audio clips are stored in the website, and linked to icons using JavaScript code. When the user clicks on an icon, the associated audio clip is played. The website can be accessed here [14] or by using the QR code shown in Figure 4.

III. Measurement CCUS

To validate the credibility of CCR, an evaluation process with appropriate criteria is essential. Since CCR has a unique concept, inventing a new and suitable measurement tool is more realistic rather than using conventional criteria without localization. Related literature about measurement design and cross-cultural adjustment are demonstrated by Benson [15], Cui & Awa [16] and Yellen [17]. Ten dimensions of cross-cultural understandings have been determined, which are:

A. Mobility

An individual's ability to find his/her way around in the foreign place is one of the most important dimensions of cross-cultural understandings. Knowing local geography and usage of public transportation systems are two potential items for this dimension. Ability to ask staff around in the face of uncertainty for directions, or usage of appropriate tools such as map application on smartphone is included.

B. Food/Diet

Although food allergy is not the case, this dimension involves being open-minded to try new food, and how he/she can be adaptable for the change of diet. Accepting foreign food and culinary manners cannot be omitted when understanding certain culture, and for many people eating food is a big aspect of cultural exchange.

C. Flexibility

As Hofstede defined "uncertainty avoidance" in his prominent work [18], more or less people from any cultural background may face culture shock and attempt to escape from that anxiety. Being flexible, patient, and tolerant for such uncertain activity or unexpected cultural norm is one dimension.

D. Knowledge

Whether he/she accepts it or not, acknowledgment of host culture is an essential aspect of cross-cultural understandings. In terms of socially appropriate behaviors, host country nationals have certain expectations as to how foreigners in their country should behave includes avoiding offensive actions. Webb et al.'s unobtrusive measure [19] could be useful in this regard.

E. Language Skills

This dimension appears consistently as a core criterion of mutual understanding as former literatures are reviewed. However, we should be aware that when cultural adaptation or acculturation occurs, an adapted individual will learn the language, but individual who learn the language may or may not adapt.

F. Interaction

The nature and frequency of interactions with host country individuals is an indication of individual's level of cross-cultural understandings. This involves one's ability to initiate interaction, as well as the extent of his/her eagerness to communicate with Japanese people, regardless of language ability.

G. Awareness of Cultural Differnce

A question such as "to what extent are you aware of Japanese culture/society is different from yours?" is asked in this dimension. Recognition of cultural difference between their own is a starting point to build mutual understanding in any circumstances.

H. Nonverbal Communication

In addition to language, there are a variety of ways to communicate nonverbally. Understanding visible gestures and appreciating personal space are some of them. Also having a reasonable repertoire of "communicative currency" may be useful as a criterion dimension.

I. Respect

Being interested in the host country citizens and casual friendliness towards them should be relevant as cross-cultural understandings. For instance, willingness to participate in activities distinctive to the host country will raise a fundamental respect for others and might lead to an appreciation of his/her current state.

J. Relationship

Inclination to establish and maintain relationships regardless of the skills is one crucial dimension. Even though this can be influenced by an individual's personal character such as being extroverted or introverted, we should be aware that every individual has his/her own pace for building it. For instance, not all introverts are weak in relationship building than extroverts; they will establish deeper and more stable relationship with others.

After the relevant literature was reviewed and dimensions mentioned above were rationalized, these new criteria were named CCUS. In the evaluation phase, measurement users score each dimensions from 1 to 10 (Figure 5), using the self-evaluation method.

```
|------|------|------|------|------|------|------|------|------|

1   2   3   4   5   6   7   8   9   10

Low --------------------------------------------→ High
```

Figure 5. Scoring system of CCUS

This evaluation is conducted twice, before and after any related experiments such as fieldwork or interview. Afterwards, two score results are compared and discussed.

IV. EVALUATION EXPERIMENT

A. Method

Fieldwork was conducted for twelve international tourists as CCR listeners, using the same scheme to explore how the cycle of CCR works as an evaluation experiment. In order to observe various cultural exchanges, we tried to select tourists who have diverse cultural backgrounds, as well as their length of stay in Japan. Fieldwork details and participants' attributes are below (Table 1).

TABLE I. FIELDWORK DETAILS AND PARTICIPANTS' ATTRIBUTES

Nationality / Code (xx)	**Participants' Attributes**		
	Age	***Sex***	***Date / Time***
China (CH1)	28	F	October 31st, 2015 / 11:00 – 13:00
Malaysia (ML)	23	F	October 31st, 2015 / 14:00 – 16:00
Taiwan (TW)	20	F	November 1st, 2015 / 11:00 – 13:00
Japan/Korea (JP)	22	F	November 1st, 2015 / 14:00 – 16:00
England (UK)	22	M	November 1st, 2015 / 14:00 – 16:00
Korea (KR)	18	F	November 7th, 2015 / 11:15 – 13:00
India (IN)	19	M	November 7th, 2015 / 15:00 – 16:30
Uzbekistan (UZ)	22	M	November 16th, 2015 / 11:00 – 13:00
China (CH2)	24	F	November 18th, 2015 / 10:00 – 12:00
China (CH3)	25	F	November 18th, 2015 / 10:00 – 12:00
Vietnam (VN)	24	F	November 18th, 2015 / 15:30 – 17:30
Russia (RU)	28	M	November 28th, 2015 / 15:00 – 16:30

B. Instruction

First, a sheet of paper was distributed to the participants as an experiment instruction. Route of fieldwork is printed and they were asked to walk and listen to the content mapped into the route in the numeric order. Before they started walking, they filled in the CCUS form. We observed and took pictures of participants while they are walking (Figure 11), and asked questions to participants for each content such as "what did you think about the place or object, which is explained in the content?" or "do you have any implication or comments compared to your home culture?"

Fieldwork was done either in English or Japanese, depending on participant's language ability. Conversation was recorded and after they listened to all content, they answered the CCUS form again.

C. Result

Figure 6 shows the average score for each dimension, the blue line shows the results prior to the test, the red line shows the results after the test was finished.

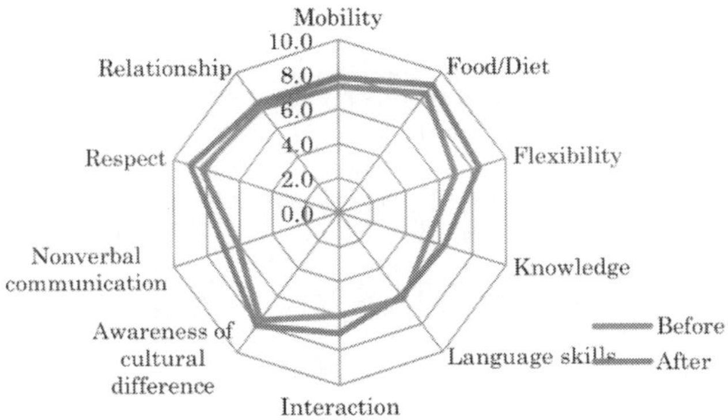

Figure 6. 12 participants' average CCUS score

Most of the dimensions are slightly improved after the fieldwork. Specifically, according to Figure 6, "Flexibility" (+1.4pt), "Knowledge" (+1.0pt) and "Interaction" (+1.0pt) have improved more than other dimensions, and "Language skills" has declined a bit (-0.2pt).

V. BEHAVIORAL ANALYSIS OF PARTICIPANTS

As shown in the result, CCR has enriched most aspects of dimensions. We will have a closer look at specific participant's score based on arbitrary choices, which recorded notable difference for "Flexibility", "Knowledge", "Interaction" and "Language skills", as well as who formed distinct shape of ten dimensions.

A. Participant CH2 (Figure 7)

CH2 is a close friend of CH3 and they took part in the evaluation experiment together. As she has never been in Asakusa before, she was a beginner tourist in a way.

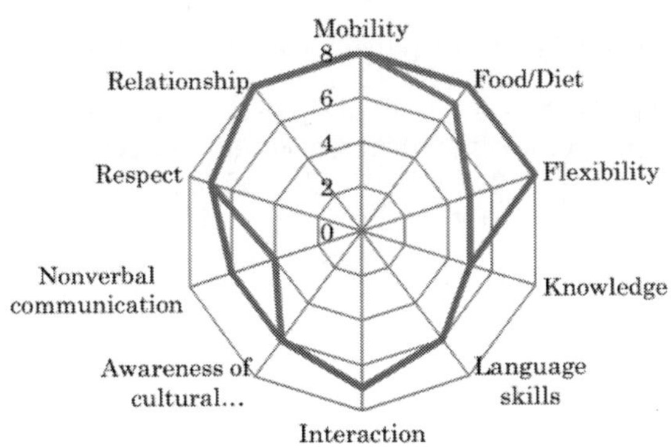

Figure 7. Participant CH2's CCUS score

Especially after listening to content "Guidebook" about small museum shows and offering of Japanese traditional handicrafts, she seemed to be interested in the place mentioned and took a couple of pictures in front of it. She had a conversation with CH3 in Chinese and invited CH3 to go into the museum. Later on, CH2 told us they were talking about the Japanese craftsmen's elaborate work and made a comparison with Chinese merchandise including price. They recalled handicrafts sold in museum were very expensive and unfortunately they were not able to purchase any, nevertheless they were surprised of their good quality.

Talking with a peer participant in home language raised satisfaction to enhance "Flexibility" and "Nonverbal communication", which represents acculturation process [20]~[22] including elimination of uncertainty towards Japanese culture. It is assumed that CH2 has faced Japanese craftsmen's "Kodawari" to their works at the museum as her tangible experience, and the content worked as the trigger of cultural encounter.

B. Participant UZ (Figure 8)

UZ is a university student who has been studying Japanese for two years, and shows a great enthusiasm towards understanding local cultures. He was particularly interested in the concept of CCR and was cooperative for taking part in the evaluation experiment. He was walking the main street of Asakusa called Nakamise-dori, and after he listened to the content where a local person discussed the future of Asakusa (Fig. 3), he mentioned his hometown Samarkand. He told he genuinely would love but because of financial reasons lots of residents are leaving the city and flowing into Toshkent, the capital of Uzbekistan and he feels sad about it. He wishes people in Samarkand will love their city just like as Asakusa locals do. Obviously he felt something in common with Japanese people and cultivated affinity toward Japanese culture. In other words, he got an idea of Asakusa locals' "Omotenashi" mind to the foreigners, as his own mindset in himself when he would feel in Uzbekistan.

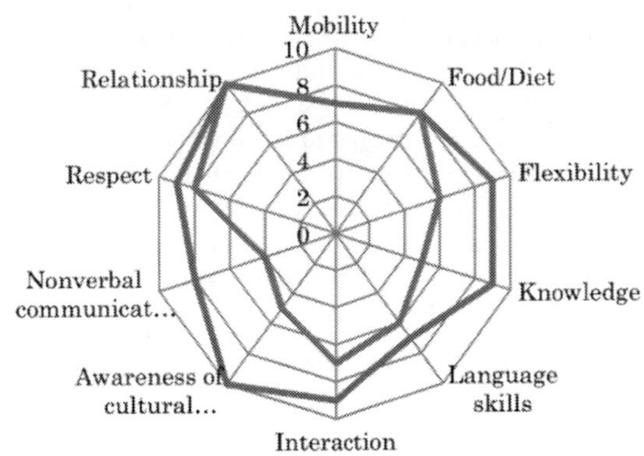

Figure 8. Participant UZ's CCUS score

He commented, "it was fun and I learned some internal/external factors of Japan, especially Asakusa city's culture and society." What he implies as internal and external factors are about the context of both content. Internal factors are invisible cultural aspects such as Asakusa locals' attitude or value to the place, in relation to his radical improvement of "Awareness of cultural difference". On the contrary, external factors are attainable by information input, corresponds to "Knowledge". The synthesis of these noticeable two dimensions has appeared as the improvement of "Flexibility".

C. *Participant JP (Figure 9)*

JP is a friend of UK and they took part in the experiment together. Although born in Japan and being a Japanese citizen, she has international background. She is half Korean and was raised in Hawaii.

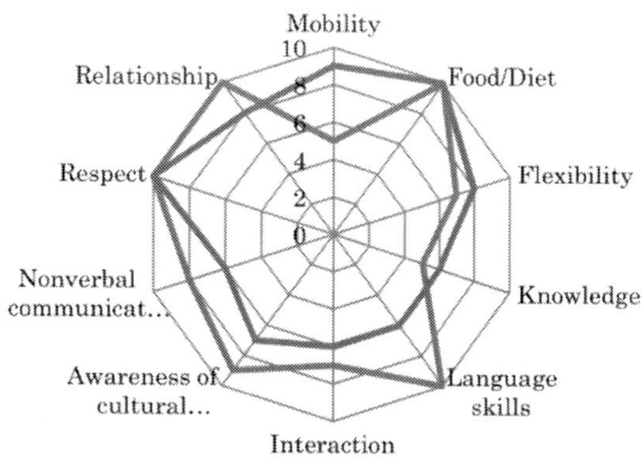

Figure 9. Participant JP's CCUS score

After she listened to "Locals" content about the founding story of Nakamise-dori and a kindergarten nearby, she remembered when she learned phonetics in her childhood in Hawaii. As she has an Asian look some peers automatically assumed that she does not understand any English, hence she had a hard time to build close friendship with them. Now English is her native language and similar circumstance occurs when she encounters Japanese people who guess she would understand Japanese perfectly whilst she actually does not. JP admits "that awkward and annoying moment" frequently happens whenever she recognizes disappointment on their faces. JP's the biggest decline "Language skills" is not irrelevant with her story. On the other hand, she improved "Mobility", explained in her comment "now I feel more confident walking in Asakusa without GoogleMaps".

D. *Participant UK (Figure 10)*

The fieldwork for JP and UK was conducted in English since we wanted to encourage the casual conversation between two peers, which enabled us to observe frequent cultural exchange. UK arrived in Japan about 2 months before the fieldwork, and had just started learning Japanese language and culture.

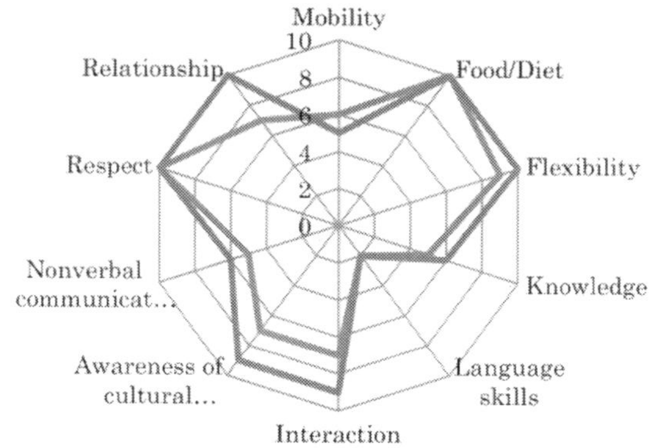

Figure 10. Participant UK's CCUS score

According to his feedback, "Locals" content was more enjoyable than "Guidebook" although he had never visited Asakusa before. JP and UK take the same courses in their studying abroad and had established a good rapport already. UK is researching theories of traditional Japanese music for his master degree, so it is reasonable to assume that he is more interested in Japanese culture than most of international tourists. He may have felt sympathy to the local people talking and that influenced his improvement of "Relationship", "Awareness of cultural difference" and "Interaction".

VI. CONCLUSION AND FUTURE STUDIES

In this paper, place oriented Internet radio called CCR was proposed by providing two types of content, "Guidebook" and "Locals" which gives an idea about real cultural aspects of Japan, represented as "cultural keywords". To validate the effectiveness of this unique media, we also suggested CCUS as new criteria set to measure the level of cross-cultural understanding. According to the overall result of evaluation experiment conducted in Tokyo for 12 participants, it is reasonable to assume CCR has contributed to the enhancement of several aspects such as "Flexibility" and "Interaction" which are cultivated by listening to local's stories, and "Knowledge" in relation to the information provided by the guidebook. Besides, through advanced behavioral analysis for individual participants, some cultural aspects were found such as;

1) Uncertainty Avoidance

Participants CH2 and CH3 both improved "Flexibility" through their conversation about Japanese culture in home language. CCR content will be more understandable when cultural uncertainty is reduced, and participants' verbal and nonverbal interaction greatly contributes to them.

2) Affinity towards Culture

For some participants, CCR content functioned as a sympathy builder. For instance, UZ listened to the "Locals" content illustrates local people's values and felt something in common with his own culture. In his specific case, his cultural appreciation enhanced "Awareness of cultural difference" and "Nonverbal communication".

3) Awareness of Language Skills

We observed the drop of "Language skills" in certain participant such as JP. Possibly this is because after the experiment she was more aware of her level of Japanese proficiency by listening to the "Locals" content, spoken partially in Japanese native speed. In addition, it is quite reasonable to say that just listening to a sequence of short audio clips will not enrich one's language skill hugely. In fact, sometimes it even causes a small decline of confidence.

For the future work, we will develop the variety of place-oriented content and add more participant of the evaluation experiment so CCUS will be more reliable. Additionally, the introduction of content "Tourists" to encourage listener's self/mutual reflection between other listeners is needed, to compare with conventional "Locals" and "Guidebook" content.

References

[1] R. Damasio, "Self comes to mind: Constructing the concious mind" New York, Pantheon, 2010.

[2] Japanese Ministry of Justice. Retrieved on March 12th 2016 from: http://www.moj.go.jp/ENGLISH/index.html

[3] Y. Yoon, and M. Uysal, "An examination of the effects of motivation and satisfaction on destination loyalty - a structural model" Tourism Management, 2005, vol. 26(1), pp.45-56.

[4] B. Bramwell, "User satisfaction and product development in urban tourism" Tourism Management, 1998, vol. 19(1), pp. 35-47.

[5] J. Alegre, and M. Cladera, "Repeat visitation in mature sun and sand holiday destinations" Journal of Travel Research, 2006, vol. 44(3), pp.288-297.

[6] Y. Ekinci, M. Riley, and J. Chen, "A review of comparisons used in service quality and customer satisfaction studies: Emerging issues for hospitality and tourism research" Tourism Analysis, 2001, vol. 5(2) pp. 197-202.

[7] M. Masuda, T. Izumi, and Y. Nakatani, "A system that promotes repeat tourists by making sightseeing unfinished" Human Interface Society, 2012, vol. 14(3), pp.259-270.

[8] S. Takagi, M. Masuda, and Y. Nakatani, "Tour navigation system using landmarks customized by personal preferences" Information Processing Society of Japan, 2012, vol. 3, pp.305-306.

[9] M. Hatala, and R. Wakkary, "Ontology-based user modeling in an augumented audio reality system for museums" User Modeling and User-Adapted Interaction, 2005, vol. 15(3), pp:339-380.

[10] S. Bodker, "Through the interface: a human activity approach to user interface design" Malwah, NJ: Lawrence Erlbaum Associates, Inc, 1990.

[11] D. Dean, "Museum exhibition: theory and practice" London, Routledge, 1994.

[12] C. Hummels, and A. Helm, "ISH and the search for resonant tangible interaction" Personal Ubiquitous Computing, 2004, vol. 8(5), pp.385–388.

[13] T. Hornyak, and R. Milner, "Lonely Planet Tokyo (Travel Guide) 9th Edition", NY: Lonely Planet, 2012.

[14] Cross-Cultural Radio. Retrieved on March 12th 2016 from: http://web.sfc.keio.ac.jp/~ayk/reradio/map.php

[15] P. Benson, "Measuring cross-cultural adjustment: the problem of crieria" International Journal of Intercultural Relations, 1978, vol. 2(1), pp.21–37.

[16] G. Cui, and N. Awa, "Measuring intercultural effectiveness: an integrative approach," International Journal of Intercultural Relations, 1992, vol. 16, pp.311–328.

[17] T. Yellen, "The cross-cultural interaction inventory: development of overseas criterion measures and items that differentiate between successful and unsuccessful adjusters" National Technical Information Service, 1975, vol. 3, pp.1-19.

[18] G. Hofstede, "Cultures and organization: software of the mind" NY: McGraw-Hill, 1991.

[19] E. Webb, D. Campbell, R. Schwartz, and L. Sechrest, "Unobtrusive measures – nonreactive research in the social sciences" IL: Rand McNally and Co, 1966.

[20] J. Berry, "Acculturation: living successfully in two cultures" International Journal of Intercultural Relations, 2005, vol. 29(6), pp. 697-712.

[21] T. Graves, "Psychological acculturation in a tri-ethnic community" South-Western Journal of Anthropology, 1968, vol. 23, pp.337-350.

[22] A. Ryder, and L. Alden, "Is acculturation uni-dimensional or bi-dimensional?" Journal of Personality and and Social Psychology, 2000, vol. 79, pp.49-65.

Figure 11. Participants taking evaluation experiment in Asakusa

Digital Services for the Aging Society: The Impact of Previous Workplace Priviliges on Mature Adults' Use of the Internet

Heiko Gewald and Robert Rockmann
Center for Research on Service Sciences (CROSS)
Neu-Ulm University of Applied Sciences
Neu-Ulm, Germany
e-mail: heiko.gewald@hs-neu-ulm.de; robert.rockmann@hs-neu-ulm.de

Abstract—**Developed economies face severe challenges from demographic change. A popular measure to counter this development is to empower the aging society for longer independent living. Digital services offered through the Internet are discussed as major enabling factor. However, although this seems the natural way to help this clientele, our knowledge on Internet usage habits of the elderly is still limited. Therefore, we conducted a quantitative study targeting the 50+ population to assess the effect previous Internet usage at work has on current private Internet use. Our findings underline the high importance which Internet self-efficacy and anxiety have on the actual use of Internet services.**

Keywords: Internet Use; Mature Adults; Computer Self-Efficacy; Computer Anxiety.

I. INTRODUCTION

Literally all developed economies face the problem of an adverse demographic structure [2]. Especially Europe has been struck by the challenge that the general population rapidly grows older and in the near future old people will have outnumbered the young ones [3]. The demographic change affects society in many ways. One of the most pressuring being a severe shortage of people working in the service industry to care for the aging generation. This applies specifically to health professionals [4] as older people tend to increasingly request health related services. But not only healthcare, also other service areas suffer from a lack of qualified personnel.

As widely propagated answer to counter this challenge is to provide digital services for the elderly to enable them to longer live autonomously. eHealth and telemedicine offerings are booming these days [5]. However, despite the numerous offerings the proof that these mechanisms are effective is still outstanding. Several studies point out that adoption rates for eHealth and telemedicine are low [2].

To a certain extent, this mismatch between supply and demand may arise from a lack of knowledge about the level of comfort elderly people have interacting with the Internet. This poses a severe challenge for current research, as there is certain ignorance about old people's attitude towards the Internet and the offerings presented via this channel. In fact, even the few IS studies that used the concept of age as a substantive variable have mostly relied on stereotypical accounts alone to justify their age-related hypotheses [6].

In order to provide digitalization to the aging society, we first need to understand more about the behavioral intention and attitudes of the elderly. This research aims to provide insights into these matters. As pointed out before, the elderly are not a homogenous group but in fact as heterogeneous as all other segments of the population. With respect to Internet use we see different shades of grey ranging from frantic users to total rejection. Reason for rejection could be that the person had no prior contact to the Internet during younger times. Therefore, we hypothesize that there is a positive relation between previous Internet experience and current use. To investigate this question we put forward the research question: What is the relationship between previous Internet usage at work and current Internet use in private life?

Our findings are assumed to help developing more suitable digitalization services for the aging society.

To shed light on this question we developed a theory-guided questionnaire that was tested with 148 participants 50 and above. As we were targeting the general population (including those who only make very limited use of the Internet) the research needed to be conducted as physical interviews to avoid bias towards those who use the Internet more frequently.

The paper is structured as follows. In Section 2, we briefly outline important individual differences found in prior literature on mature adults' technology use. In Section 3 we develop our research model and derive according hypotheses how mature adults' private Internet usage is influenced by prior workplace Internet usage. Thereafter, in Section 4, the research method is described in detail and participants' demographics, as well as results are discussed. Following that, the findings are presented and limitations explicated in Section 5. The paper closes with an outlook to further research and the conclusion in Section 6.

II. LITERATURE REVIEW

Research identified several sources of individual differences in IT related behavior. These are demographic factors (age, gender, income, level of education, etc.), situational variables (knowledge, expertise, etc.) or IT-specific individual characteristics [7][8]. Naturally, the latter are regarded as prime candidates in explaining and predicting individual differences in IT-related behavior [8][9]. Specifically Computer Self-Efficacy and Computer Anxiety have previously shown to assert a severe impact towards human behavior on IT-related matters, both, in general [8][9] and in the context of mature adults [10][11]. Within this section, we briefly outline these two distinct individual characteristics – Computer Self-Efficacy and Computer Anxiety– and their importance for mature adults.

A. *Computer Self-Efficacy*

Computer Self-Efficacy (CSE) is defined as the "judgment of one's capability to use a computer" [12, p. 192]. The concept originated from Bandura's Social Cognitive Theory [13][14] where general self-efficacy reflects "the belief in one's capability to organize and execute the courses of action required to manage prospective situations" [14, p. 2]. Self-efficacy thereby acts as a key determinant of behavioral control [14][15]. It has been consequently incorporated into the Theory of Planned Behavior (TPB) by reflecting internal control beliefs [16].

IS researching utilizing CSE consequently theorized about the role of CSE as determinant of IT-related behavior from different perspectives [17][18][19]. Consequently, CSE has been found to play an important role in individual's technology-directed behavior by influencing adoption decisions and actual use both directly and indirectly [20][21][22]. For instance, CSE significantly influences ease of use and usefulness perceptions and thereby indirectly influences behavioral outcomes such as intention or actual use of a given technology [23]. Likewise, several direct effects of CSE have been reported in the literature, whereby CSE significantly individuals' intention to use or to continue using a technology [15][22][24][25].

With respect to Internet usage, Davis and Mun [26] revealed that CSE highly predicts the extent to which individuals utilize the web by means of how frequently certain functions such as online-shopping or social networks are used. Wang, Li and Hsieh [27] show that CSE acts as a strong contingent effect on how individuals found innovative uses of IT. In contrast to these findings Mcelroy, Hendrickson, Townsend and Demarie [28] found that general self-efficacy does not predict how often users surf the Internet or visit chat-rooms, but that it predicts whether users are willing to shop online or not, thereby reflecting an absolute measure of an extended use case.

In the realm of mature adults, research likewise emphasized the important role of CSE on elderly individuals' technology behavior. By drawing on Social Cognitive Theory, Lam and Lee [11] have shown how CSE among with outcome expectations predicts Internet use intentions. In a recent study investigating the predictive power of major technology acceptance models, Niehaves and Plattfaut [29] reported that CSE constitutes the strongest predictor by outperforming other important factors.

Given these insights about the importance of CSE in explaining general and mature adults' Internet behavior, it becomes important to understand how CSE is actually determined. Hereunto, Marakas, Yi and Johnson [30] identified in their literature review a broad variety of environmental, cognitive and behavioral influences on CSE, such as training, experience, social persuasion, but likewise individual factors, such as age, gender, emotional states, or personality.

B. *Computer Anxiety*

Computer Anxiety (CA) reflects the tendency of individuals to be uneasy, apprehensive or fearful when confronted with using computers. Typical fear comprises data loss or irrevocable mistakes by the user (e.g., deleting a file or formatting a hard drive) [31][32]. Individuals with computer anxiety often possess feelings of helplessness [33].

In a review of two decades of research on CA, Powell [34] found a variety of antecedents for CA. For instance, the broad trait of neuroticism and other emotional forms of anxiety have been found to predict one's CA while computer training and experience have been found to be countermeasures in decreasing –especially older– individuals' anxiety [11][35][36]. CA is an established, important anchor how individuals form ease of use perceptions and thereby indirectly influences technology-directed behavior [17][37].

The relationship between CA and CSE has been consistently reported to be negatively associated [8][10][12][30] indicating that individuals with higher anxiety tend to pose decreased self-beliefs in their ability to use a computer. Considering CA's relevance for mature adults' computer behavior, CA was commonly found to increase with higher age [34].

III. Research Model

Our study seeks to investigate the sources and effects of individual differences in mature adults' use of computer technology and in our specific case: the use of the Internet in private settings. Based on the aforementioned reflections on prior literature, we pose that CSE and CA as factors accounting for individual differences directly influence mature adults' Internet usage. Although these two factors have been found to be of importance for adults' technology use behavior, less is known how these factors are determined. Most of todays' available studies observed the impact of explicit training interventions [11][35][36] that are likewise generically applicable to other populations.

Consequently, existing studies fall short in explaining these differences with factors distinct to mature adults, leading researchers frequently to call for further unique studies how CSE and CA are determined for mature adults [6][29]. Therefore, our research seeks to investigate the effect of prior working environments on mature adults' current Internet use behavior. Our research model in Fig. 1 depicts our research model graphically. We elaborate on the constructs and hypothesized relationships between them in the following paragraphs.

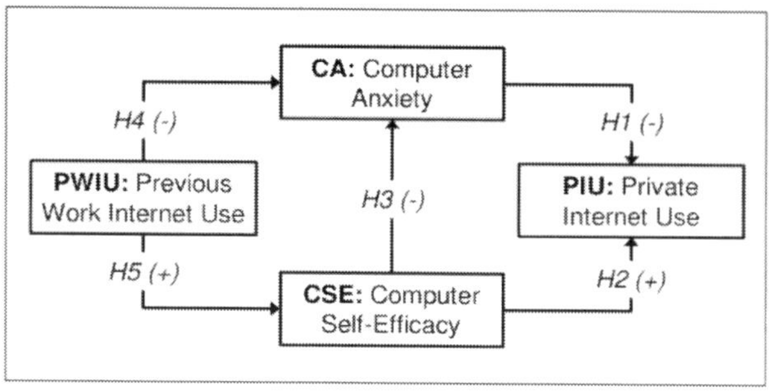

Figure 1. Research Model.

Private Internet Use (PIU) acts as the dependent variable in our research model and is hereunto defined as an individuals' utilization of the Internet in the last period (i.e., six months) in a private setting. Our PIU measure considers important dimensions of actual technology behavior [38] by incorporating the dimensions of duration (i.e., how much time spent), frequency (i.e., how often), and intensity (i.e., extent of Internet-related activities) [39][40].

The Internet has become an ubiquitous tool with the potential to support nearly all mature adults' life aspects. It serves not only as a knowledge base, but likewise as a handy tool for communication purposes, commerce activities or banking. Many mature adults only partially take advantage of the broad spectrum of features the Internet offers and remain at lower level uses, such as information retrievals. As such, we expect that especially the dimension of intensity is heterogeneously distributed among mature adults. To understand these differences in Internet usage, we draw on above outlined factors accounting for individual differences in technology behavior: CA and CSE.

As outlined, CA reflects the tendency of individuals to be uneasy, apprehensive or fearful when confronted with using computers, such as data losses and other mistakes by the user [31][32]. Individuals with computer anxiety often possess feelings of helplessness [33]. CA is a IT-specific derivate of the broad the broad trait of neuroticism and other emotional forms of anxiety [34]. Our review of prior literature in Section 2 indicated that CA both, in general and especially in cases of mature adults, directly and indirectly influences individuals' technology usage. It has been shown that mature adults generally possess higher anxieties towards technologies compared to younger counterparts [34]. Since our study is concerned with Internet usage, we adapt CA to this context and denote CA as the fear or apprehension that individuals experience when using the Internet [41][42]. Based on prior evidence, we expect that mature adults with high computer anxiety feel insecure and try to avoid using the Internet and vice versa. We consequently position CA as a direct determinant of PIU by hypothesizing:

H1: *Computer Anxiety negatively influences Private Internet Use.*

CSE generally reflects an individual's judgment about her/his capabilities to use a computer [12, p. 192].

As outlined above, CSE reflects an important individual differentiator of mature adults' technology use. For our study purpose we adapt CSE similar to CA to the Internet context by defining it as one's ability to make use of Internet websites. We assume that people with high degrees of CSE are more actively engaged in their Internet usage. Given the high importance and prior evidence for CSE's general role, we hypothesize that:

H2: *Computer Self-Efficacy positively influences Private Internet Use.*

According to Social Cognitive Theory [13][14], emotional arousal and self-efficacy are reciprocally determined; depending on which variable acts as a stimulus, an effect in the other variable can be observed [17]. Prior research on CSE and CA provides evidence that both effects also occur in the context of technologies [8][22][43]. CSE thereby might act as an important coping mechanism in dealing with negative emotions in technology use [37]. In our study context, we assume that mature adults with a higher degree of CSE have a lower degree of CA as they are more confident in working with computers and the Internet. Users who reached that status are usually not afraid of computers or the Internet as they know what to do and which actions to avoid. This level of security is assumed to decrease feelings of anxiety. Therefore, we hypothesize:

H3: *Computer Self-Efficacy negatively influences Computer Anxiety.*

Despite the reported important role CA and CSE play in mature adults' technology usage, little is known how these factors specifically for mature adults are determined leading researchers frequently to call for dedicated research [6][29].

Both factors –CA and CSE– are argued to be dynamic in nature, as that they be altered by dispositional and environmental factors [8][33]. As outlined in Section 2, especially computer training and experience have been frequently found to be of importance as that these factors are able to increase CSE and decrease CA of mature adults [11][34][36].

In a different, yet related research context of the digital divide among pupils, Wei, Teo, Chan and Tan [44] revealed that school IT access and usage "had a significantly stronger impact on CSE for students without home computers than students with home computers" (p. 179). The study indicates that IT-related behavior can be in part determined through distinct types of experience gained in dedicated environments giving greater insights into the causal, underlying mechanisms of individual differences in IT use.

Adults in general or 'digital immigrants' today often receive dedicated computer training and gain thorough experiences in handling digital media at their working places, where working with computer technologies and the Internet has become a natural routine. In contrast to that, however, a lot of mature adults are naturally already in retirement. As Tams, Grover and Thatcher [6] state, most of those mature adults, received their, if any, computer education in times where information technologies were far less multifaceted than today.

Following the rationale that CA and CSE can be altered through environmental factors, the preliminary evidence of the effects from dedicated environments, and given that many workplaces increasingly relied computer and Internet use for the last two decades [10], some mature adults might have gained their computer and Internet experience during their last years of work affecting their CA and CSE.

Consequently, we propose the factor of Previous Work Internet Use (PWIU), defined as an individuals' utilization of the Internet in the last period at her/his workplace (time frame of six months) that encompasses the dimensions of duration and frequency of Internet use [adapted from 45]. For those being retired, this definition denotes the last six months before retirement. Based on the above outlined discussion, we hypothesize that:

H4: *Previous Work Internet Use negatively influences Computer Anxiety.*

H5: *Previous Work Internet Use positively influences Computer Self-Efficacy.*

Based on these theoretical considerations and hypotheses, we conducted our empirical research as described in the following Section 4.

IV. Research Methodology

A. *Questionnaire Development*

In order to test our research model, we conducted a quantitative survey-based research approach. We developed a questionnaire with measurement items drawn from previously published information systems research. The measurement instrument for our core constructs is depicted in Table 4 at the end of the paper. For CSE and CA, available items were carefully transferred from the context of general computer interactions, to the Internet use context.

CSE was measured with a 5-item version [21][46] based on the original CSE scale of Compeau and Higgins [12] and adapted to the context of using a new Internet service. Measures for CA were taken from Compeau and Higgins [12] and adapted to using the Internet. PWIU was assessed with two items along the dimensions of duration and frequency [45]. Duration of PWIU measures the average amount of time a person spent using the Internet (i.e., how long) in a typical week in her/his last period at work [adapted from 45]. Frequency, in contrast, asks respondents how often one used the Internet at work in a typical week in her/his last period at work. PIU asked respondents about their Internet use in a private context and was assessed along three dimensions of duration, frequency and intensity. While duration and frequency are assessed similar as to those of PWIU, we additionally measured intensity by asking respondents typical Internet offerings they use, such as (e.g. information search, communication, online shopping, etc.). Based on binary values (yes/no) of features used, we calculated intensity with values ranging from 1 to 7.

As most items were originally published in English they have been translated in to German first. In several iterations, we validated the instrument with a total of 18 respondents from the target group to ensure readability, clarity and proper wording. The questionnaire was modified until the pre-tests did not bring up any new suggestions for improvement.

B. *Data Collection*

Access to the target group has been frequently shown to be difficult [e.g. 2] and using an online-survey might attract rather technology-savvy adults causing potentially biased results. Therefore, we employed a convenience sampling method using a paper-and-pen based field survey approach that has been shown to be successfully in gathering data from the target group [e.g. 47]. Like other studies before [e.g. 36], we collected data at public places such as pedestrian zones, libraries, gyms, adult schools, and senior citizen centers.

Three independent researchers conducted the field study from May to October 2015 in southern Germany by randomly asking people (who appeared to be 50+) to participate in the survey. The researchers ensured the participants for anonymity and that there are no 'wrong' or 'right' answers for the survey questions asked while collecting data [48]. We only addressed participants that actually used the Internet at least once in their lifetime. The reason for this was that only people who had seen the Internet before are able to answer the questions correctly.

To motivate participation, a tablet computer was raffled amongst all participants who provided contact details. The latter data were kept on a separate sheet and destroyed after the winner received the price.

C. *Participants' Demographics*

In total, we collected 165 surveys, whereby 19 surveys were incomplete and needed to be dropped from the dataset. The remaining 146 surveys constitute the dataset of our analysis. Table 1 outlines the demographics of our dataset.

V. Results

To validate our research model, the data was analyzed as structural equation model using the partial least squares (PLS)

TABLE I. Participants' Demographics (N=146)

Age		Gender		Retired		Marital status		Household's (net) income p.m.	
40's	4%	Male	33%	Yes	65%	Single	12%	< 1 k Euro	1%
50's	22%	Female	67%	No	34%	Married	65%	1–2 k Euro	20%
60's	42%			n.a.	1%	Divorced	8%	2–3 k Euro	23%
70's	26%					Widowed	13%	3–4 k Euro	23%
80's	6%					n.a.	1%	4–5 k Euro	7%
n.a.	1%							> 5 k Euro	10%
								n.a.	16%

TABLE II. Measurement Model Validation

Construct	Mean	S.D.	AVE	CR	CRA	1	2	3	4
1 CA	1.84	1.29	0.613	0.888	0.842	**0.783**			
2 CSE	5.07	2.46	0.689	0.917	0.887	-0.307	**0.830**		
3 PWIU	3.13	2.65	0.918	0.957	0.912	-0.075	0.159	**0.958**	
4 PIU	3.50	1.66	0.637	0.840	0.715	-0.536	0.321	0.134	**0.798**

method with the software package SmartPLS 3.0 [49]. Although the dataset with 146 responses seems to be small, it is sufficiently large to analyze the model according to the rule of ten [50]. Following the two-step procedure as proposed by Chin [1], we first analyzed the measurement model, followed by an assessment of the structural model.

The measurement model represents the relationships between the observed data and the latent variables. Table 2 reports the results of the measurement model that can be interpreted as follows.

All item loadings are above 0.70 and each item loaded on its construct significantly ($p < 0.001$); items with insufficient loading have been dropped [51]. To ensure further construct quality, we assessed whether values for composite reliability (CR) and Cronbach's Alpha (CRA) are above 0.70 [52], values for average variance extracted (AVE) are at least 0.50 [53]. Sufficient discriminant validity is given since construct correlations are smaller than the square root of the AVE [53][54]. In sum, the results demonstrate adequate psychometric properties of the measurement model allowing us to proceed and test the structural model.

The structural model represents the relationships between the latent variables. To evaluate the structural model we assessed the coefficients of determination (R^2) and the significance levels of the path coefficients [1]. For our dependent variable the model explains 31.5% of the variance in private Internet use. The results on all hypothesized relationships are illustrated in Table 3 and Fig. 2 below.

Finally, we checked typical control variables. We controlled for effects of gender and age on Internet use. No effects of age (-0.118; p=0.140) or gender (-0.104; p=0.187) were observed.

TABLE III. STRUCTURAL MODEL RESULTS

Path	Path Coefficient	t-value	Effect Size[a]	Result
PWIU → CA	-0.026	0.303	–	Not supported
PWIU → CSE	0.159*	2.015	0.026 (small)	Supported
CSE → CA	-0.303***	3.922	0.099 (small)	Supported
CA → PIU	-0.483***	7.244	0.309 (medium)	Supported
CSE → PIU	0.172*	2.417	0.039 (small)	Supported

*** p < 0.001; ** p < 0.01; * p < 0.05

a. Effect size interpretations according to Chin [1]

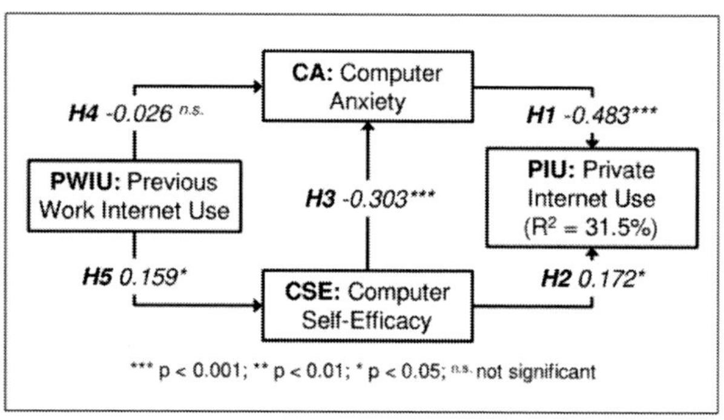

Figure 2. Research Model Results.

VI. DISCUSSION

A. Findings

Our research model is able to explain about 30% of the variance in mature adults' private Internet usage. Although these values might seem to small, the results correspond with research that relied on such factors related to individual differences in explaining technology use with reported R^2 values of 20% [11], 25% [26], or 34% [22].

We see that CA has a highly significant negative effect on private Internet use, thereby supporting our hypothesis (H1). This forges the obvious explanation that mature adults who are more anxious of the Internet do not like to use it. In the same vain, we see a significant positive effect going from self-efficacy towards private Internet use as hypothesized (H2). Although we would have expected this relationship to be stronger and higher in significance, the hypothesized relationship still finds good support: mature adults with a higher level of self-confidence towards an action are likely to perform it. Moreover, we found a highly significant negative path from self-efficacy towards anxiety giving support for the hypothesized negative effect of CSE on CA (H3). Hence, mature adults with higher confidence in their own abilities significantly decrease their fears towards the Internet.

We further sought to unravel the distinct influence of prior exposure to IT from a workplace (i.e., PWIU). Our underlying hypothesis is that the influence is positive, i.e., people who used the Internet as part of their (previous) work routines have a higher CSE and lower CA.

In this study, we did not find a significant relationship between PWIU and CA leading us to reject our hypothesis (H4), yet we found solid support for the effect of PWIU on CSE supporting our hypothesis (H5). Given the strong effect of CSE on CA, in turn, our results indicate that CSE acts as a mediator between PWIU and CA as that PWIU poses indirect effects on CA.

B. Implications

In this study, we sought to unravel the effects of individual differences on mature adult's Internet usage. In our research model, we incorporated CA and CSE as direct antecedents of Internet usage and positioned PWIU as a novel and distinct determinant for these differences in mature adults. We empirically tested our model with 146 adults aged 50 and above. Drawing on these results, we can derive the following contributions and implications.

First, prior research highlighted the role of self-efficacy beliefs and emotional fears as predictors for mature adults' technology behavior. Our results indicate, that CA and CSE solely account for 30% of the variance in mature adults' Internet usage. Our study thereby supports prior research and highlights again that these two factors must be taken into account to understand mature adults' technology behavior. Prior research that likewise solely on individual differences as predictors of Internet usage frequently observed younger adults. Comparing our results with those studies, we observe that CA is indeed of higher relevance for mature adults than for younger adults. In sum, our study supports prior research about the importance of CSE and CA for mature adults.

Second, given the importance of CSE and CA for mature adults, less is known about the sources for these individual differences of mature adults. Although training interventions and general experience have been found to be of predictive relevance, researchers frequently urged for further research on distinct sources as outlined in above. Given this gap in research, we conceptualized PWIU as a distinct source of mature adults' CA and CSE. In contrast to explicit training interventions, PWIU reflects a rather salient source of 'mastery experience', an important source of one's self-efficacy. Our results demonstrate that PWIU indeed determines CSE meaning that people who used the Internet on the job are likely to have a higher self-confidence towards using the Internet. In contrast, we did not found support for PWIU's impact on CA. The absence of the direct effects of PWIU on CA is, however surprising and contrary to our hypotheses. A potential explanation is that PWIU poses rather indirect effects of CA with CSE serving as a mediating factor; PWIU increases mature adults' CSE, which, in turn, decreases their anxieties towards the Internet.

Another potential explanation for the insignificant relationship between PWIU and CA might be the frequent media coverage on the dangers of using the Internet could play a role. Especially in the last years, several threats in the dynamic Internet environment emerged, such as fraud, scams, and phishing. Given that most of our study's participants are already retired, we suggest that they gained their experiences in interacting with the Internet in times were such dangers were less wide spread or of less great concern than today. As such, our results suggest that mature adults' anxieties towards the Internet are frequently adapted to novel and emerging threats of the Internet and that their prior experiences are not supportive in dealing with such endangering situations of the Internet. This issue might further amplify the longer individuals have left the working environment respectively the longer they are retired.

Based on our findings and discussion, the derived implications of our research are manifold. We were able to show that the ageing generation is by far not Internet-adverse. On the contrary, the behavioral mechanisms are very similar to those of other age clusters. We see that people need a certain level of self-efficacy in order to use the Internet and when they possess this confidence then they are more actively using it. Practice needs to be aware that although the Internet became widespread already 15 years ago, most individuals of higher ages started using the Internet at a far later time. While some of those 'senior surfers' got in touch with the Internet already during their working time that resulted in higher self-confidence in their abilities to navigate through the Web, others did not have the chance to gain earlier experience. Thus, practice needs to be aware of these differences and should either provide Internet-based solutions that do not require sophisticated Internet skills or policy makers that are in charge to foster Internet education for the elderly. Prior research has shown that even rather simple computer and Internet training interventions are highly effective for mature adults in increasing their CSE and significantly decreasing their CA [11][36]. However, given that not all mature adults are necessarily willing or have the chance to take part in dedicated training interventions, we further suggest that media should not only cover the threats of the Internet but should likewise offer educational material on countermeasures in dealing with those issues in a format that is easily understandable and applicable for older individuals.

From a theory perspective we were able to increase our knowledge on Internet-related behavior of the aging society. Our results first of all underline the general applicability of individual differences in explaining technology-related behavior and highlight the importance these factors play for the aging segment of the population. Second, as outlined, we offered a novel source accounting for these individual factors that is distinct to mature adults: previous work Internet use. We thereby enriched our understanding on the important behavioral factors of mature adults' Internet usage and a novel, yet salient, source accounting to the digital divide.

C. *Limitations*

Our research is not without its limitations and these must be taken into account when interpreting the results. First, we had to rely on a convenience sampling approach given the difficulties in access to the target group. Therefore, we surveyed mature adults at public places and institutions thereby potentially mitigating those individuals, which are less outgoing or have severe issues forcing them to stay at home. Although our sample size of 146 responses is sufficiently large to calculate our research model, these can be no means be regarded as representative for the general population. Consequently, our results and contributions are limited in their generalizability. Moreover, we measured all independent and dependent factors at one time, which might have primed the participants about the purpose of our study [48]. We further employed self-reported usage measure that involve subjective judgments and individuals often tend to over- and underestimate their actual usage behavior [38]. This poses a problem specifically in previous work Internet use as in some cases (the older population) the work experience dated back several years (sometimes decades).

Second, although our explained variance of about 30% for mature adults' correspond with those of related studies drawing primarily on factors accounting for individual differences [11][22][26], we acknowledge that there are obviously further influential factors causing for mature adults' Internet usage. We only relied on two important individual factors accounting for variance and left out technology-related beliefs about usefulness or ease of use.

Third, given that –to the best of our knowledge– our research is one of the first that sought to understand the effects prior Internet exposure at the workplace, our study is best positioned as exploratory in nature. We only observed the direct effects of PWIU on CA and CSE and left out potential moderating effects such as the length of retirement.

Fourth, since our technology under investigation was the Internet, we adapted the measurements to the Internet context, which consequently limit our results to the specific Internet context.

To address these shortcomings of our study, we outline our further steps and additional potential avenues for further research next.

VII. Conclusion and Future Work

This research elaborated on the influence of previous work Internet usage on current private Internet usage. We selected computer anxiety and computer self-efficacy as mediating constructs. In a quantitative research with 146 valid responses, we targeted an audience of 50+, i.e., people who did not grow up with widespread Internet experience.

Our findings underline the strong influence of the chosen constructs, CA and CSE. We were able to show that "the elderly" are not a homogenous group of people not using the Internet. However, digital services need to be presented in a way that mature adults feel they possess the right skillset to use it and do not fall for anxiety. This calls for easy solutions and creative training mechanisms.

However, taking the stated limitations into account, our future goal is to enlarge the interview base and recruit informants on a global basis. We expect novel insights when comparing national differences in elderly's Internet use.

Furthermore, we suggest that more research is needed to elaborate on the mechanisms accounting for mature adults' technology behavior. In a recent review on mature adults' technology usage, Chen and Chan [55] outlined literature on studies of that draw on the well-known Technology Acceptance Model (TAM) [56][57] and reflect that usefulness and ease of use perceptions constitute important factors for older adults' technology use as they often consider novel technologies as irrelevant and unnecessary for their daily life leading them to reject technologies. The authors echo that these usefulness beliefs are likewise derived from their perceptions about the efforts with which the technologies can be used (i.e., perceived ease of use) [55]. Given that, as outlined in Section 2, CA and CSE both act as important anchors of these traditional TAM factors, incorporating CA and CSE among TAM factors should consequently lead to greater explanations in terms of explained variance (i.e., higher R^2 values). However, TAM-based models are likewise generically applicable in other research contexts and for other target groups. We suggest that other, rival theories are needed to derive distinct insights into mature adults' technology behavior. We suggest that age-related theories, such as from the domain gerontology, could be worth of further research to observe in the domain of adults' technology acceptance and use.

Acknowledgment

This research received funding from the German Federal Ministry of Education and Research (BMBF) under grant code 01FR14021. The responsibility for the content of this publication lies with the authors.

VIII. References

[1] W. W. Chin, "The partial least squares approach to structural equation modeling," Modern methods for business research, vol. 295, no. 2, pp. 295-336, 1998.

[2] T. Heart and E. Kalderon, "Older adults: Are they ready to adopt health-related ict?," International Journal of Medical Informatics, vol. 82, no. 11, pp. e209-e231, 2013.

[3] World Health Organization, "Strategy and action plan for healthy ageing in europe, 2012–2020", 2012

[4] N. Crisp and L. Chen, "Global supply of health professionals," New England Journal of Medicine, vol. 370, no. 10, pp. 950-957, 2014.

[5] H. Eren and J. G. Webster, The e-medicine, e-health, m-health, telemedicine, and telehealth handbook, CRC Press, 2015.

[6] S. Tams, V. Grover, and J. Thatcher, "Modern information technology in an old workforce: Toward a strategic research agenda," The Journal of Strategic Information Systems, vol. 23, no. 4, pp. 284-304, 2014.

[7] R. Agarwal and J. Prasad, "Are individual differences germane to the acceptance of new information technologies?," Decision Sciences, vol. 30, no. 2, pp. 361-391, 1999.

[8] J. B. Thatcher and P. L. Perrewe, "An empirical examination of individual traits as antecedents to computer anxiety and computer self-efficacy," MIS Quarterly, vol. 26, no. 4, pp. 381-396, 2002.

[9] C. Maier, "Personality within information systems research: A literature analysis", Proceedings of the Twentieth European Conference on Information Systems (ECIS), 2012

[10] N. Wagner, K. Hassanein, and M. Head, "Computer use by older adults: A multi-disciplinary review," Computers in Human Behavior, vol. 26, no. 5, pp. 870-882, 2010.

[11] J. C. Y. Lam and M. K. O. Lee, "Digital inclusiveness-longitudinal study of Internet adoption by older adults," Journal of Management Information Systems, vol. 23, no. 4, pp. 177-206, 2006.

[12] D. R. Compeau and C. A. Higgins, "Computer self-efficacy: Development of a measure and initial test," MIS Quarterly, vol. 19, no. 2, pp. 189-211, 1995.

[13] A. Bandura, "Self-efficacy mechanism in human agency," American Psychologist, vol. 37, no. 2, pp. 122-147, 1982.

[14] A. Bandura, Self-efficacy: The exercise of control, New York: Freeman, 1997.

[15] J. P.-A. Hsieh, A. Rai, and M. Keil, "Understanding digital inequality: Comparing continued use behavioral models of the socio-economically advantaged and disadvantaged," MIS quarterly, vol., no., pp. 97-126, 2008.

[16] I. Ajzen, "Perceived behavioral control, self-efficacy, locus of control, and the theory of planned behavior1," Journal of Applied Social Psychology, vol. 32, no. 4, pp. 665-683, 2002.

[17] V. Venkatesh, "Determinants of perceived ease of use: Integrating control, intrinsic motivation, and emotion into the technology acceptance model," Information Systems Research, vol. 11, no. 4, pp. 342-365, 2000.

[18] S. Taylor and P. A. Todd, "Understanding information technology usage: A test of competing models," Information systems research, vol. 6, no. 2, pp. 144-176, 1995.

[19] S. Taylor and P. Todd, "Assessing IT usage: The role of prior experience," MIS quarterly, vol., no., pp. 561-570, 1995.

[20] V. Venkatesh and F. D. Davis, "A model of the antecedents of perceived ease of use: Development and test*," Decision sciences, vol. 27, no. 3, pp. 451-481, 1996.

[21] V. Venkatesh, M. G. Morris, G. B. Davis, and F. D. Davis, "User acceptance of information technology: Toward a unified view," MIS Quarterly, vol., no., pp. 425-478, 2003.

[22] D. Compeau, C. A. Higgins, and S. Huff, "Social cognitive theory and individual reactions to computing technology: A longitudinal study," MIS Quarterly, vol. 23, no. 2, pp. 145-158, 1999.

[23] R. Agarwal and E. Karahanna, "Time flies when you're having fun: Cognitive absorption and beliefs about information technology usage," MIS Quarterly, vol., no., pp. 665-694, 2000.

[24] L. R. Vijayasarathy, "Predicting consumer intentions to use on-line shopping: The case for an augmented technology acceptance model," Information & Management, vol. 41, no. 6, pp. 747-762, 2004.

[25] J. He and L. A. Freeman, "Understanding the formation of general computer self-efficacy," Communications of the Association for Information Systems, vol. 26, no. 1, p 12, 2010.
[26] J. M. Davis and Y. Y. Mun, "User disposition and extent of web utilization: A trait hierarchy approach," International Journal of Human-Computer Studies, vol. 70, no. 5, pp. 346-363, 2012.
[27] W. Wang, X. Li, and J. P.-A. Hsieh, "The contingent effect of personal IT innovativeness and IT self-efficacy on innovative use of complex IT," Behaviour & information technology, vol. 32, no. 11, pp. 1105-1124, 2013.
[28] J. C. Mcelroy, A. R. Hendrickson, A. M. Townsend, and S. M. Demarie, "Dispositional factors in internet use: Personality versus cognitive style," MIS Quarterly, vol., no., pp. 809-820, 2007.
[29] B. Niehaves and R. Plattfaut, "Internet adoption by the elderly: Employing IS technology acceptance theories for understanding the age-related digital divide," European Journal of Information Systems, vol. 23, no. 6, pp. 708-726, 2014.
[30] G. M. Marakas, M. Y. Yi, and R. D. Johnson, "The multilevel and multifaceted character of computer self-efficacy: Toward clarification of the construct and an integrative framework for research," Information Systems Research, vol. 9, no. 2, pp. 126-163, 1998.
[31] R. K. Heinssen, C. R. Glass, and L. A. Knight, "Assessing computer anxiety: Development and validation of the computer anxiety rating scale," Computers in Human Behavior, vol. 3, no., pp. 49-59, 1987.
[32] S. Parasuraman and M. Igbaria, "An examination of gender differences in the determinants of computer anxiety and attitudes toward microcomputers among managers," International Journal of Man-Machine Studies, vol. 32, no. 3, pp. 327-340, 1990.
[33] G. M. Marakas, R. D. Johnson, and J. W. Palmer, "A theoretical model of differential social attributions toward computing technology: When the metaphor becomes the model," International Journal of Human-Computer Studies, vol. 52, no. 4, pp. 719-750, 2000.
[34] A. L. Powell, "Computer anxiety: Comparison of research from the 1990s and 2000s," Computers in Human Behavior, vol. 29, no. 6, pp. 2337-2381, 2013.
[35] K. V. Wild, N. C. Mattek, S. A. Maxwell, H. H. Dodge, H. B. Jimison, and J. A. Kaye, "Computer-related self-efficacy and anxiety in older adults with and without mild cognitive impairment," Alzheimer's & Dementia, vol. 8, no. 6, pp. 544-552, 2012.
[36] A. Chu, J. Huber, B. Mastel-Smith, and S. Cesario, "Partnering with seniors for better health: Computer use and Internet health information retrieval among older adults in a low socioeconomic community," Journal of the Medical Library Association, vol. 97, no. 1, pp. 12-20, 2009.
[37] G. Hackbarth, V. Grover, and Y. Y. Mun, "Computer playfulness and anxiety: Positive and negative mediators of the system experience effect on perceived ease of use," Information & management, vol. 40, no. 3, pp. 221-232, 2003.
[38] A. Burton-Jones and D. W. Straub Jr, "Reconceptualizing system usage: An approach and empirical test," Information Systems Research, vol. 17, no. 3, pp. 228-246, 2006.
[39] V. Venkatesh, S. A. Brown, L. M. Maruping, and H. Bala, "Predicting different conceptualizations of system use: The competing roles of behavioral intention, facilitating conditions, and behavioral expectation," MIS Quarterly, vol. 32, no. 3, pp. 483-502, 2008.
[40] M. Z. Lallmahomed, N. Z. A. Rahim, R. Ibrahim, and A. A. Rahman, "Predicting different conceptualizations of system use: Acceptance in hedonic volitional context (facebook)," Computers in Human Behavior, vol. 29, no. 6, pp. 2776-2787, 2013.
[41] C. Presno, "Taking the byte out of Internet anxiety: Instructional techniques that reduce computer/Internet anxiety in the classroom," Journal of educational computing research, vol. 18, no. 2, pp. 147-161, 1998.
[42] J. B. Thatcher, M. L. Loughry, J. Lim, and D. H. Mcknight, "Internet anxiety: An empirical study of the effects of personality, beliefs, and social support," Information & Management, vol. 44, no. 4, pp. 353-363, 2007.
[43] J. Davis, L. Lee, and M. Yi, "Examining the relationships among personality traits, IT-specific traits, and perceived ease of use," AMCIS 2007 Proceedings, vol., no., p 295, 2007.
[44] K.-K. Wei, H.-H. Teo, H. C. Chan, and B. C. Tan, "Conceptualizing and testing a social cognitive model of the digital divide," Information Systems Research, vol. 22, no. 1, pp. 170-187, 2011.
[45] S. S. Kim, N. K. Malhotra, and S. Narasimhan, "Research note—two competing perspectives on automatic use: A theoretical and empirical comparison," Information Systems Research, vol. 16, no. 4, pp. 418-432, 2005.
[46] V. Venkatesh and H. Bala, "Technology acceptance model 3 and a research agenda on interventions," Decision Sciences, vol. 39, no. 2, pp. 273-315, 2008.
[47] X. Guo, Y. Sun, N. Wang, Z. Peng, and Z. Yan, "The dark side of elderly acceptance of preventive mobile health services in china," Electronic Markets, vol. 23, no. 1, pp. 49-61, 2013.
[48] P. M. Podsakoff, S. B. Mackenzie, J.-Y. Lee, and N. P. Podsakoff, "Common method biases in behavioral research: A critical review of the literature and recommended remedies," Journal of Applied Psychology, vol. 88, no. 5, p 879, 2003.
[49] C. M. Ringle, S. Wende, and J.-M. Becker, "Smartpls 3", SmartPLS GmbH, Boenningstedt, 2015
[50] J. F. Hair, C. M. Ringle, and M. Sarstedt, "PLS-SEM: Indeed a silver bullet," Journal of Marketing Theory and Practice, vol. 19, no. 2, pp. 139-152, 2011.
[51] J. F. Hair, R. E. Anderson, R. L. Tatham, and W. C. Black, Multivariate data analysis, 5th ed., Upper Saddle River, NJ: Prentice Hall, 1998.
[52] J. C. Nunnally, Psychometric theory, 2nd ed., New York: McGraw-Hill, 1978.
[53] C. Fornell and D. F. Larcker, "Evaluating structural equation models with unobservable variables and measurement error," Journal of Marketing Research, vol., no., pp. 39-50, 1981.
[54] J. Hulland, "Use of partial least squares (PLS) in strategic management research: A review of four recent studies," Strategic management journal, vol. 20, no. 2, pp. 195-204, 1999.
[55] K. Chen and A. Chan, "A review of technology acceptance by older adults," Gerontechnology, vol. 10, no. 1, pp. 1-12, 2011.
[56] F. D. Davis, "Perceived usefulness, perceived ease of use, and user acceptance of information technology," MIS Quarterly, vol. 13, no. 3, pp. 319-340, 1989.
[57] F. D. Davis, R. P. Bagozzi, and P. R. Warshaw, "User acceptance of computer technology: A comparison of two theoretical models," Management science, vol. 35, no. 8, pp. 982-1003, 1989.
[58] M. Limayem, S. G. Hirt, and C. M. Cheung, "How habit limits the predictive power of intention: The case of information systems continuance," MIS Quarterly, vol., no., pp. 705-737, 2007.

TABLE IV. MEASUREMENT INSTRUMENT (TRANSLATED FROM GERMAN)

Items		Source
Computer Self-Efficacy (CSE)		
	I could use a heretofore unknown website…	Adapted from [12][21][46]
CSE.1	if I had previously used similar websites for the same purpose.	
CSE2	if someone showed me how to do it first.	
CSE.3	if I had just the built-in help facility for assistance.	
CSE.4	if I had never used a website like it before.	
CSE.5	if there was no one around to tell me what to do while using it.	
Computer Anxiety (CA)		
CA.1	I feel apprehensive about using the Internet.	Adapted from [12]
CA.2	It scares me to think that I could lose data by mistake by using the Internet.	
CA.3	It scares me to think that I could inadvertently reveal sensitive information on the Internet.	
CA.4	I hesitate to use the Internet for fear of making mistakes that I cannot correct.	
CA.5	The Internet is somewhat intimidating to me.	
Past Work Internet Use (PWIU)		
PWIU.FRQ	If you think (back) about your job, how often did you use the Internet on average in the last 6 months of your career in your job?	Adapted from [45][58]
PWIU.DUR	If you think (back) about that period, how many hours did you spend using the Internet on average in a typical week at your job?	
Private Internet Use		
PIU.FREQ	On average how often did you use the Internet in your private life in the last 6 months?	Adapted from [45][58]
PIU.DUR	If you think about the last 6 months, how many hours did you spend using the Internet on average in a typical week in your private life?	
PIU.INT	For what do you use the Internet in your private life? Check all that apply: (1) Information searching, (2) Reading news, (3) Online shopping, (4) Communication (e.g., e-mail, chat, telephony), (5) Entertainment (e.g., videos or games), (6) Online banking, (7) Browsing/Surfing	

Scale for Duration (DUR): (8) Several times a day, (7) Approx. once a day, (6) Several times a week, (5) Approx. once a week, (4) Several times a month, (3) Approx. once a month, (2) Less, (1) Not at all

Scale for Frequency (FRQ): (7) More than 30 hours, (6) 20-30 hours, (5) 10-20 hours, (4) 5-10 hours, (3) 1-5 hours, (2) Less than 1 hour, (1) Not at all

Scale for Computer Self-Efficacy (CSE): 10-point ranging from 'Not at all confident' to 'Totally confident'

Scale for Computer Anxiety (CA): 7-point ranging from 'Strongly disagree to 'Strongly agree'

Design and Evaluation of a "Play Place Sound" service that Changes the Image of a City by Music and Sound

Saori Aisawa
Graduate School of Media and Governance
Keio University
Kanagawa, Japan
e-mail: saoaiai@sfc.keio.ac.jp

Katsuhiko Ogawa
Faculty of Environment and Information Studies
Keio University
Kanagawa, Japan
e-mail: ogw@sfc.keio.ac.jp

***Abstract*—According to *The Image of the City*, which is one of the most representative works of Kevin Lynch, paths, edges, districts, nodes, and landmarks are important elements that constitute the image of a city. Actually, these elements are very strong and seem to influence not only the image of the city but also our actions. Therefore, we propose to add sounds to a city experience as new elements could make a great impact that can change the existing strong image of the city. We call this "change" the city. We developed a Web service called Play Place Sound (PPS). By using this service, users can hear the sounds plotted for an arbitrary spot on the website automatically when they approach that spot in the real world. Then, we performed an experiment to define the differences in the cognitive map between walking in the city while using the PPS or without it. A cognitive map is the collection of beliefs, experiences, and information that a person uses to orient himself or herself within an environment such as a social setting. As a result, when people use the PPS, the cognitive map is more detailed. Furthermore, when the content increases significantly, edges tend to appear in the cognitive map.**

Keywords-sound scape; cognitive map; urban design.

I. INTRODUCTION

In Japan, there are several places where we can see people who walk, jog, or run alone while listening to music on their portable music players or mobile phones. However, it is a fact that jogging in the same way while listening to the same music becomes boring as time passes, and there is no novelty. We feel it is regrettable that the act becomes usual and boring though we come in touch with the real city.

In *The Image of the City* [1], which is one of the most representative works of Kevin Lynch, he proposed that the role of the scenery of the city is to be seen, memorized, and please people. With that in mind, to consider the configuration of the image of the city, he performed an experiment with a cognitive map in three cities of the United States of America—Boston, Jersey City, and Los Angeles. Then, he stated that the following are important elements to configure the image of the city: paths, districts, nodes, edges, and landmarks, and these make for a study about whether he can change the appearance of the city and its importance.

After this, in Japan, there have been several studies to consider spatial awareness through the cognitive map, and there are many studies about the association of sound and image, and their point of interest is also different [2]-[5]. In addition, studies about harmonization of the image and music have done [6][7]. However, there are few studies that consider changing the existing cognitive map by adding new elements to the city.

Therefore, using a new form of art that redesigns the city by sounds, we propose a Play Place Sound (PPS) service for individuals to enjoy the experience of the city. Instead of simply enjoying music, the PPS is a service for enjoying the sounds that can be heard only at a particular location. So, the user can listen to the sounds attached to a certain location only by going to the place. Information services that display a message according to the location have already been used in art museums, but there are few studies that add a sound to a particular place.

This way, by adding sounds as a new fascination of the city, we examine how this novel factor can affect the existing image of the city and what are the changes as represented by the cognitive map.

This paper describes the concept of PPS and service design. Then, we pick the peripheral port of Yokohama as the sample spot and consider the relationship of the pasted sound content and location through some samples. Section 2 describes the concept of the PPS, and in Sections 3 and 4, we describe our experiments. Finally, we present the conclusion and future work in Section 5.

II. THE CONCEPT OF "PLAY PLACE SOUND (PPS)"

Like *The Image of the City*, when we undertake city planning or investigate the existing city, especially in the architectural field, paths, buildings, and open spaces like parks are emphasized as elements of the city. The same may be said when we consider what kind of impression of the city people have. Actually, these elements are very strong, and our actions and impressions regarding the city are strongly influenced by them. As a result, our actions and images tend to be limited or patterned. Therefore, by adding sounds as a new element, we want to change the city and its rules that have been made by the existing physical environment such as paths and buildings.

A. Usage of the PPS

PPS is intended to be used with smartphone. When the user approaches a spot, he or she can hear the installed sound through the earphone connected to his or her smartphone.

Figure 1 shows an example of the use of PPS. In this sample, users who are jogging on the same route every day follow this routine with PPS. With regard to the relation between the area and sound, four sounds are assigned to each area, from area 1 to area 4, and the user can hear sounds in each area. This way, we expect that the user will feel like going on a different street from his or her usual routine or spend more time jogging.

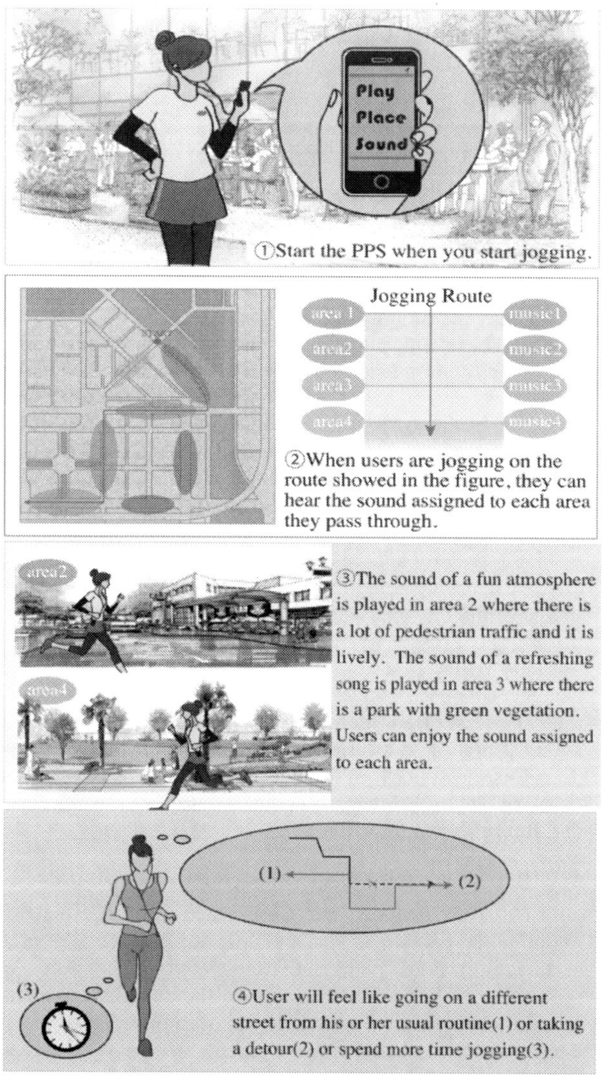

Figure 1. How to Use the PPS

B. System Configuration

The mechanism that should be prepared in advance is a system to plot sound files on the map. This system acquires the positional information of a place, plots sounds using JavaScript, and plays these sounds in HTML5. The flow chart of this system is shown in Figure 2.

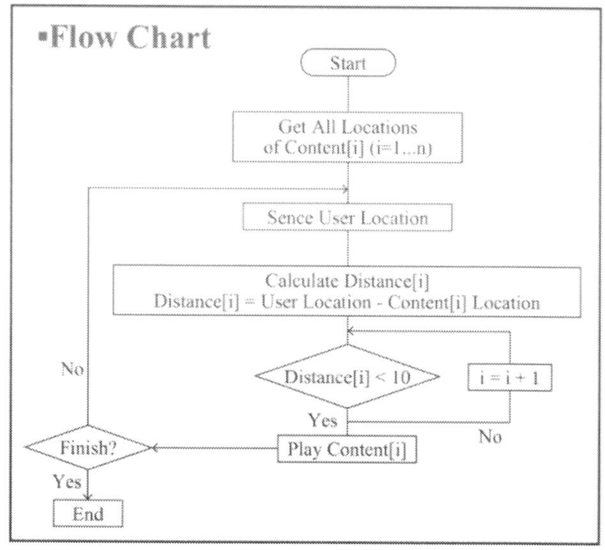

Figure 2. Flow Chart of PPS

This system sends the present location of a user, as detected by the Global Positioning System (GPS) function of the cellphone, to the Web server. When the user approaches the place where the sound has been plotted, it is played automatically.

III. PRELIMINARY EXPERIMENT

In proposing the PPS, it is necessary to consider what kind of sound is suitable for what kind of place. We performed a pre-experiment as the first step. In this experiment, we prepared sounds used in a movie as content and posted these sounds along two plot patterns. Then, we investigated how the PPS affects our behavior and what kind of impression was provided when we walk in these areas. Three people were the subjects of the first pattern and five of the second pattern. Both areas were near the port of Yokohama. This area is called Minato Mirai and is being continuously developed since 1965. We show the famous view of Minato Mirai in Figure 3.

Figure 3. Image of Minato Mirai

There are not only offices of various companies, but also amusement facilities such as an amusement park, concert hall, hotels, and a large shopping mall. Hence, this area is one of the most famous sights of Japan.

A. Sound Content

Before conducting this experiment, we considered the sound content. In this experiment, we took up three kinds of sound— music, sound effect, and dialog—used in the movie *Star Wars*. Michel Chion carefully considered what sound to be used in a movie, and we refer to his consideration [8][9]. Generally, a movie is being edited a lot, even if it is a live-action movie. Thereby, the producer can convey something that cannot be represented only through pictures, such as the atmosphere of scenes, feelings of characters, or clues. This research is intended for an experience in real space. We consider that the way of sound arranging in a movie is similar to the way of sound arranging in this study. A movie director removes unnecessary noise and adds various sounds.

First, the music we used as content included not only famous theme songs such as "Main Title" or "Imperial March" but also various music used in the movie as Background Music (BGM). Then, for sound effects, for example, the subjects could hear the sounds of warriors wielding their weapons, ray guns, robots waking up, and so on. Each of these sounds had a characteristic feature, and we could understand the sound source just by hearing the sound. Finally, dialog could be heard through the voices of characters. Humans and many other characters, including robots and aliens, appear in *Star Wars*. In many cases voices are edited, and they resemble a sound effect. However, the primary difference between dialog and sound effects is that there are meanings to the former. For example, in this experiment, we used a line of one of the main characters, C-3PO: "Help!!!". In this case, it was not only an electronic sound but also meant that someone is asking for help.

B. Plot Pattern

As a sample of the change in Minato Mirai area by sounds, we proposed two plot patterns of content. We show the map plotted with sound along pattern 1 in Figure 4.

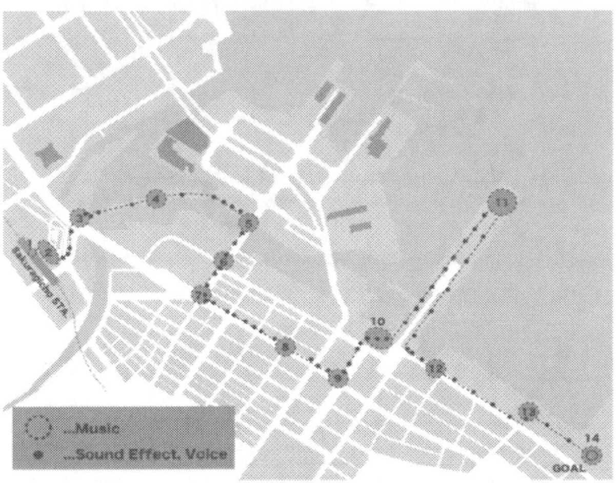

Figure 4. Plotting Map of Pattern 1

In pattern 1, we plotted sounds along the street in the order of their use in the movie and kept the story arbitrary for the user. In this sample, the user started from Sakuragicho Station and walked to the Yamashita Park via the Canal Park, Nippon Boulevard, and Osanbashi (international passenger terminal).

For the second pattern, we plotted sounds, in particular sound effects and dialog that were not limited by existing ways. In this design example, we designated two areas, a good area with a focus on the hero and a bad area with a focus on the old enemy. For example, sounds that are used in the hero's hometown scene were plotted near the center of the good area, the theme music of the evil side was plotted near the center of bad area, and the sounds used in the battle scene were plotted along the contact surface of each area. We expected that the user will feel, "What kind of sound will I hear if I go to that place?" We show the map plotted with sound content along pattern 2 in Figure 5.

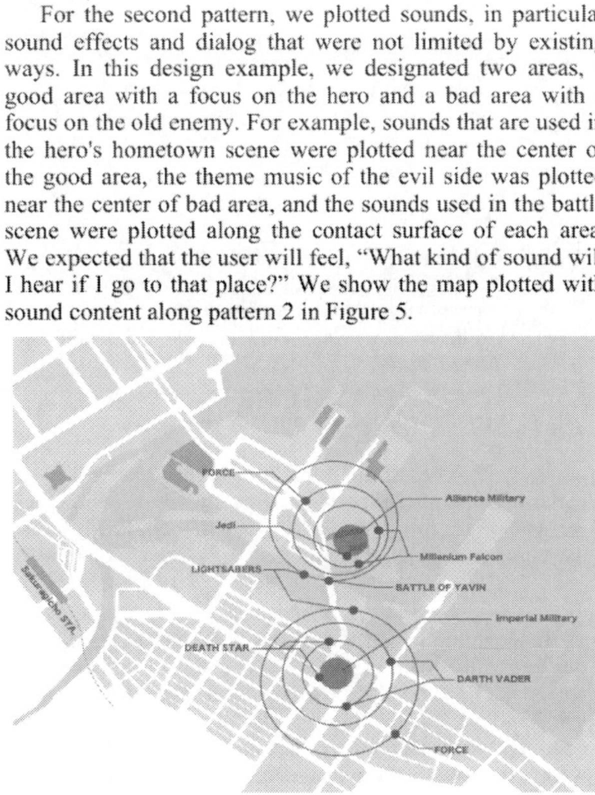

Figure 5. Plotting Map of Pattern 2

C. Result of the Preliminary Experiment

In pattern 1, although we supposed that users will walk down the street with plotted sounds, we wanted to give arbitrary instructions using only automatic sounds. Then, we started the experiment without notifying users which street has the plotted sounds. As a result, three users who completed this experiment could not find the street to go to and had lost their way. Obviously, since six users were scheduled to participate in this experiment, we were stopped unavoidably. This experiment underlined that it is too difficult to guide a person to the intended way only by sounds. Of course, to prevent users from getting lost, we plotted sounds at about 10m intervals in a straight line and at about 20m intervals at the corner of the street. Yet, there were many spots where we could not hear anything, and hence, the user became anxious each time. As a result of walking here and there, users got lost. In addition, in this case, PPS became a tool to find a specific way desperately rather than making town walking fun.

Similarly, in the second pattern, users walked around the area with plotted sounds. In this pattern, we informed where the sounds were plotted in advance, and it took about 15 minutes per person. The following is a list of opinions about this experiment.

Postive Opinions

- A sound of the breathing of Darth Vader is similar to that of snorkeling. I associated it with a snorkeling partly because the area was close to the sea.
- When I heard the voice say, "Run Luke, run," I was on the lawn, and I wanted to run unintentionally.
- As for me, it was interesting because I didn't know what kind of sound I would hear next.

Negative Opinions

- There is not much association with this place. It may be because the sphere of *Star Wars* is space.
- I felt uneasy when I heard nothing.
- I didn't know what kind of rule the sounds were plotted along.
- These sounds were boring for me because I am not very knowledgeable about *Star Wars*.

With this result in mind, we considered a new plot pattern for the next experiment. Specifically, we thought that we would inform subjects of the way to walk in advance and use content of a longer duration.

IV. Main Experiment

In keeping with the result of the pre-experiment, we performed the main experiment. The aim of this experiment was to define the difference between walking the city as usual and while using the PPS. In this experiment, we used a cognitive map as a method, because it was used by Lynch, as well to investigate the spatial perception of the city.

The plot pattern of this experiment was designed to address the negative opinions of the pre-experiment. First, about the relation between sounds and the place, the user had obtained information from both eyes and ears. When the hearing information deviated from the sight information, this system might have become boring. Next, in order to remove uneasiness, we plotted sounds along a predetermined street, similar to the first pattern of the pre-experiment, and informed users of this street. About the content, when we used film music, the impressions of the system varied depending on whether the user knew the movie or not. Hence, we used music that everyone knows or can enjoy even though they do not know it.

A. Experimental Method

The area of this experiment was Minato Mirai (refer to Figure 3.), as in the case of the pre-experiment. We chose the route beforehand and plotted three pieces of content along it. The subjects of this experiment were eight people with ages between 20 and 50 years old, and we divided them into two groups, A and B. The subjects of group A only followed the guide and walked the route. The subjects of group B followed the guide while using the PPS and listening to the music content. The subjects of both groups drew a cognitive map on A3 paper just after the walk. This experiment was conducted from the beginning to the middle of December, 2015. In Japan, sunset occurs at about 16:30 during this time, and when we performed the experiment, the area was already dark, and the illuminations of the city were turned on.

B. Sound Content and Place

The first piece of content was "The Phantom of the Opera Theme Song" from *The Phantom of the Opera*. This content started at the half-way mark of Kishamichi Promenade where we can view Minato Mirai at night and ended at Navios Yokohama Hotel, which is a hotel in the shape of an arch. This content is in a minor key and is made magnificent by the powerful operatic singing voice. It shows an upsurge steadily towards the climax. We wanted to research how the strangeness of this content fitted the existing atmosphere and influenced the impression of the town.

The second piece of content was the BGM of *Pocket Monster*, which is a handheld video game developed and manufactured by Nintendo Co., Ltd. This content is heard when users walk through the area where there is nothing but lawn. This BGM is electronic music, which reminds us of an 8-bit game. We wanted to investigate the change of impression that resulted from plotting funny BGM at a dull place.

The third piece of content was a medley of Christmas songs that included "Santa Claus is Coming to Town" and "We Wish You a Merry Christmas". Both these are basic Christmas songs in Japan and almost all Japanese people know them. The place we plotted was the open space between two warehouses. It was Christmas season when we carried out this experiment, and a Christmas market and a skating rink reproduced a European setting. We wanted to define the change of the impression of the place that already had a Christmas atmosphere by adding festive songs. The map plotted with the sound content in Figure 6.

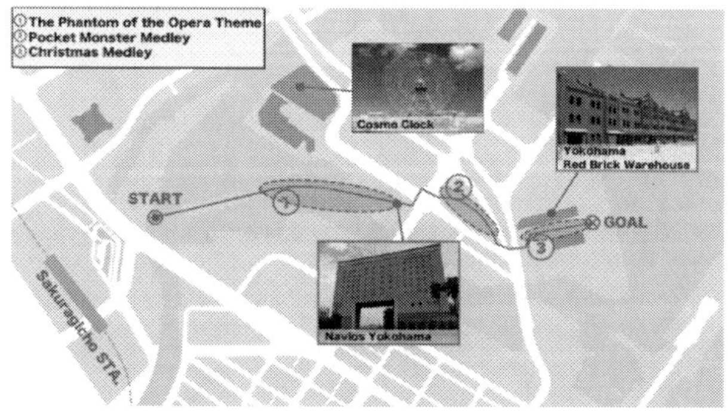

Figure 6. The Map of the Main Experiment

C. Result

It is true that there were individual differences in the ability of the subjects to grasp nuances about the space and their drawing skills. However, there were many common points in the elements and the form drawn on the map, and we were able to clarify some tendencies by examining these points. First, we counted the elements that the subjects wrote on a blank paper one by one and arranged them to ascertain which subject wrote what. We assumed the elements that were written by more than four subjects were a major element and assumed anything other than that to be a minor element. We assigned serial numbers from 1 to 28 for each element and alphabetical letters A to H for each subject. In addition, subjects A, B, C and D did not use PPS, and subjects E, F, G, and H used PPS. We show this in Tables 1 and 2.

TABLE I. MAJOR ELEMENT

Major Element		Type of element	No PPS				Use PPS			
			A	B	C	D	E	F	G	H
1	Yokohama Red Brick Warehouse	Landmark	*	*	*	*	*	*	*	*
2	Navios Yokohama Hotel	Landmark	*	*	*	*	*	*	*	*
3	Cross Walk	Node		*	*	*	*	*	*	*
4	Cosmo Clock ;wheel	Landmark	*	*	*	*	*		*	*
5	Queen's Square ;shopping mall	Landmark	*	*	*	*		*		*
6	World Porters ;shopping mall	Landmark				*	*	*	*	*
7	Railroad Bridge	Landmark		*	*	*	*	*		
8	Landmark Tower ;office building	Landmark			*	*		*		*
9	The Other Side of Warehouse	Edge					*	*	*	*
10	Skating Link	District	*				*	*	*	
11	Inter Continental Hotel	Landmark	*	*	*	*				
12	Christmas Tree in Market	Landmark					*	*	*	*
13	Anniversaire ;wedding hall	Landmark	*			*	*		*	

TABLE II. MINOR ELEMENT

Minor Element		Type of element	No PPS				Use PPS			
			A	B	C	D	E	F	G	H
14	Illumination for Kishamichi	Path		*		*		*		
15	Christmas Tree of World Porters	Landmark		*				*	*	
16	Right side of Kishamichi	Edge			*	*		*		
17	Shape of Kishamichi	Edge							*	*
18	Arch of Christmas Market	Landmark				*			*	
19	Asuka ;luxuly liner	Landmark						*	*	
20	People met on the way	Landmark					*		*	
21	Nipponmaru ;exhibited ship	Landmark								*
22	Reflection on the surface of water	District					*			
23	Lawn	District						*		
24	Sound Source of the City BGM	Node						*		
25	Christmas Market Stalls	Path							*	
26	Santa Clause in Christmas Market	Landmark							*	
27	Objrct near the World Porters	Landmark							*	
28	Cosmo World ;amusement park	District								*

For example, Yokohama Red Brick Warehouse and Navios Yokohama Hotel are elements written by all subjects. The note about the far end of the Yokohama Red Brick Warehouse is characteristic in Table 1. All the subjects of Group B did a note about the square or sea or ship spread to the other side of warehouse as well as the warehouse. On the other hand, Group A did not have the person who made a note about scenery of the other side of the warehouse. There is the goal in the place where they have finished passing through the open space of the warehouse, and it is the scene which is completed while the Christmas medley that is the third contents becomes lively at the climax when they use PPS. In Table 2, there are many numbers of elements that subjects of Group B write in at cognitive map, and they wrote in unique elements that were not cover by others. In Tables 1 and 2, we classify these elements into 5 types proposed by K. Lynch. Most elements recorded are classified as "landmark", and as it becomes the unique element, the ratios of other type increase. In particular, the element classified as "edge", is written in the cognitive map of only the subjects of Group B. We show the example of the cognitive map that a subject really made. Figure 7 is the cognitive map of a subject who did not use PPS, and Figure 8 is the cognitive map of a subject who used PPS.

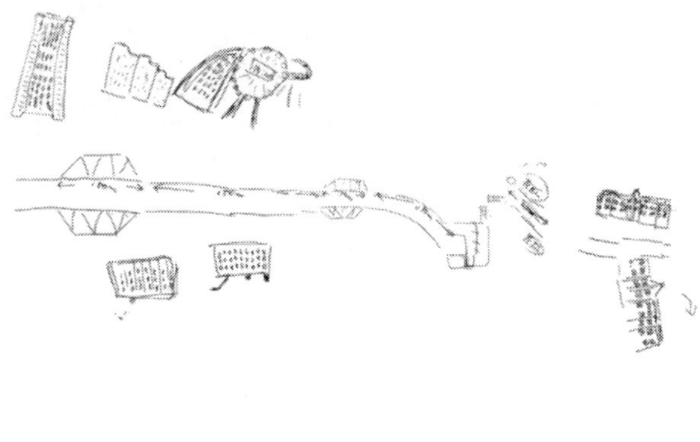

Figure 7. Cognitive Map of Subject C

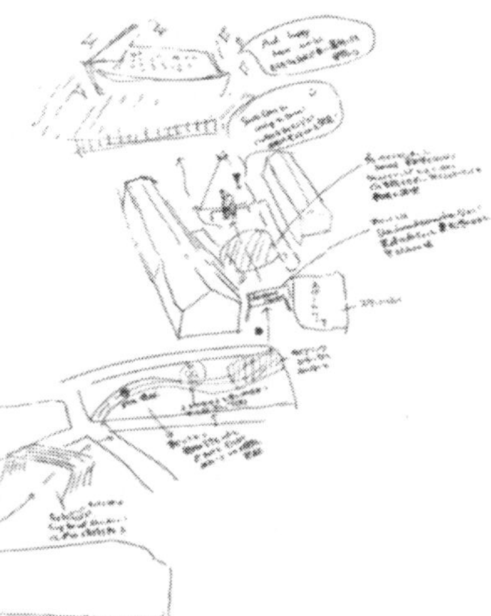

Figure 8. Cognitive Map of Subject G

As seen in Figure 7, all the subjects of Group A expressed elements by an illustration or a letter. On the other hand, as for the subject of Group B, three of four people left not only the illustration but also comments.

D. Consideration

We compared the cognitive maps of Groups A and B and analyzed them. First, the primary feature was that the subjects of Group B made their cognitive maps in more detail than those of Group A. When we walk the city, we depend on our sight for the most information, and though we always hear some sounds, we are not conscious of hearing them unless they are very loud. However, when we use PPS, the subject walks the city while being conscious of not only the sight information but also the hearing information because of the clear music. In this way, meanings and impressions are added to elements that had no meaning for the subjects when they just looked. Although music might not necessarily harmonize with scenery, there is a previous study that even if a feeling is incongruous BGM affects to remember the image [10]. Actually, almost all of the comments written in the cognitive map of Group B were descriptions that the subjects gave not only through sight but also through the image of the music. For example, a certain subject left a comment that she associated a kidnapped bride with the marriage ceremonial hall, because she had been listening to "The Phantom of the Opera Theme" when she looked at the hall. As a result of the questionnaire, we deduced that the reason why the cognitive map of group B has more comments with expressive sentences is because the best way to express the feeling in suit is to leave comments.

Next, we considered the notes about the other side of the warehouse that was featured only in the cognitive maps of Group B. Though the city does not have an area and a boundary line, we predicted that the cognitive maps of Group B have three areas divided by content. However, there was no cognitive map to show that.

However, when subjects heard the content reach a climax and end, they tended to draw an edge at that spot. There is a study that termination feeling of the music affects the termination of the video product [11]. In this experiment, the first and third pieces of content corresponded to that.

As mentioned earlier, the first piece of content played at the Navios Yokohama Hotel. This landmark has a very impressive external appearance and shape and all the subjects experienced this; not only subjects of Group B but also Group A did not forget to draw it.

Though this hotel is just a landmark for Group A, for Group B, it tended to perform a role as the end of the first area. This is because three subjects of Group B left notes on this hotel and perceived it as the end of the first piece of content.

About the point that subjects of Group B drew edges for the other side of warehouse, we considered that they grasped the range where they could hear the third piece of content as one area, and also, it was a spot where the music increased and concluded in a particularly impressive manner. Therefore, edges were expressed there.

V. Conclusion and Future Work

We performed some experiments using the new form of art that changes the city through sounds. As a pre-experiment, we proposed two patterns of PPS. The first was a pattern that plotted sounds used in *Star Wars* in a sequence along the street. The second was a pattern that assumed a good-man area and a bad-man area and plotted sounds focused on the sound effect and character's voice. Based on the outcome of the pre-experiment, we performed the experiment with the cognitive map. In this experiment, we defined the difference between the cognitive maps while walking the city as usual and while using PPS. The contents used were "The Phantom of the Opera Theme", *Pocket Monster* BGM, and a medley of Christmas songs. These contents were plotted for Kishamichi, a lawn, and the square of a red brick warehouse. As a result, we defined that the cognitive map drawn by the PPS user has more information, and when the PPS user hears the content reach its climax and end, he or she tends to draw an edge at that spot.

We inspected the movement of the PPS. We confirmed whether the sound played at the desired volume automatically when the user approached the assigned spot. Although sometimes it took several seconds for the sound file to be read, we confirmed that the service functioned normally. An aim of PPS is to create a fun experience and add fascination for a city where we do not feel novelty any more. We want to ensure that every user can plot sounds that will make a place more fun and create an original channel of PPS. Then, a user who is an audience can search for a favorite channel made by another user. In sharing the channels with each other, PPS will become a communication tool through the real space that uses sounds. For that, we want to first show a guideline for the user to plot sounds.

In the pre-experiment, we defined that user's feelings are influenced by the content. However, the change of feelings was not tied to the image of the city. As a result, the image of the city did not change. In the next experiment, we found that the sound could not change the image of the city, but amplified that. However, this fact is dependent on this city. In the future, we need to perform a qualitative and quantitative evaluation such as a required time and junction on the cognitive map. In addition, the number of combinations of sound content and plotted places was not enough. It is necessary to examine more content and plotted spots and define more differences of the image of the city by adding sounds. Then, we want to define the guide of what kind of sound is suitable for what kind of place.

References

[1] K. Lynch, "The Image of the City," MIT Press, 1960.

[2] S. K. Marshall and A. J. Cohen, "Effects of musical soundtracks on attitudes toward animated geometric figures," Music Perception, vol. 6, 1988, pp. 95-112.

[3] S. D. Lipscomb and R. A. Kendall, "Perceputual judgement of the relationship between msical and visual components in film," Psychomusicology, vol. 13, 1994, pp. 60-98.

[4] A. J. Cohen, "Associationism and musical soundtrack phenomena," Contemporary Music Review, vol. 9, 1993, pp. 163-178.

[5] M. G. Boltz, "The cognitive processing of film and musical soundtracks," Memory and Cognition, vol. 32, no. 7, 2004, pp. 1194-1205.

[6] V. J. Bolivar, A. J. Cohen, and J. C. Fentress, "Semantic and formal congruency in music and motion pictures," Effects on the interpretation of wisual action. Psychomusicology, vol. 13, 1994, pp. 28-59.

[7] S. D. Lipscomb, "Cognition of musical and visual accent structure alignment in film and animation," Proceedings of 4th

International Conference of Music Perception and Cognition, 1996, pp. 309-313.

[8] M. Chion, "The Sound in Cinema," New, revised and corrected edition. [N. p.]: Cahiers du Cinema Livres.

[9] M. Chion, "The Music of Cinema," Les chemins de la musique. Paris: Fayard.

[10] M. Boltz, M. Schulkind, and S. Kantra, "Effects of background music on the remembering of filmed events," Memory and Cognition, vol. 19, no. 6, 1991, pp. 593-606.

[11] W. F. Thompson, F. A. Russo, and D. Sinclair, "Effect of underscoring on the perception of closure in filmed events," Psychomusicology, vol. 13, 1994, pp.9-27.

Design and Evaluation of "Social Networking Radio" To Provide Voice and Sound of the Location Based Information

Kosuke Miyasaka
Keio University
Graduate School of Media and Governance
Fujisawa, Japan
e-mail: mikko@sfc.keio.ac.jp

Katsuhiko Ogawa
Keio University
Faculty of Environment and Information Studies
Fujisawa, Japan
e-mail: ogw@sfc.keio.ac.jp

Abstract—**People in a city are usually seen spending a lot of time on their smartphones. By developing information technologies, we have become able to access information on the Internet and get in touch with friends anytime and anywhere. However, there is also the possibility that such behaviors make people a "cocoon" in social spaces. Therefore, we propose a new service called -social networking radio (SNR), which provides voice and sound of location-based information. By setting the voices in the city and listening while walking, we expect to encourage a user's interest around the town. This paper describes the concept of SNR, the system design, and from the experimental results, considers the playing method and contents of comments.**

Keywords-Radio; Navigation; Speech synthesis; Smartphone.

I. Introduction

Owing to the development of information technology, city walking and driving habits have changed. Before the inception of the smartphone and car navigation systems, we relied on a paper map and enquiries for navigation. Strolling the streets while studying maps and meeting people on routes, we were able to discover the attractiveness of the towns and experience the atmosphere of the town.

Today, by the evolving location service, it has become possible to reach specific destinations quickly and easily. However, it inhibits the chance to encounter the city and people. Furthermore, when we use the location information application of smartphones, we concentrate fully on the smartphone screen by looking downward, which isolates one. It is, therefore, necessary to research on city walking with interesting media that are different from existing navigation systems. There exists previous research that is related to interesting city walk; here, we introduce some of this research.

Kori developed a blog car radio system that presents blog entries in auditory style using speech synthesis [1]. He discussed a method of extracting text contents that is suitable for speech synthesis; he also verified the effectiveness of the method. This system collects information from a local blog, and summarizes the information to some "entry," which gives it the ranking for users. This ranking method helps to screen the content that is associated with the users' location. However, blog contents used in this system are not suitable for sightseeing, and its use for sightseeing based on location is not mentioned.

Nakatani proposed a new tourist navigation system that does not provide detailed route information [2]. By not presenting a specific route, attempts to induce a chance encounter and detour of the city were made. A navigation system that only provided a path and landmark was developed and experiments were conducted by actually walking around with this navigation system. By using this, subjects had a detour in the city. In his research, he discussed the route and time subjects walked around; however, there was no mention of how subjects changed their cognition of the town.

Suda proposed the system "GBvoice" to take advantage of leaving a characteristic old locality [3]. GBvoice recorded the voice of town dwellers who were interviewed and provided this to walking users. In this research, it was found that local contents led to user's motivation to discover new things about contents. However, this was not related to the location of users. It was also not possible to provide a voice that corresponded to the user's location.

We intend to develop a new navigation system that provides interesting comments that only locals know and provides it to the user depending on their location. We created this system to discuss how a change in user's route would change a cognitive map.

Therefore, we propose a news service—social networking radio (SNR), which provides information based on the route of walking. SNR provides interesting location-based information. By listening to information that only locals know, we are able to make users walk around normally.

This paper describes the concept of SNR, the system constitution, and by the experimental results, considers a playing method and comments. In addition, we discussed the changing of a subject's perspectives in the town by a cognitive map written by subjects.

II. Concept

Collecting and vocalizing local information of the city, and playing it automatically corresponding to a user's location would enable users to walk around with ease. This is the fundamental concept of SNR, which is shown in Fig. 1. To achieve this, we propose two elements.

The first element is to provide local information that only locals know. By providing local information rather than the information that is listed on the Internet, SNR promotes user interest in the city. If users listen to this information, they look around and try to find the location indicated by the information. It promotes a detour, thereby, making walking around fun.

The second element is to set the sound in the city and images of the city given to users, which also change. When we try to search location information and route in an existing web map, it is displayed in a text. Consequently, the user's point of view is downward unlike SNR, which provides users with local information by speech, thereby, allowing users to face upward. For example, when we hear the voice of a male while walking, we look up and see around to search his voice. This is unlike an image from the usual path. Forming a different image from the usual path could promote fun in city walking.

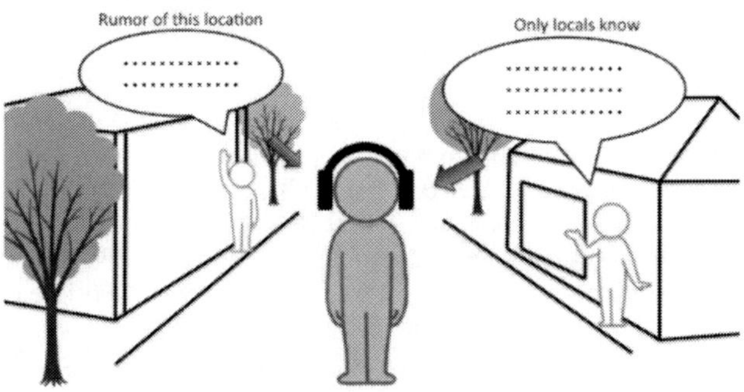

Figure 1. Concept of SNR.

III. System Design

The system design of SNR is configured in three sides (input side, output side, and vocalizing and processing side). In Figs. 2 and 3, the image of the system design and flowchart are shown .

A. Input Side

The informant enters the text in the text box, and the input system stores it in the input database. The comments of input are id, Name, and Text. These are stored in the MySQL database. Anyone can enter comments to this system because it is online (consists of Javascript and PHP).

B. Vocalizing and Processing Side

The vocalizing and processing side load text from the database, and converts the text to sound data with the speech synthesis system. This converts sound files that are stored in a local folder. This local folder associates local latitudes that are predetermined to play the sound file. If the text in database id is updated, this side loads the latest text automatically, and generates a new sound file.

C. Output side

The output side extracts the location of the user's information and measures the distance of this position together with the local latitude where the audio file is placed. When approaching a certain location, audio files placed in this position are automatically played. Here, we define "Rad" as a certain distance, which is the radius of the circle to be displayed on the map. In other words, if the marker indicating the current location is entered in a circle on the map, a sound file that is placed in its position is automatically played.

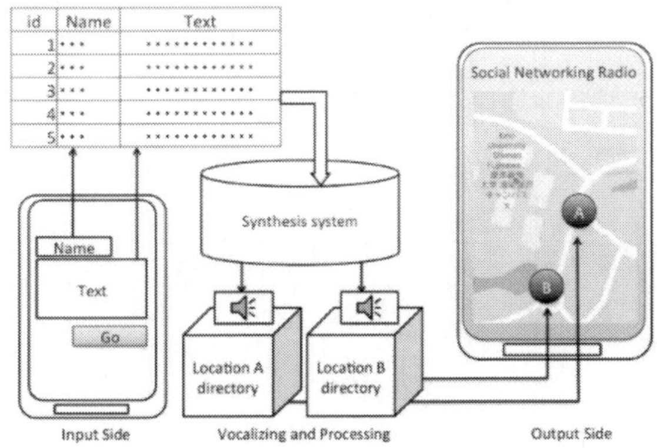

Figure 2. System design.

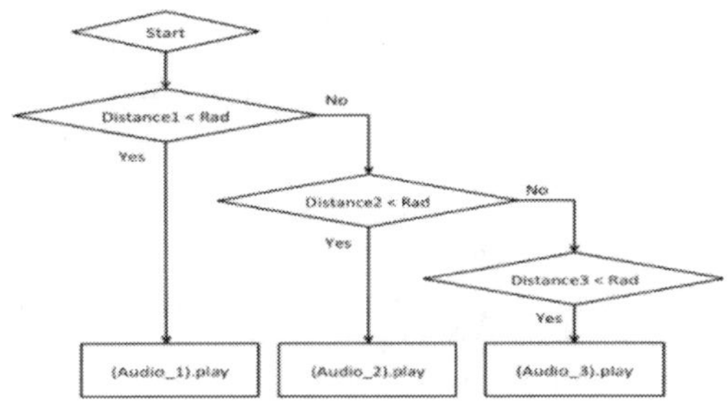

Figure 3. Flowchart.

To play an audio file automatically, an automatic playing permission button in SNR was installed. When users start the SNR and press this button, SNR will load the audio file on the server, which will be played automatically and corresponds to the location of the user.

Based on this system design, a prototype was implemented. In Figure 4, two prototypes are shown. The prototype on the right is the new version that has the automatic playing permission button installed.

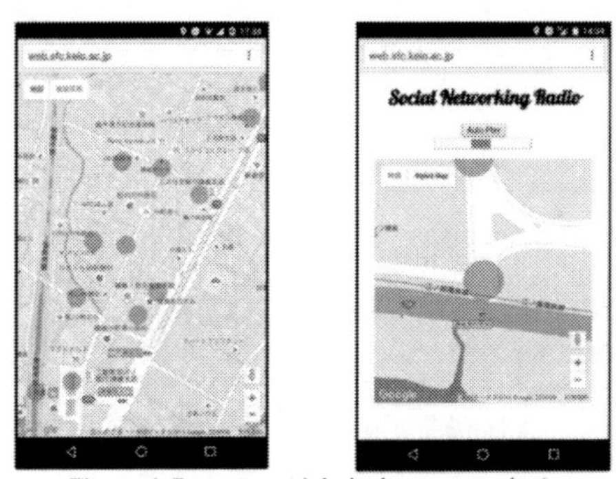

Figure 4. Prototype (right is the new version).

After the prototype implementation, the arrangement intervals of the comments were examined owing to simultaneous activation of the first and second audio in some cases. The average walking speed of people is said to be 1.5 m/s. If the length of one of the audio file used in the SNR is 10 to 25 s, the distance between the comments must be at least 37.5 m. Therefore, when the comments on the SNR are arranged, it is necessary to consider the distance. In Figure 5, the sample interval between the first comments and next comments is 25 seconds, and the speed of walking is 1.5m/s is shown.

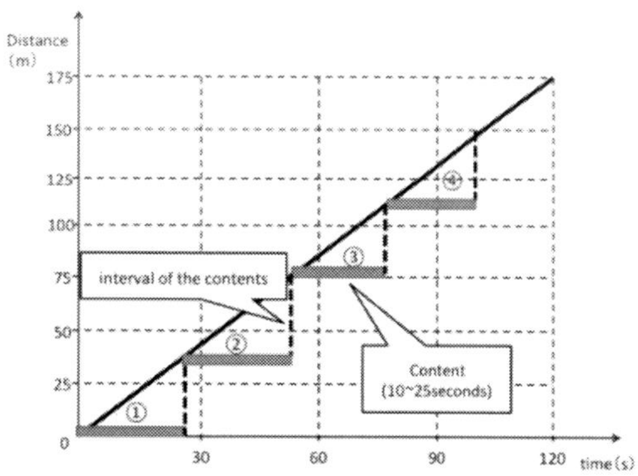

Figure 5. the sample Interval of comments.

IV. Comments For SNR

In this experiment, the type of comments suitable for the SNR system is discussed.

A. Comment Collection and Grouping

In order to collect local information of the city, we interviewed people of the city. The location chosen was at the wayside of Enoshima Railway.

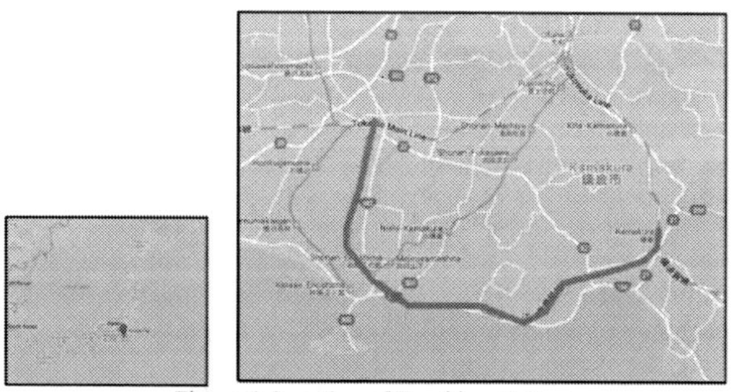
Figure 6. Location of Enoshima Railway.

Many tourist spots and fashion shops are located in this location, which attracts 12 million tourists per year. Apart from being a popular tourist location, the locals are warm and familiar with the many attractive spots.

The interview was carried out by 40 team members from our laboratory. To facilitate the interviewing process, three pieces of information were focused upon:

- Recommended Shops
- Recommended Place
- Other recommendations

We were able to collect 159 pieces of comments through this fieldwork. We studied the text of all comments and grouped them based on the technique of HCD (Human Centered Design). After grouping, it was found that the groups could be classified into four quadrants.

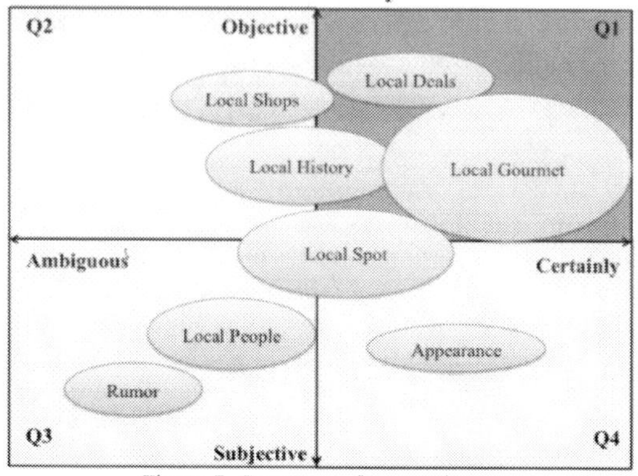

Figure 7. Comments four quadrants.

B. Evaluation

1. Evaluation Method

SNR of Enoshima Railway was created for all 15 Stations with 10 comments per station. These audio comments were created by speech synthesis, and the subjects were students of the laboratory. The comments placed on the map were heard, and the comments in the free description were evaluated. Fig. 8 shows an experimental SNR in the Kamakura station.

Figure 8. Experimental SNR in the Kamakura station.

2. Results and Discussion

From the results of the free description evaluation, opinions were summarized as shown in Table1.

TABLE I. List of Description

- On the street, reliable information is better because it is easy to understand.
- Ambiguous information is bad to hear.
- Information of the local gourmet food increases motivation to go shopping or visit a restaurant.
- Long comments are too long and difficult to listen to.
- Local information of shops and restaurants that only locals know is interesting to hear.

From these results, two points for SNR comments were noted.

1) The length of the comments

It becomes difficult to hear the voice of the speech synthesis if the comments are very long.

2) The contents of the comment

It is better to include specific comments to present reliable information.

In light of these points, Q1 in Fig. 7 is deemed to be the most suitable quadrant for SNR comments. However, by context of the situation of users and the city, other quadrant comments such as Rumor or Appearance may generate interest for users in the town.

V. EXPERIMENT

SNR based on system design was developed, and a demonstration was performed. Users of SNR and users without SNR walked on the same street and the difference between walking and the user's perspective were verified.

A. Experimental Method

Three students (one male and two females) of KEIO University were subjects. Subjects A and B use the SNR while subjects C did not use the SNR but rather, used Google Map. The experimental location was between Kamakurakokomae Station and Shichirigahama Station in Fujisawa (Kanagawa). This is same place of the comment experimental. The shortest distance of this section is about 950 m, which can be covered in 10 min. This section is also a famous location of SlamDunk - a famous animation in Japan. In this section, there is a branch point to either choose to walk by the sea or climb to hills but most people choose the coastal road. However, there exists many beautiful places along the hills. For example, the location of beautiful views of the sea is lined with beautiful houses that make the walk interesting.

In this section, each subject walked from Kamakurakokomae Station to Shichirigahama Station after which they had drawn a cognitive map.

B. Comments

Comments that were used in the experiment, based on the discussion of the recorded comments were originally created. Comments on both the coastal side street where many tourists visit and the hillside street where locals live were placed. Arrangement intervals of the comments were based on the comment distance of system design. In this experiment, 20 comments were placed on this section. Fig. 9 shows the SNR used in the experiment, while Table 2 shows some example of comments.

Figure 9. SNR in the experiment.

TABLE II. COMMENTS EXAMPLE

If you go up the hill there is a place from where you can see a beautiful view of the sea.
There's a dead end sign but this road leads to the Enoden railroad.
Restaurant Shichirigahama. Drink a beer and enjoy the view of the sea at this restaurant.

C. Behavior Observation

Fig. 11 shows the route that subjects walk around the town. The behavior of each subject is summarized below.

1. Subject A (SNR)

Subject A visited this location once. In Fig. 11-1 we showed the route of Subject A. At Point A, SNR provided the voice "let's go to the hill" and the way of the hill was chosen by the male subject A. At Point B, the directions chosen by the SNR was also chosen. The interest of the male subject was in the local information that "this is the stage of drama" and "beautiful location of scenery", and at Point C, when the location introduced by SNR was found, the subject took a photo. The male subject also reacted to the word "these is Aloe" but it could not be found by the subject. At Point D, SNR provided "There are Stop Signs, but you can come out to Enoden Line". The male subject went through the route and arrived at Shichirigahama Station.

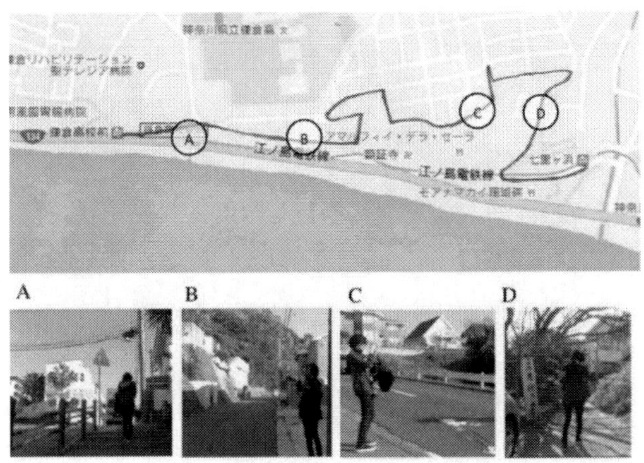

Figure 11-1. Route of Subject A.

Fig.11-2 shows the cognitive map of Subject A. In this cognitive map at Point 1, Subject A recorded a nice view of the sea. At Points 2, 3, and 4, elements that SNR provided were recorded especially at the side of the hill. The "edge" that meant Enoden Line was recorded, but was exceeded in the cognitive map. It was observed that more points could be located than we expected.

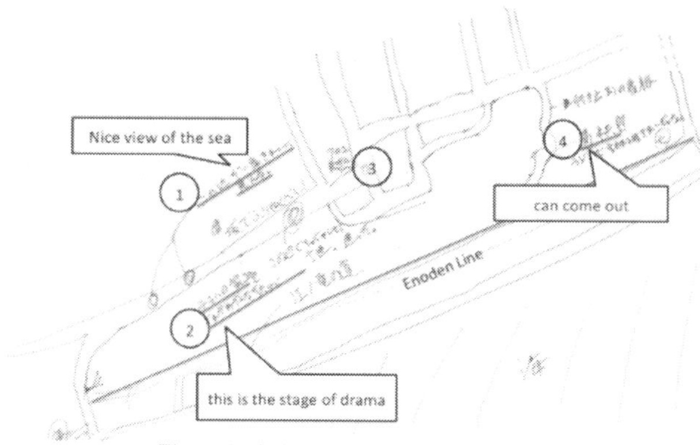

Figure 11-2. Cognitive Map of Subjects A.

2. Subject B (SNR)

Subject B also visited this location once. In Fig. 12-1, the route of subject B is shown. At the branch Point A, SNR provided the voice "let's got to the hill" similar to that of subject A, which was selected by Subject B. At Point B, the street that was further at the top of the hill was selected, which was reached via a walking trail in the woods. When she arrived at the walking trail in the woods, the subject's path was crooked in the forest but a picture was taken at the middle point of the trail denoted as Point C, which overlooked the Sagami Bay. After the walking trail, at Point D, the subject was behind Shicirigahama Station by chance.

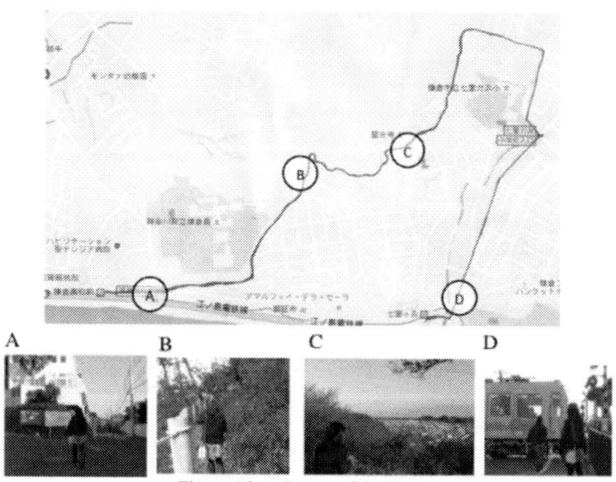

Figure 12-1. Route of Subject B.

In Fig. 12-2, we showed the cognitive map of Subject B. At Point 1, the comment "I wanted to see the view of the sea from the hill" was recorded. Point 2 is where the female subject could see the sea, which she also recorded on the map. Though the subject was lost for a while after this point, the subject recorded "relieved" at Points 3. In this cognitive map, however, the female subject did not write Enoden Line.

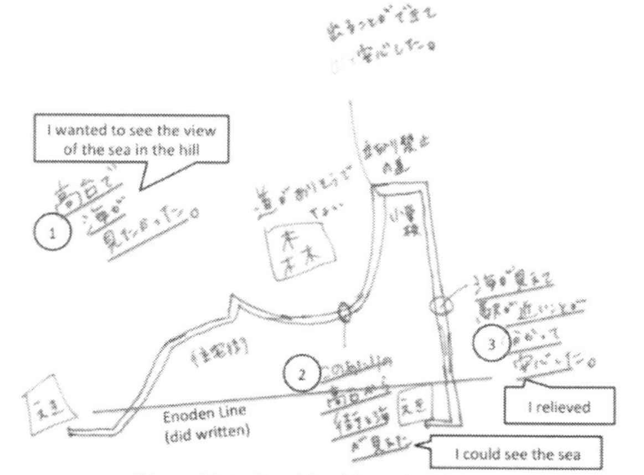

Figure 12-2. Cognitive Map of subject B.

3. Subject C (Google Map without SNR)

Subject C was at this location once as the other subjects. In Fig. 13-1, the route of the Subject C is shown. On the start location, the subject used Google Map to check for the route to Shichirigahama Station, which was found at Point A. The subject decided to choose the way of the seaside and walked a while to Point B before looking over sea and hill. Though the female subject was lost at the branch point of Point C, the female subject used Google Map and found the route to the Station(Point D) instantly. By using Google Map, the shortest route was selected and the female subject arrived at the station in 15 min.

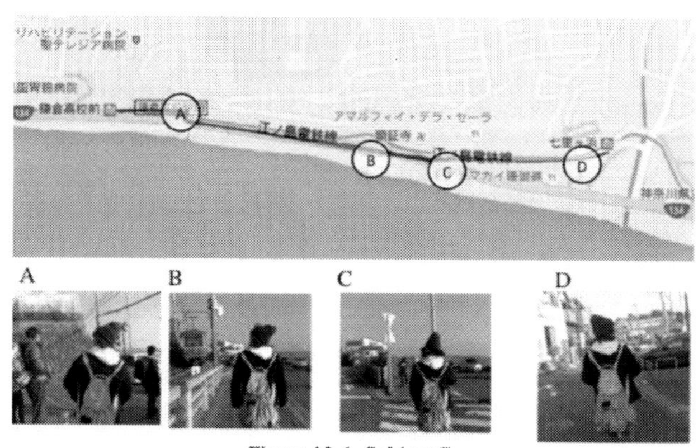

Figure 13-1. Subject C.

Fig. 13-2 shows the cognitive map of Subject C is shown. At Point 1, the female subject commented "There would be residential areas". At Points B and C (Fig.13-1), the female subject also commented forecast too and at Points 2 and 3, elements that were seen by the subject were also recorded. At Point 4, the female subject commented "There would be pizza shop". This female subject also wrote Enoden Line clearly.

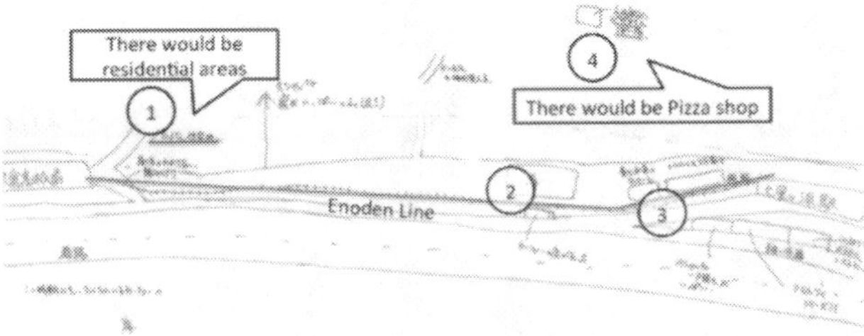

Figure 13-2. Cognitive map of subject C.

VI. DISCUSSION

A. the Effect of SNR

Two effects of SNR were deduced from this experiment.

- A way that was different from usual was chosen.

Subjects of SNR chose a way different from usual. Subject A walked around based on the speech provided by the SNR. By walking via the streets while listening to the local comments in the SNR, the male subject was able to walk through a route that was not provided in Google Map. In addition, Subject B selected the street of hills, and walked via the forest road that was not in the map. In a later interview about walking, the subject noted that the choice was selected because SNR provided a comment "The view of the sea is beautiful from the top of the hill." This comment was created by author intentionally, in order to lead users to choose uncommon routes.

- Change the cognition of the city

From the experimental cognitive map, the most uncommon record of the SNR user was "exceed the edge". Subject C wrote "that may be residential area" near the starting point. Subject C suggested this from the road and line. It is assumed that line of Enoden is "edge" for users who are walking in city.

However, comparing the two subjects of SNR and the subject C, SNR users could exceed this edge. In addition, there is a little difference in height between the hills and the line, and this could be an edge. However, SNR users could exceed beyond the line unconsciously. From this fact, it was found that SNR users could change their cognition and could change behavior from the usual.

B. Know-how of SNR

From this experiment, we can discuss some knowhow about creating SNR.

1. The location and comments

From this experiment, it was discovered that SNR is useful in the two situations of the user, which could either be on the Path or on the Node. On the Path if SNR provides comment about its location, users will look for its comment position and find new discoveries. For On the Node, SNR can provide direction on the node for users to find new routes and be more motivated to walk around than usual. In Fig. 14, the image of these two instances is shown.

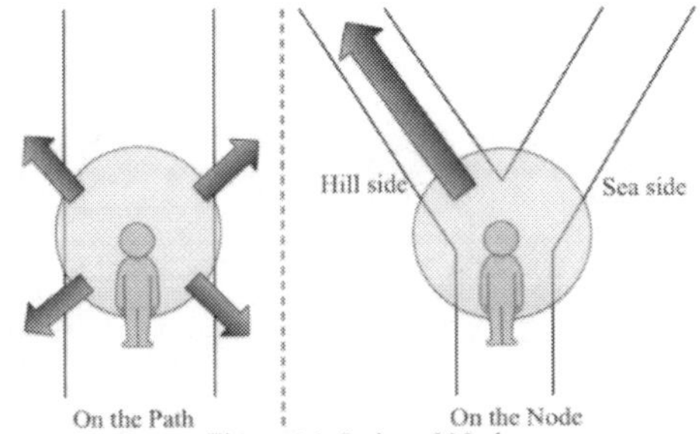

Figure 14. Path and Node.

2. Story of the comments

From the interview results, it was found that users seek to listen to the story of comments. For example, the first comment was about gourmet food, the second comment was also about gourmet food or provided more detailed for the first comment. Relevant comments are easier to hear than independent comments.

VII. CONCLUSION AND FUTURE WORK

In this paper, the concept of SNR was described and its system design. By experimental results, discussion on the effect of SNR and the playing method and comments, it was found that SNR changes both the usual route and the cognitive map of the city. It was also found that using SNR could lead to detour. Furthermore, from experiments, a suitable location to play comments could be found and contents of comments could then be selected.

On the other hand, some improvements about SNR were identified, which can only provide comments to walking users at the moment. However, since there are many people on the move, driving cars, riding on bikes or, in the future, automatic operation vehicles, SNR would have to be suitable to many users on the city who would enjoy the city by detour Therefore an improvement on system design and comments to various users has to be sought for.

VIII. REFERENCES

[1] H. Kori, "Text Extraction and A User Interface for Regional Blog Sonification" Proc. of the 2nd International Special Workshop on Databases for Next-Generation Researchers (SWOD2006), 2006.

[2] Y. Nakatani, "Tourist Navigation System that Induces Accidental Encounter" Human Interface Symposium, 2008, pp.1033-1038.

[3] M. Suda, "The Development of Audio Contents for Conveying Characteristics of Local Regions and a Proposal of Distributio nSystem for Them" IPSJ SIG Technical Report, 2013, pp.13-18.

[4] K. Lynch, The Image of The City, The MIT Press, 1960.

[5] P. Thorndyke, and H. Barbara, "Differences in spatial knowledge acquired from maps and navigation" Cognitive psychology 14, 1982, pp.560-589.

[6] H. Mallot, and G. Sabine, "Route navigating without place recognition: What is recognised in recognition-triggered responses?" Perception 29, 2000, pp.43-56.

[7] F. Redlick, M. Jenkin, and H. Laurence, "Humans can use optic flow to estimate distance of travel" Vison research 41, 2001, pp.213-219.

[8] F. Kato, "Experiencing the City through Podwalk: A Medium for Flâneur" Pervasive Image Capture and Sharing Workshop, 2006.

AUTHOR INDEX

International Academy, Research,
and Industry Association (IARIA)
412 Derby Way
Wilmington, DE 19810

ISBN 978-1-5108-2308-2

CURRAN ASSOCIATES INC.
proceedings
.com